FLICKERING LIGHT
A HISTORY OF NEON

CHRISTOPH RIBBAT

REAKTION BOOKS

Published by Reaktion Books Ltd
33 Great Sutton Street
London EC1V ODX, UK
www.reaktionbooks.co.uk

Flackernde Moderne. Die Geschichte des Neonlichts
Christoph Ribbat
© 2011 Franz Steiner Verlag, Birkenwaldstrasse 44,
70191 Stuttgart, Germany
All rights reserved

The translation of this work was funded by Geisteswissenschaften International – Translation Funding for Work in the Humanities and Social Sciences from Germany, a joint initiative of the Fritz Thyssen Foundation, the German Federal Foreign Office, the collecting society VG WORT and the Börsenverein des Deutschen Buchhandels (German Publishers & Booksellers Association).

First published in English 2013

Translated by Anthony Mathews
English-language translation © Reaktion Books 2013

Printed and bound in China

British Library Cataloguing in Publication Data
Ribbat, Christoph.
Flickering light : a history of neon.
1. Neon — History.
2. Neon lighting — History.
3. Neon signs — History. 4. Neon lighting — Social aspects.
I. Title
621.3'275'09-dc23
ISBN 978 1 78023 091 7

CONTENTS

Neon signs, Paris, 1931.

1 READING NEON

A Call from Rattlesnake Gulch

The town seemed to be burning. The telephone rang at the fire department headquarters in Missoula, Montana, way out on the American prairie. A man was calling from Rattlesnake Gulch, 26 km away. He reported a glow right over Missoula; he was so beside himself that the fireman had trouble calming him down. Then he asked the caller whether what he thought was a blaze was long and rectangular. When he said it was, the fireman assured him that it was not flames lighting up the night but the neon sign of the Florence Hotel in Missoula. It had turned the night sky red in that year of 1928.[1]

In its natural state neon gas is unremarkable, without colour or smell, something for the chemist rather than firefighters. Its symbol in the periodic table is Ne. Its density is 0.838 g/l; its boiling point −246.08 degrees centigrade. Like helium, argon, krypton, xenon and radon, it is one of the 'noble' gases that are derived from air and which British scientists identified in the late nineteenth century. These gases are called 'noble' because, like noble metals, they resist chemical reaction. For a long time scientists thought that it was impossible for them to combine with other elements. This theory was, however, disproved in 1962. In French they refer to *gaz rare* rather than *gaz noble* since in the air we breathe neon amounts to only 0.00046 per cent.[2]

The neon signs associated with modernity are less rare: those tubes all over the world shining out over hotels, bars and casinos or advertising the sale of beer. It all started in Paris in 1912, when the first-ever neon advertising sign lit up a barber's with the words 'PALAIS COIFFEUR'. Then it was the turn of the 'FAHRSCHULE VIENNA' to get this kind of advertisement, for the Vienna Driving School. 'STAR NOODLE FRIED SHRIMP' in Ogden, Utah, was similarly promoted, as was 'CARTA BLANCA' beer in Mexico City. In East Germany, the state-owned 'EISENHÜTTENKOMBINAT J. W. STALIN' (J. W. Stalin Ironworks Combine) lit up Communist nights in neon – at least for a while. At the Gare du Nord, the same sort of lights held out the prospect of 'PARIS À LIÈGE 367 KM EN 4 HEURES SANS ARRÊT', and in Hong Kong they made it easier to find the 'RAM LUNG NIGHT CLUB' and the 'ITALY FRANCE JAPAN FOOD PLAZA 24 HOURS'. In Schöneberg, Berlin, people were likewise reminded about 'BESTATTUNGEN KLUTH' (Kluth Funerals).[3] It's worth noting that English uses the general term 'neon lights' for all fluorescent light tubes, even when these are filled with other gases (argon produces violet, helium pink, xenon pale blue and krypton silvery white, while a mixture of mercury and argon radiates blue).[4]

The uniquely designed tube that is blown by mouth and shaped by hand became an advertising medium, an element of architecture and eventually a favourite material for installation artists. It has played a highly individual role in the whole story of modernity. It challenges what countless cultural critics have been saying in the last few decades about how, in the course of the twentieth century, our culture has become increasingly less concerned with the material object and with human agency. For a time it seemed as if every new technology and every new medium would make our everyday existence more artificial, more remote from the body and from objects. For historians this process began during the heyday of modernism, during the early years of the cinema, fluid architecture and flickering advertisements.[5] In the era of artificial lighting and illuminated signs the city was becoming more and more superficial and theatrical, clamouring for more and more effects.[6] Going along with the ideas of a thinker like Guy Debord, one could read the flashing light shows as part of the overall hypnotization of passive consumers, continually dazzled by light in a capitalist 'society of the spectacle'.[7] From this perspective the postmodern metropolis

Erecting a neon sign, Fargo, North Dakota, *c*. 1940.

represents a 'fantasy city' dedicated to nothing but pleasure and sales gimmicks. It has its roots (if it has roots) in the period when illuminated advertisements first transformed the streets.[8]

A closer look at the handmade neon tube, however, discloses a technology of modernity which did not turn everyday life into a virtual reality. On the contrary, it created a new craft product. This was not made in anonymous, automated factories but in down-to-earth workshops where glass blowers and sign writers produced these new signs using their breath, mouths and hands and all their own acquired knowledge and skill. Contrary to the blatant scorn heaped upon the flashing of advertising slogans by cultural critics and theorists, neon workshops reveal the kind of characteristics described by Richard Sennett in his study *The Craftsman*: artisans using both head and hand, mind and material.[9] The neon signs they created, often unique objects of exceptional originality, shine out as representative of a form of creativity, of craftsmanship. The philosophers Hubert Dreyfus and Sean Kelly argue that well-made objects create meaning in a secular world – since creative engagement with the material brings out the best in the human being.[10] From this point of view the history of neon stands out against the overly pessimistic story of the ongoing dematerialization of our cities and the virtualization of our everyday life. The letters glowing in the dark may seem to be disembodied, as if capitalism itself was emblazoned across the sky, but in fact the neon tube brought the handmade object back into the city. And indirectly to Rattlesnake Gulch, too.

The Most Beautiful Pig in Winnemucca

In March 2004 Vera Lutter, a 44-year-old from Munich, climbed up every morning on to the roof of a Pepsi factory in the borough of Queens, New York, heading for a shed there. The wooden structure, 2 m wide and 3 m high, had been built by the artist herself. She had drilled a hole measuring 2 mm in its front wall. On arrival in the morning she spread out three sheets of highly sensitive paper on the back wall inside. After four hours she took them down again and transported them in a totally light excluding container to her studio in Manhattan.

The artist had set up the shed as a camera obscura in order to record the dismantling of a neon sign. The words 'Pepsi-Cola' had shone out in red over the East River, almost unchanged, since the days of Franklin D. Roosevelt. Harshly glowing tubes were mounted on the steel letters of flowing handwriting. In the dark they concealed the metal construction behind them. They appeared to be floating in the night air over Queens. Now all this was being removed. And Vera Lutter did not want to miss a single moment of the work in progress. 'First they took the bottle down, then the P, E, P, S, and I – and then the hyphen', the artist recalls. Her observation of the process led to the series of images, 'The Deconstruction of Pepsi-Cola'.[11] It consists of non-reproducible originals: the photographic papers of the camera obscura on the factory roof. But the neon writing itself was a unique original for the artist, an object possessing what Walter Benjamin calls 'aura', the passing of which appears to be celebrated by her images.

The success story of neon is short. This advertising technique spread throughout the world in the 1930s, dwindling in the benighted Europe of the war years. In the post-war period it saw a short revival, until by the 1950s and '60s it began its unstoppable decline, replaced by backlit plastic structures that were becoming considerably easier to use, more flexible and more durable than fragile glass.[12] For a long time the brightly coloured tubes were not seen as signs of innovation and commercial success, particularly in the United States. They became the typical advertising medium for those cheap, rather run-down bars, hotels and restaurants which could not afford brand-new advertising displays. Then, between the 1950s and '70s, Las Vegas developed into a neon oasis. In that period its casinos went in for spectacular innovations in order to attract gamblers. A later flowering sparked by the enormous success of contemporary light art brought about a revival of interest in these glowing letters and signs. But even this postmodern renaissance was marked by a desire to rescue a dying technology from obscurity. Thus Vera Lutter's photographs of the slow disappearance of the

P, E, P, S and I appear to fit seamlessly into the gloomy story of neon advertising, with its short rise up to the heights and its long decline.

But Vera Lutter was not the only one hooked on that piece of writing on the East River in the spring of 2004. Instead of being all for the dismantling of an advertising symbol of a worldwide consumer product, various politically active New Yorkers campaigned to keep the advertisement. For a while it sparked heated political debates over town planning issues. Citizens wrote letters and signed petitions, discussions took place and involvement escalated until the sign's supporters got their way. This New York City landmark was saved and the letters were reinstalled some hundred metres from their original location. There the lights shine still, just as in Roosevelt's time.

The demise of neon has met with similar counter-reactions on a number of occasions. In the late twentieth century various American cities experimented with preserving their traditional bright lights. Neon museums, coach tours and tax concessions for the renovation of advertisements with cultural significance all served to save the most popular of the urban icons. Despite the fact that the advertising industry always preferred the most up-to-date and cheapest of techniques, fans of sophisticated neon lights were passionate in the struggle to preserve them.[13] Supporters were also fighting to save a trade skill. In 1950s Philadelphia, for example, there were still around 40 neon producers at work blowing, shaping and filling the glass tubes. By 1989 the city only had six of these specialists left and five of them were old enough to be retired. This state of affairs prompted collectors and conservationists to take over the threatened workshops.[14]

On both coasts of the United States there were quite enthusiastic fans of neon. None of them were more active than Rudi Stern, the painter who had studied under Hans Hofmann and Oskar Kokoschka and developed psychedelic light shows for the LSD guru Timothy Leary in the 1960s. In 1972 Stern set up a New York City gallery called Let There Be Neon. He also produced a lavishly illustrated eponymous volume outlining a history of the topic. In the book he hailed neon lights as a form of folk art that needed to be championed alongside the claims of sculpture.[15] In one particular interview Stern announced that he had plans for 'neon sidewalks, neon highways, neon tunnels, neon on bridges and under water'. Even his first daughter's name was part of the project: Stern named her Lumière.[16] On the West Coast, in Los Angeles, the light artist Lili Lakich founded the Museum of Neon Art in 1981. It was designed to be 'the Disneyland of the Fine Arts', showing off the spectacular light effects of neon art along with the practical skill of their producers.[17] For the historian Michael Webb, neon activists like Lakich and Stern are part of a general cultural movement of the 1970s and '80s that brought colour, ornament and glamour back into architecture.[18] Among them was the Austrian Dusty Sprengnagel, who in the late twentieth century was always off on his travels in search of the bright lights. Sprengnagel captured the best of neon advertising around the world on his camera. At nightfall, he wrote in 1999, the cities of the world reveal themselves. They turn into a 'dark playground for shining dragons, cowboys, fish, lobsters, palms, naked bodies'.[19] Sprengnagel's illustrated volume Neon World shows the results of such games. Its pages reveal a world of shining advertisements reaching all the way from Las Vegas to Bangkok. (The last part of the book consists largely of advertising for Sprengnagel's own neon productions – but that is part and parcel of the world of neon.) His colleague Rudi Stern called Sprengnagel a sort of 'neon archaeologist', documenting an 'electric Pompeii for future visitors to our planet'.[20]

Many neon fans prefer to stay local rather than global in search of neon lights. In the 1970s Sheila Swan and Peter Laufer, a married couple living in Nevada, set out to explore their home state in a quest to scout out neon art. In the little town of Elko, Swan and Laufer found an advertisement for Shorty's Club which put a caricature of the somewhat vertically challenged owner of the bar up in lights. It even remained there long after Shorty had sold his club to a slightly taller entrepreneur.[21] In Winnemucca, halfway between the towns of Reno and Jackpot, Laufer and Swan came across a neon pig with wings, on the Flyin' Pig Bar-B-Q. It switched on and off in such a way that the hog pictured in blue neon lights

Manufacturing neon tube signs, 1933.

appeared to take off on its yellow wings. The authors dubbed it 'Pigasus'. The general feeling in Winnemucca, according to the luminous animal's owner Lee Armstrong, was that this was the most beautiful neon sign in the town.[22] The book by Swan and Laufer detailing 'neon' tours around Nevada begins with a picture of a simple neon heart on the wall of their home, symbolizing their passion for the shining tubes and for one another. It ends with a visit to Tom Romeo in Las Vegas, one-time head of the 'neon boneyard' there – a graveyard of neon signs where the advertisements for casinos such as the Golden Nugget, the Silver Slipper and the Aladdin were laid to rest.[23]

At first glance it looks as though the story of the glowing tubes can be left to the enthusiasts. Those who, like Vera Lutter, build sheds on factory roofs in order to document the dismantling of a much-loved advertisement. Those boffins who know all there is to know about the tubes that once were available in 40 different colours. Those who are therefore just as at home with ruby red illuminated advertisements as they are with midnight blue, uranium green and noviol gold. Those who have actually fixed the rubber hose on to the glass tube and know how and when to blow through the hose to keep the tube open, and how to shape letters, hearts, dragons and flying pigs, fill the vacuum with noble gas, apply the electrodes and seal the tube.[24] Their stories apparently give the last word on the subject of neon. Almost, that is.

Neon as Metaphor

Anyone taking on the subject of neon can't stick to the technical issues. Because, however short-lived the glory days of the tubes filled with noble gas, there is no way of ignoring the welter of literary texts, music and artworks to which the glow and the flicker have given rise. In the same way as Shorty in Elko and Lee Armstrong in Winnemucca adorned their businesses with neon signs, writers, intellectuals, musicians and scientists have been just as eager to set out their stalls by putting neon up in lights – that is, in the titles of their works.

This has been especially true of American writers. In 'Good Old Neon', one of the key stories by author David Foster Wallace (published in the collection *Oblivion* in 2004), neon advertisements highlighting letters and lighting up words become a symbol for the notion that there can be real communication in the afterlife.[25] In the novel *The Neon Bible*, written half a century before and un-published within the lifetime of its author, John Kennedy Toole, the glowing words of the Bible shine out red, yellow and blue from a church steeple, forming a living symbol of the banality and narrow-mindedness of a town in the deep South.[26] The glowing tubes were introduced to literature in 1947 by the novelist Nelson Algren in *The Neon Wilderness*, his narrative cycle devoted to the life of prostitutes, alcoholics and small-time crooks in Chicago.[27] Algren's book was in turn followed a few years later by John D. MacDonald's novel *The Neon Jungle*, which combined the locale of a run-down city with the gripping story of senseless violence.[28] From then on there was no stopping American writers from giving new works titles incorporating the word neon. From Mark McGarrity's *Neon Caesar*, Tony Kenrick's *Neon Tough*, James Lee Burke's *The Neon Rain* and Dick Lochte's *The Neon Smile* through to Matt and Bonnie Taylor's *The Neon Flamingo* – they all chose the symbol of our glowing tubes to evoke a world of violence and crime.[29] The fashion managed to cross the Atlantic. Beate Stein, the heroine of the novel *NeonNächte* by the German whodunnit author Sabine Deitmer, investigates a series of murders of tram conductresses.[30]

In other genres, too, the metaphor of neon has been high up there in the popularity stakes. North American poetry in particular seems to go in for titles based on neon advertising. *Neon Vernacular* is the title of a volume of poems by Yusef Komunyakaa; another is *Foreign Neon* by Daniel Halpern, while Tony Moffeit has a collection called *Neon Peppers*. The Canadian singer-poet Lucien Francoeur plumped for *Neon in the Night* and the American slam poet Michael Salinger kept to a simple *Neon*.[31] The poem 'Poetics', by the contemporary American August Kleinzahler, deals with childhood memories of a store called 'Shop-Rite Liquor' and highlights the 'unsuccessful neon' of this booze outlet as a key metaphor for his writing.[32]

In the main it is writers at the beginning of their careers who seem to find neon very attractive (particularly appropriate given that the Greek word means 'new'). *In Neon*, first performed in spring 2010, is the title of the first play by Julia Kandzora, born in Germany in 1982.[33] *Neon* was the title given in 2000 to his first novel by the then 23-year-old Dutch writer Niels Carels, while in 1953 the Austrian poet Alois Hergouth, 28 at the time, called his first collection of poems *Neon und Psyche*.[34] The title *Neon* was given to an unsuccessful literary journal for new American authors, founded by the writer Gilbert Sorrentino in New York in 1956, which folded in 1959 after its fifth edition.[35] The autobiography by Cherie Currie, lead singer of the '70s teen-rock band The Runaways, is entitled *Neon Angel* and was her first publication.[36] The debut film by Taiwanese director Tsai Ming-Liang glories in the title *The Rebels of the Neon God*.[37] *Néons* is the title of the debut novel by the French writer Denis Belloc, describing the experiences of a hooker in 1960s Paris.[38] This is certainly not the only neon story set in a red-light district, by either debut or experienced writers. 'The Neon Express', a poem by Claude Pélieu, describes among other things an ejaculating neon-man in a night-club called Wives & Whores.[39] In the poem 'Die Neonikone', by German writer Thomas Rosenlöcher, an apparently sensitive voyeur observes a prostitute in Amsterdam, who 'sticks out' her 'long, livid' tongue at him (whereupon the lily-livered passer-by beats a hasty retreat to Saxony).[40] A poem in Charles Plymell's 1970 collection *Neon Poems* pictures New York as an 'ecstatic asshole sucked like steaming clams'.[41] The poem 'BANGKOK [neon lights]', by the Vietnamese-American poet Mong-Lan, observes Thai dancers insert-ing table-tennis balls, small birds, needles and razor blades into their vaginas and then withdrawing them.[42]

Given these kinds of associations it is not surprising that cultural criticism, too, has turned its attention to the subject of the noble gas. 'The Neon Telephone' is the title of an essay by the American intellectual Theodore Roszak, in which he states his rejection of an American society dominated by consumerism and technology. An essay by the American art critic Dave Hickey about Las Vegas, where he lives, entitled 'A Home in the Neon', lambasts the elitist, middle-class, educated East Coast of America. In the book *Beneath the Neon*, the journalist Matthew O'Brien reports on homeless people living in the sewers under the streets of Las Vegas. In his much-quoted essay 'Neon Cages', the social scientist Lauren Lang-man argues that the modern consumer paradise – typified by the shopping mall – could give rise to an 'amusing techno-fascism'.[43]

Theodor W. Adorno would no doubt come to a similar con-clusion. In his *Philosophy of New Music*, art is associated with darkness, challenging the 'all-powerful neon-light style' of the culture industry.[44] Despite what Adorno says, however, musicians are often the biggest fans of neon. The sound recording data bank of the American Library of Congress has 77 entries in its catalogue for pieces of music with the word 'neon' in their titles. These include titles such as 'Neon Fool', 'Neon Women', 'Neon Lady', 'Neon Madonna', 'Neon Café', 'Neon Fire', 'Neon Moon' and 'Neon Zebra'. Not included in the data bank are songs by major musical figures such as Elton John ('In Neon'), Björk ('All Neon Like'),

Kraftwerk ('Neonlicht'), Black Sabbath ('Neon Knights') and Iggy Pop ('Neon Forest').[45] They – and several others – are nevertheless available on iTunes, which in 2011 offered 5,860 results for the search term 'neon'.[46] One of the most successful albums from the start of the twenty-first century is *Neon Bible*, by the band Arcade Fire.[47] The Neonboys, a band from the 1970s New York scene, paved the way for punk and New Wave (their singer, Richard Hell, later became the frontman for the influential band Television).[48] In 1981 Dirk Timmermans and Frank Vloeberghs, alias Dirk Da Davo and T. B. Frank, founded their electronic rock band The Neon Judgement.[49] In 'The Sound of Silence' (1964) Paul Simon and Art Garfunkel sang of neon as the god of the age.[50]

The American boxer Leon Spinks does not exactly fit into this idiosyncratic cultural history. Dubbed 'Neon Leon', he beat the ageing world champion Muhammad Ali in Las Vegas in February 1978 and lost the return match seven months later.[51] And in the animal world, the freshwater fish *Paracheirodon innesi* (from the Upper Amazon) has an iridescent red stripe along the rear half of its body and is commonly known as the neon tetra.[52]

Fans of boxing and tropical fish are as nothing compared to sculptors and installation artists in their particular devotion to neon. Unlike the photographer Vera Lutter on the factory roof in Queens, they do not stop at simply recording the flowing signs (or their disappearance). They do the shaping or get others to shape the shining tubes to realize their artistic projects. The erotic associations of neon tubes were recognized as early as the 1930s by the first neon artist, the Czech Zdeněk Pešánek, whose sculptures featured light from coloured neon tubes playing on intimately entwined male and female bodies.[53] At the start of the 1950s, using abstract neon objects, Luciano Fontana realized his concept of 'Spazialismo', the three-dimensional effect of the image.[54] In one exhibition of his work, the artist Mario Merz installed a saying of the famous Vietnamese military commander Võ Nguyên Giáp in shining neon letters on an igloo. This read: 'If the enemy masses his forces, he loses ground; if he scatters, he loses strength.'[55] One of the neon signs of the American artist Bruce Nauman, installed in the window of his studio in 1967, declared: 'The true artist helps the world by revealing mystic truths'.[56] A work by the artist Richard Serra, otherwise known for his heavyweight steel sculptures, announced this good news in neon letters: 'God is a loving father'.[57] South African artist Kendell Geers represented another theological position at the art biennale in Lyons in 2005 with a neon sign bearing the words 'HOLY FUCK'.[58] A neon work by the English artist Katie Paterson consists of her telephone number (07757-001122). If you call the number, you can listen to the Icelandic glacier Vatnajokull melting.[59] Less neon-friendly, on the other hand, is the Clan du Néon, a French environmentalist group that achieved notoriety in 2008 under their slogan: 'For cities of light, against neon cities'. To save energy and avoid unnecessary light emission, their members secretly switched off neon advertising on shops at night.[60]

A Cultural History of the Glow and the Flicker

Faced with this barrage of literary works, music compositions and performances, a cultural history of neon light should home in on the way in which people – not just those of Rattlesnake Gulch – reacted to this key example of modernist technology. It should ideally discuss the ways in which the glowing tubes have been judged by those witnessing their development, including those who were all for them and those who saw them as emblematic of the decline of Western civilization. It should also discuss how art, literature and music have developed out of the world of neon and commented upon it. Cultural historians have demonstrated how valid it is to place the night and night lighting in a historical context, at the same time analysing the ways in which writers, journalists and artists of earlier periods have arrived at their contrasting views, fantasies and nightmares in illuminated environments.[61] At this point the views of the cultural historian Andreas Bernard seem particularly useful. He recommends seeing everyday technologies in relation to the 'aura of alienation', tracing them back to their key historical turning points – that is, not focusing on the humdrum normality of technology but its 'disconcerting force'.[62]

And indeed, neon can be disconcerting – and this is the basis of its force as a metaphor. The colours of neon light are as glaring as popular culture. The flashing light of advertisements and the conditioned responses to their programmed effects seem to cultural critics to be representative of the hysteria and the programmed (and programming) nature of media banalaties. Neon advertising, blown by mouth and shaped by hand, exists in order to attract the attention of the masses. Its writing is intended to be seen and read, its invitation to buy to be acted upon. It is this very simplicity that strikes critics of mass culture as typical of modern commerce. Those who feel alienated by neon light, or react to it with incomprehension or disgust, do so as a result of an overall hostility towards triviality and technology. They do not care whether neon lights send out a multicoloured glow. For them the tubes represent nothing but superficiality.

Those who consider themselves to be more kindly disposed towards the glowing signs, be they neon geeks or neon poets, do so because they get a buzz out of modernity. They are all for the dazzle of popular culture, the dynamism of urban life and individual creativity, programmed effects and simple messages. They hanker after individual creativity expressed both in the production and consumption of neon light. In the twentieth century, writers, artists and intellectuals continually ventured into the neon jungle in a bid to get away from the cultural elite and from what they saw as their self-important pretensions. Artists sought the glow of such objects and the practical skills associated with creating advertising signs, keen to make a bold public declaration of their love for what frequently symbolized a run-down city environment. American essayists identified themselves with Las Vegas in order to put as much distance as possible between themselves and the East Coast establishment. Poets took up the glow and the flicker so that the dynamism of the present might somehow rub off on their poems. Neon has always functioned in such a programmatic way.

To understand the reasoning behind such shifts of scene one could do no better than try to blur the distinction between fiction and biography and treat both texts and writers as historical actors in the world of neon.[63] This book tells the life stories of individual writers, artists and commentators – but in so doing it is not based on the dated view that the biographies of their creators can explain texts and works of art. Instead this micro-historical perspective serves to portray neon lights, artworks and writers as equally interesting characters in the world of neon. This enables us to describe more accurately the confrontations and interactions between flashing tubes and people in the street.

For one thing, the writers, musicians and artists captivated by neon mostly did not fall for the temptation of seeing the city as disembodied and post-human. They were interested (and exceptions prove the rule) above all in the people they came across: men and women bathed in this light. These were often the losers of modernity, the underprivileged inhabitants of troubled inner-city areas. In the world of neon, writers found what they were looking for: the would-be naked, seemingly authentic existence of drunks, hookers, gamblers and small-time crooks.

This is the ironic twist in the story of the glowing tubes. They were developed as an element of business technology to advertise hairdressing salons, cinemas and department stores and boost commercial success. But when they lost the charm of the new, they became a symbol of urban decay, their light shining above all on those looked down upon as losers. Thus neon light became the favourite metaphor of those observers of the city who based their defiant traditionalism on naked reality. 'Unsuccessful neon' on liquor stores, once upon a time hailed by the American poet August Kleinzahler, shines out over this study of the glow and the flicker, and so lights up reality.

Mark Bilbanke, *Sir William Ramsay*, 1913, oil on canvas.

2 ROSES ARE BLOOMING IN MANHATTAN

'I Should Call It Novum'

On Tuesday 7 June 1898, in a laboratory at University College London, chemistry professor William Ramsay and his assistant Morris Travers were experimenting with liquefied air. They were on the track of noble gases, up until then undiscovered elements which they reckoned to be there in the atmosphere. Four years earlier Ramsay, along with his colleague Lord John William Rayleigh, had already discovered argon, three years earlier helium and, one week earlier, on 31 May 1898, a gas he called krypton.[1] He was convinced that he would find more of these gases, so filling the last places left in the periodic table established by the Russian chemist Dmitri Mendeleev in 1869.

Using a new air-liquefying apparatus, the duo of Ramsay and Travers made giant leaps forward around this time. It was on this Tuesday in early summer that they also managed to extract an unknown substance from liquid nitrogen. They tested to see how it reacted with oxygen and finally analysed its emission spectrum. They could make out quite unremarkable violet, red and green lines, but they knew they were dealing with a new gas. The same afternoon, Willie Ramsay, the chemist's thirteen-year-old son, paid a visit to the laboratory. Actually he had come to see krypton for himself. Instead he was immediately confronted with the latest discovery. 'What are you going to call it?', his father asked him. 'I should call it Novum', Willie answered. 'I think that we had better go to the Greek, and call it Neon', his father opined. And Willie had to go along with that.[2]

This was the eureka moment. But the true story of neon light did not really begin until William Ramsay and Morris Travers filled what is called a Plücker tube with the new gas, causing an electrical discharge. Ramsay threw the switch of the detonator coil on the apparatus. He and Travers then reached for the prisms that were always lying at the ready on the laboratory table in the case of such experiments. With these they were hoping to make out particular rays of colour in the spectrum. But the two chemists had no need of technical aids to see what was taking place in the Plücker tube. As Morris Travers remembered later, a 'blaze of crimson' flooded from the tube – a glowing colour, holding the two chemists 'for some moments spell-bound' on seeing the result. Ramsay and Travers called two colleagues working in the basement of the lab. All four men stared transfixed at this glowing red phenomenon. And so in this 'dramatic way', as Travers later explained, the long sought-after substance made its appearance. In the lab log Ramsay and Travers noted the 'magnificent spectrum' of the gas. Then they called an end to their day's work in the lab, Ramsay inviting Travers to his home where, after dinner, they wrote an article on their latest discoveries, sending it in a sealed envelope to the Royal Society.[3] Six years later, William Ramsay travelled to Stockholm as the first British person to receive the Nobel Prize for Chemistry for his work on the discovery of noble gases.

Neon light has become a standard metaphor of modern technology. And at first glance Ramsay's lab comes across as typical of the places where such technology was forged. Historians describe the era in which Ramsay attained international notoriety as a key period for science. In the late nineteenth century physics and chemistry labs almost became factories. There developed what was, in the twentieth century, to be termed Big Science – the close association of industry and scientific research and a whole closed world largely impenetrable to non-specialists.[4] The discovery of X-rays in 1895 and radioactivity in the following year brought new relationships to physical bodies and the material world. A universe of mysterious flows and rays was born, overturning common perceptions.[5] We can see the lighting up of neon tubes in the context of this historical moment, a new sort of glow the source of which is a total mystery to those of us who are not experts.

After the turn of the century, William Ramsay also began to get involved with radioactivity, thus turning his attention to the brave new world of chemistry. But in fact the British scientist belonged more to an earlier strain of science associated with its nineteenth-century empirical and positivist origins. The era is seen as the golden age of chemistry, when the discipline enjoyed an enormous amount of authority and marked up success after success, discovery after discovery. However, it found itself challenged by new approaches and the daring theories of nuclear physics and lost ground.[6] (This is supported by a historian of science who shows that the selection committee of the Nobel Prize for Chemistry, awarded since 1901, favoured this traditional approach over the more theoretical tendency.[7])

Neon, discovered during the golden age of chemistry, was sought after and not theorized, discovered and not developed. In the quest for still unknown noble gases extending over several years William Ramsay continually undertook research on new minerals obtained from the British Museum. Along with Morris Travers he heated meteorites and investigated their gases with a spectroscope. Their work involved advanced hands-on expertise. The two men blew their own glass containers (Travers was particularly adept at this) and they honed their instruments so that they could work with the smallest possible quantities. They acquired samples from hot springs in England and Scotland. They travelled to Cauterets in the Pyrenees, to collect substances in that area not far from Lourdes. Ramsay went to Iceland, extending the search to the hot springs there. The decisive new development in the discovery of additional noble gases was a technological innovation: the apparatus put together by Carl von Linde (and copied by William Hampson) for the liquefaction of air.[8] However, in the case of Ramsay's research one was dealing with the discovery of natural substances rather than synthetic developments. Instead, his experiments developed out of those of the eighteenth century in which the British naturalist Henry Cavendish discovered air residues, very accurately predicting their proportion in the atmosphere. Ramsay possessed a copy of a biography of Cavendish of 1849 and in the 1880s put a note 'look into this' against the passage in which that experiment of almost a century before was described.[9]

Ramsay's own statements fit in with the more traditional discoveries of the nineteenth century, more than with highly theoretical twentieth-century science. In one personal essay the chemist traced his successes back to the simple curiosity of a man interested in the details of the natural world. He wrote: 'The beginning is in small things . . . A drop of water; a grain of sand; an insect; a blade of grass.'[10] Neon, the rare gas, was of the same order for him. Ramsay compared its glow to the phenomenon known for millennia – the aurora borealis or Northern Lights. They too were products of an electrified atmosphere, and admired not only by experts in the labs of triumphant modern science. In the far north they shone in the night sky, visible to everyone.[11]

The Unreal City

Those who discovered noble gases were creatures of the modern, nineteenth-century metropolis, and yet were so struck by neon light that at times they described it in terms of elemental imagery taken from the natural world. So, William Ramsay likened the glow of neon light to the Northern Lights, as an amazing natural phenomenon. This comparison was rather nostalgic, considering that artificial light had long ago transformed the city into an increasingly *un*natural, artificial world – an electric glare had become the norm in urban centres by that time. In London, sixteen years before Ramsay and Travers stood in amazement at the sight of the flaming red substance in the Plücker tube, the first modern illuminated pre-neon advertisement had put Edison's name up in lights using 100 light bulbs. Electrification and modern illuminated advertising went hand in hand, there as much as in other metropolitan centres. In the high streets of towns and cities the gas lamps of the past were replaced by tall, brightly lit arc lights.[12] Paris boulevards came alive with them in the 1870s. Electric light came to St

Stephen's Cathedral Square in Vienna in 1882. The new electrical industry and advertising experts maintained extremely close contact. Shop windows and the fronts of buildings were lit up and the new electric light was used to put trade logos and goods clearly on show. During the late nineteenth century, advertising artists developed newer and newer techniques for creating and playing with slogans and images that used tubes flashing in sequence.[13] European metropolitan centres vied with one another for the unofficial title of 'city of light' and defined the existence of modern illuminated advertising as a key feature of attractive urban spaces.[14]

Cultural historians of such electrically lit metropolitan centres interpret these developments in very different ways. Wolfgang Schivelbusch argues that the former 'warm light' of the gas lamps was replaced by 'cold' electric light. Instead of a natural flame, urban people were exposed to artificial lighting. In addition, electrification brought about a focus on increasing commercialization. Control over energy became centralized.[15] Joachim Schlör, too, reads the spread of urban lighting as a move towards cultural uniformity, robbing what were previously dark streets of their mystery.[16] According to John Jakle, electric lighting brought about a 'nocturnal geography' – redefining thoroughfares, casting important buildings in a new light and transforming urban experience.[17] The cultural historian Janet Ward sees the 1920s, with its advertising and light effects, as a precursor to postmodernity with its apparent view that there is nothing left but superficiality, there being no distinction any more between light and dark, profundity and spectacle.[18] Different critics, on the other hand, see the electrification of city lighting as the birth of a new, possibly liberating, urban culture. The illuminated metropolitan centre, according to an analysis by the historian Lewis Erenberg, became a kind of collective dream available to urban dwellers of all social strata since it combined commercialization and cultural emancipation.[19]

Critics are unanimous in the view that the effects of electric light and illuminated advertisements made the cities of Europe and North America appear less and less real. In the last two decades of the nineteenth century, street lighting and advertising signs turned cities into almost imaginary spaces. In New York as early as the 1890s, an advertisement for the company Heinz consisted of a 15-m-high gherkin made up of green light bulbs.[20] In the early twentieth century, lights created gigantic bouquets of flowers on the walls of buildings. A larger-than-life-size man made of light poured water on to a 'stainless-steel corset'. People in the street watched gin made up of dots of light being poured into glasses made up of dots of light and a bird of light stretch its wings at the behest of Budweiser beer.[21] Above a hotel on 38th Street, 20,000 tubes formed a Roman chariot pulled by galloping horses, including the driver wielding a whip and the wheels flashing as they turned. While advertising in colour did not appear in American magazines until the late 1920s, the streets of urban America gave birth to the 'age of light and colour' in which the neon tube was to play such a key role.[22]

In Germany, and particularly in Berlin, there was a similar development, if on a smaller scale. In 1898 the advertising slogan 'Raucht Manoli' (Smoke Manoli), surrounded by rotating bulbs, was the first moving illuminated advertisement in Berlin. The lights flashed so furiously that the cigarette brand's name, 'manoli', caught on as a popular term for 'crazy'.[23] A number of 'Leibniz-Cakes' illuminated signs advertised biscuits made by the firm of Bahlsen. An advertisement installed on Friedrichstrasse in 1912 represented drops of sparkling wine made up of light bulbs while a glass was filled from a bottle of 'Kupferberg Gold'. One bubble consisted of 1,600 bulbs – which the technology historian Günther Luxbacher considers an 'image resolution . . . of enormous quality'.[24] On the Potsdamer Platz a glass was filled with Odol mouthwash. On the Kurfürstendamm there were thousands of bulbs in an advertising installation weighing 10 tons that proclaimed the qualities of Scharlachberg brandy. The washing-powder slogan 'Persil bleibt Persil' (Persil Is Still Persil) was put across by means of yellow, red and green light bulbs plus, to complete the light spectacle, appropriately shining white tubes showing a dirty shirt being washed.[25] The media historian Anne Hoormann has described the world of the new illuminated advertisements as a key feature of culture in the roaring '20s – a network spreading throughout the city and developing its

The Kurfürstendamm at night, West Berlin, 1950s.

very own 'cinematography'. The flashing lights contributed to the 'cultural predominance of the visual' and thus to the increasing unreality of urban life.[26]

Shocking Red or Green with Envy

Neon light only became a standard image for writers and journalists around the middle of the twentieth century. However, the light bulb had attracted various earlier intellectuals, in particular those who poured scorn on the glaring lights and flashing letters. The writer William Dean Howells, one of the leading American novelists of the late nineteenth century, considered the new urban signs per se to be in bad taste and advertising to be an offence to any concept of beauty in architecture.[27] The poet Vachel Lindsay – a fan of the early cinema – was inspired to write a 'Rhyme about an Electrical Advertising Sign' on seeing the electric light installation of an advertisement for shirt collars. He described the installation as at first satanic like a snake, then suddenly appearing to be exotic in an African way, as: 'Blatant, mechanical, crawling and white / Wickedly red or malignantly green'.[28] For his part, George Moore described the neon advertisements at London's Piccadilly Circus as totally primitive and a 'disgrace to any planet'. Like the poet Vachel Lindsay, Moore went to town on the exotic associations. 'A cannibal feast is not more absurd', he wrote, stating that these 'monstrosities in flamboyant lights' were 'more ridiculous than anything savages ever invented'.[29] Undoubtedly such critical observers, however modern and shining their environment was, were going along with traditional motifs of writing about cities. In their day the *flâneurs* of the nineteenth century had described the city as a jungle, a haunt of the primitive.[30]

As was the case later in the age of neon, not all earlier observers of the glow and the flicker were critical. The Bauhaus artist László Moholy-Nagy, for example, based the development of his ideas on the association of art, public spaces and socialist utopias on film and luminous advertising.[31] Among architects, the concept of the 'architecture of light' signified a formal language combining streams of light and fluid lines in the frontages of buildings, thus producing a new, cinematographic form of architecture.

In the early twentieth century, both enemies and supporters of urban lighting noticed that the street was 'composed of nothing but light bulbs', as Wilhelm Hausenstein observed in Germany. The city appeared to be dominated by fantasy, to be 'lacking in substance'.[32] This perception was accompanied by the judgement that the harsh reality of urban poverty formed an increasingly stark contrast to the ever more spectacular flashing light shows. In 1928, Max Epstein wrote: '*Kriegskrüppel lässt man auf Strassen frieren, / Aber man lässt diese Strassen illuminieren*' (They leave war cripples to freeze in the streets, / But they light up these streets), thus highlighting the extremely superficial nature of the new mechanisms of illumination.[33] The chances were, neon advertising would simply add to this process.

Georges Claude's Light

In the well-illuminated Paris of the early twentieth century the chemist and engineer Georges Claude worked on a reasonably cheap method for producing oxygen required by hospitals and welders.[34] The by-products of this process, the noble gases discovered by William Ramsay and his British colleague, were used by Claude for further research. In the course of this he achieved the amazing red that the four London chemists had been so impressed by in 1898. For Ramsay and his colleagues the colour of the charged neon had been simply an interesting side effect. But Claude could not get over this effect. He experimented with the diameter of the tubes, and finally with tubes of only half a centimetre, thus intensifying the red of the neon. He also worked on the other noble gases and their light production, finding the blue of argon particularly rewarding. In addition he increased the possible varieties of brightly coloured glow by colouring the inside of the tubes. In December 1910 he presented the first neon lighting that he had created himself. It decorated the front of the Grand Palais during the Paris Salon de l'Automobile et du Cycle using tubes 35 m long.[35] It was another five years before Claude managed to produce a non-corrosive electrode, making the illuminated tube so simple and practical that there was no bar to everyday use. In the meantime he achieved great fame by developing new methods for employing gas in the First World War. This work won him the highest military honours and membership of the Academy of Sciences.[36]

Georges Claude – self-promoter, entertainer and later collaborator with the Nazis – is an ideal figure for the story of the development of spectacle. Whereas William Ramsay had followed a lifelong career as a chemist right up to winning the Nobel Prize, Claude broke off his study of chemistry after a short while out of boredom. Instead he started a career as an engineer. Also, unlike the more 'natural scientist' Ramsay, Claude did not see insects, drops of water or blades of grass as the source of his scientific curiosity. He was inspired by reading Jules Verne's fantasy novels. According to Claude, that was where research was to be found in 'an amusing

Water chute at Luna Park, Paris, 1936.

and entertaining form', whereas so many scientists were 'boring and single-minded'. Only Jules Verne's science fiction had awoken him to science. 'Without hesitation', he recognized the novelist as 'his master'.[37] As an engineer, he tried to live by Jules Verne's fictions, applying his inventions beyond the sphere of science.[38]

Claude's enjoyment of effects closely influenced his work on the gas-filled glass tubes. He presented his new neon tube at Luna Park, an amusement park in Paris, in 1911. Alongside the roller coaster, the ghost train and the water chute he set up a stand to show off his latest discoveries. He sent the steam from liquefied air aloft and dipped tennis balls in it, thus causing them to burst. It goes without saying that he treated visitors to the fairground with a demonstration of the phantasmagorical light effects of the noble gases, glowing in their various colours.[39] His research work brought him just as much spectacular credit as at Luna Park when he joined the right-wing extremist group Action Française and stood as a candidate for parliament in the constituency of Fontainebleau. At an election meeting in December 1927 he arranged for a 5-ton truck to pull up in front of the theatre in Fontainebleau to deliver containers of liquefied gas, oxygen, transformers and other equipment.[40] For the benefit of his politically aware audience Claude lit up corn-flowers draped across the stage with red neon light, thus making them appear to be black. He also flooded a bouquet of roses with mercury light, making this too appear as black. Then, finally, he switched off the current to the tubes to communicate the message that the members of parliament would, after all, have to transform themselves just as quickly according to the will of the voters in the same way as these flowers had changed colour. The aim of the performance, as of Claude's overall political programme itself, was support for technocracy. What was needed – according to Claude – were men of action, inventors, men of discovery, to bring an end to the cosy coterie of professional politicians.[41]

The New Tube

Georges Claude's bid for a seat in parliament was unsuccessful.[42] Nevertheless, neon was to catch on more and more, becoming a new lighting technology employed in a variety of contexts. In 1911, for the celebration to mark Normandy's 1,000-year birthday, Claude's coloured tubes illuminated the church of Saint-Ouen in Rouen.[43] From 1919 neon lit up the main entrance at the Paris Opera. Soon neon tubes were used at airports and for routes in-volving night flights, particularly since they were extremely easy to see in fog and could be employed on a permanent basis given their low running costs.[44] In the auditoriums of theatres neon tubes were placed near the floor, showing the audience the way in the dark. Prob-ably less of a boon to humanity were the cocktail glasses developed by Charles Lee in the 1930s, the stems of which lit up whenever they were put down on the bar.[45] The German engineer Paul Möbius promoted the effective use of neon tubes to light up ancient castles and stalagmite caves.[46] It is hardly surprising that, in Holland in 1931, hothouse cucumbers and strawberries were flooded with light from neon tubes instead of the sun.[47] Neon was even used in the early development stages of television sets – in 1929, in fact, when the development of television was being heralded by the *New York Times* as a 'new radio age'.[48]

But it was mainly in advertising that neon gained particular significance. Jacques Fonseque, a friend of Claude, was the first to market illuminated tubes, shaped as letters and symbols, as advertising signs. In 1912 the Palais Coiffeur barber's shop on the Boulevard Montmartre, Paris, was the first business in history to have a neon advertising sign. In 1913 the first building to have its roof adorned with neon writing displayed white letters over a metre high advertising 'CINZANO'.[49] By only the following year there were 160 neon advertisements in Paris;[50] by 1927 over 6,000. On the corner of the Champs-Elysées and the Rue Pierre Charron a beaming neon sun shone out from the roof of a building from 1930 onwards – neon letters in English encouraging local passers-by and tourists to 'VISIT EGYPT' and promising them 'ETERNAL SUNSHINE' and a 'LAND OF WONDERFUL TREASURES'.[51] (The most prominent advertising installation of this period, the name 'CITROËN' emblazoned in huge letters down three sides of the Eiffel Tower, was admittedly not made up of neon lights but of 250,000 light bulbs.[52]) Advertising artists created sophisticated silhouettes made of neon and supplied them to the owners of businesses, tradesmen, restaurants and churches. At Novilux in Paris in 1935 a neon sign in blue in the shape of a cross cost 625 francs; in pale pink 725 francs. A red or blue sign showing a pig, a hat, an umbrella or a goose was yours for 650 francs; a sign showing a lady's glove or a pair of spectacles cost 585 francs.[53] As for the illuminated writing to be seen everywhere in the French capital, Josephine Baker sang that 'tout Paris' were enjoying themselves beneath it. The artist Fernand Léger, on the other hand, in an essay on the 'giant letters', objected to them being projected into his apartment and to the 'unheard-of excess' and disorder causing the 'walls to explode'.[54]

The new tube quickly spread all over the world. In Germany the neon lights only caught on in the late 1920s since the direct current network held up their progress.[55] But then flowing neon writing gradually replaced open-air advertisements that used combinations of different light bulbs.[56] By this time a variety of noble gas advertisements were already installed in Tokyo. One of the largest Japanese daily papers had an advertising sign in front of the Imperial Palace, while in the entertainment quarter of Asakusa a sign proclaimed the 'HQ of Beef Stew'.[57] In Mexico City, Havana, Melbourne, Wellington and Shanghai, neon firms were also in business by 1930.[58]

In the USA the new technology travelled from Los Angeles to the east. In 1923 a car dealer from Los Angeles purchased two neon signs in Paris. From then on, high above the streets of the Californian metropolis they proclaimed the Packard make of cars in orange letters.[59] The roofs of Californian Standard Oil service stations were equipped with neon tubes in 1927, their silhouettes lighting up the night.[60] Over 60 churches and cathedrals made themselves known by means of neon crosses by the end of the 1920s.[61] In Pittsburgh, Pennsylvania, a neon installation like a vast film set advertised fridges for the Frigidaire company, an enormous model of which opened and closed its doors all night long. For the amateur gardeners of Worcester, Massachusetts, there was an advertisement showing an illuminated lawnmower with a yellow handle, blue wheels and red cutting blades on green neon grass.[62] In Los Angeles the Olympic Rings were already shining out red, white, blue, gold and green a year and a half before the opening of the games in 1932. This neon sign, in its day the largest, had been turned on by the mayor himself on 4 February 1931 at 8 p.m.[63] After the end of prohibition in 1933 neon advertisements spread like wildfire, above all advertising beer.[64] In 1934 alone nearly 20,000 neon advertisements went up in Manhattan and Brooklyn.[65] The economic crisis accelerated this spread even further. Neon was cheap and seemed to be the most practical method of advertising a business in hard times.[66]

The picture palaces, too, in the American cinema boom of the 1930s could not do without neon lights.[67] The noble gas represented glamour and glitz, radiating its reflected elegance over the cinema audience. The Earl Carroll Theater in Hollywood, totally framed by neon effects, announced this connection in 1938 in glowing letters: 'Through these portals pass the most beautiful girls in the world'.[68]

The advantages of neon advertising were obvious. It was more restrained and on a smaller scale than the monumental illuminated advertisements of the early twentieth century but impressively colourful all the same.[69] It did not require expensive equipment to be turned on and off in order to simulate movement as in the case of light bulbs. The neon tube provided five times as much red light for the same amount of current. Into the bargain it gave a unique brilliance, particularly on rainy evenings.[70] The wide choice of colours and extreme malleability made it possible to produce any number of names, logos and effects. In 1936 the newspaper boys of the *Los Angeles Times* became running headlines for this flexibility. They wore aprons with flashing neon signs on them. These protected them against the traffic – and in addition advertised the 'streamlined news' of the paper, as the editorship put it proudly.[71] Neon literally put movement into advertising.

One might see the boom for these tubes in the 1930s as a further stage in the history of modernity's gradual ushering-in of a society of spectacle. In the 1930s neon letters even created advertising slogans up in the night sky on zeppelins.[72] Neon was part of a culture of skyscrapers and airship flights seemingly without any connection to the material world. Modernization and Americanization, a frenetic popular culture, the elevator, the aeroplane, flowing neon signs flashing as if by magic . . . all this came together in the Jazz Age of the interwar years as part of what seemed like this era's lack of lasting substance.[73] For Wolfgang Schivelbusch, the relation of neon advertising to the previous methods of illumination is 'like a streamlined racing car to the first petrol jalopy'. Before, only flashing single dots of light were visible. Now the city was flooded with modern, dynamic streams of light.[74]

Yet the real advantage of neon light was that its effect was not too glaring and overly spectacular. Claude's coloured tubes provided a considerably more pleasing light than the light bulbs that had been used previously in illuminated advertisements.[75] That was the secret of their success. They did not dazzle people. They could be read with ease. When they were new, neon signs represented luxury and security. Even credit agencies were supplied with lavishly glowing neon signs.[76] Also, neon letters made possible a more extensive formal vocabulary than signs made up of single dots of light. The borders of the letters and the lines appeared rounded. In fact, the general 'streamline' style of the 1930s derived its aesthetic nature and appeal from, among other things, the animation of neon tubes giving illuminated signs a three-dimensional, sculptural quality.[77] Contemporary witnesses judged the neon advertisements to be less frenetic – that is, not as vulgar – as the countless dots of light of other types of installation.[78] In their book *Die elektrischen Leuchtröhren* of 1933 Walter Köhler and Robert Rompe recommended a combination of neon tubes and ordinary light bulbs. This gave what they called 'an extremely warm light like candlelight'.[79] And the author of a manual published in 1939 contrasted the 'harsh disconcerting glare' of light bulbs with the 'soft' light, 'pleasing to the eye', of the neon tube.[80] The new technology thus seemed to be able to make the spectacular more acceptable.

Not Just 'Any Ordinary Mortal'

The magazine *Claude Neon News* had a circulation of 17,000 in the USA in 1929.[81] It reported on the continuing triumphs and blessings spread throughout the world by the firm of Claude Neon – created by Georges Claude – and its installations. It just as roundly condemned the enemies of the organization – that is, the companies and individuals who had, without permission, appropriated Claude Neon techniques and made neon advertisements themselves. There was a good reason why Claude Neon could afford its own magazine. In order to spread the technology developed by Georges Claude throughout the world he had developed an early form of franchising

– the company magazine further advanced this model. Claude sold to partners all over the world a licence to use the electrode patented by him, giving them a discount on the gases neon and argon. Thus it became a globally represented concern, including in countries such as Canada, Cuba, New Zealand, Australia, Japan and China. It was the USA, above all, that was covered by a network of franchisees. The advertising signs of nationwide companies such as Packard, Standard Oil and Lucky Strike were developed by Claude Neon.[82] Restaurants, hotels, cinemas and amusement parks advertised using their tubes. Coca-Cola signs, designed by Claude's sub-contractors, appeared in every American city. Florists, bakeries, carpet stores and sausage factories adorned their buildings with them. The firm had a near monopoly.[83] Georges Claude had become a businessman recognized all over the globe. He missed no opportunity to add to his personal fame. 'Claude Neon' was a household name in American English. Many people thought that this was what the founder of the company was called: first name, Claude; surname, Neon.[84]

This myth was not put about by *Claude Neon News*. But the magazine of course only rarely reported on events that cast even a slightly questioning light on the new illumination technology. (A short article of 1929 represents the pinnacle of journalistic neutrality with its report that a Claude Neon skull had been taken down again at a crossroads in Detroit as it had struck passers-by as 'a bit too gruesome'.[85]) In general, *Claude Neon News* acted like the publication of an evangelical organization. The magazine printed all sorts of evidence in favour of conversion to the cause, such as reports, letters and statements by business people emphasizing the decisive, massive influence of neon advertising on their life and enterprises. On 1 August 1929, for instance, the magazine quoted the manager of the Sagamore Hotel in Rochester, New York, who praised his new advertisement bought from Claude Neon: 'Its dignity, attractiveness and its visibility have been commented upon favorably both by our transient and permanent guests.'[86] From Chicago came the enthusiastic message from the manager of the Sheridan Plaza Hotel saying: 'I now believe in signs!' And he believed these were 'Signs of prosperity, signs of progress'. He declared that: 'I believe sincerely that it is actually bringing us in an additional revenue of $50,00 a day.'[87] The automotive dealer Edward Bartholomew, of North Troy in New York State, set an example of great enterprise, the editors thought, in the face of the 'most vociferous calamity howlers' bemoaning the worldwide economic crisis then unfolding. On 13 August 1930 Bartholomew praised the qualities of his new illuminated Ford sign in a letter to the Claude Neon branch in nearby Schenectady. His advertisement had admittedly been a bit more expensive than the imitations otherwise available. But, he stated, it had been worthwhile getting hold of it. Bartholomew emphatically lauded the 'artisticness of the entire job'. Since the installation of the sign, the number of customers had increased.[88] In the same edition the management of the Mandarin Restaurant in Miami, Florida, announced with a mixture of humility and pride that: 'We think we were very fortunate in being one of the first in Miami to have one of your displays.'[89] Florenz Ziegfeld, impresario of the 'Ziegfeld Follies', the most famous dance troupe in New York, on the other hand, proved to be a little less modest. 'The name of Ziegfeld', Ziegfeld said, 'looks mighty good to me in those alluring tubes of color.'[90]

Of course *Claude Neon News* also celebrated the inventor of the neon tube himself. A man such as Georges Claude was not just 'any ordinary mortal' but in the public perception almost a 'mythical super-being'. His story was 'more interesting than fiction' – but he nevertheless retained 'the human qualities that make him loved and trusted by those who know him'. The world was forever indebted to this 'French Edison'. His story was the story of progress. It was 'an honour', the magazine informed the franchisees, to be associated with the activities of Georges Claude.[91]

At home in France Georges Claude in fact became a star – albeit, as the French historian Christine Blondel puts it, a 'star of collaboration'. In the Second World War Claude came out clearly on the side of Nazi Germany. In a number of newspapers he argued for collaboration, and put forward his views in public appearances. As was fitting for the father of neon he was happy with any effect he could produce. In one of his pro-German speeches, for example, he talked about the self-sacrifice of Christ and of Joan of Arc. He declared that it would take a personal sacrifice on his part to convince the public of the sincerity of his political position – and to emphasize this argument, he swallowed an allegedly lethal quantity of strychnine in front of the audience (he survived, it was said, as a result of the hearty dinner he had consumed before the speech).[92] After the liberation of France, Georges Claude was arrested in Nancy in August 1944, condemned to life imprisonment after the end of the war and released on 2 January 1950 at the age of 79, thanks to the involvement of influential friends.[93] Whereas William Ramsay, the one who discovered the red flare, was awarded the Nobel Prize at the end of his career, Georges Claude, once a 'mythical super-being' and the father, as it were, of the neon light, died a partly despised, partly forgotten figure.[94]

Neon in the Plural

Given Claude's biography it is tempting to read the success of neon light as a typical episode in the history of global capitalism, devoid of content but continually exploiting effects. Spectacle and consumption thus go hand in hand. The *Claude Neon News* that churned out stories of ever more prosperous global commerce through the most desperate years of worldwide economic crisis comes across as a caricature of modern marketing, totally divorced from individual and material realities. Neon light, its effects and its salesmen seem to fit seamlessly into the commercial and entertainment apparatus of modernity, transforming twentieth-century cities in particular into spaces dominated by hyper-reality and sales techniques. According to Guy Debord, in the society of the spectacle the world is reduced to one of products. (The 'signs of the dominant organization of production', Debord says, are 'at the same time the ultimate end-products of that organization'.[95]) We could apply such a view to the neon city. These brightly coloured lights promoted by Georges Claude's aggressive sales techniques simultaneously advertised goods and of course themselves as well. They seem to illuminate an ugly period in this social transformation.[96]

But the story of those new neon advertisements can also be read in a different way. Of course Georges Claude built up a worldwide company network, fought off his competitors with every means at his disposal and constructed his own quasi-religious company mythology. Nevertheless these new brightly flashing advertisements were in the main installed by small enterprises such as hairdressers, hotel managements, and restaurant owners. Neon offered them the opportunity to put up attractive advertising signs at a relatively low cost. And the technology not only caught on because it could go one better than glaring city advertising but because it made it possible for small companies and outfits to put up sophisticated signs on every main street. Even in small, remote American towns the public spaces did not look uniformly bland but were often lit up in a variety of colours and shapes. At the same time, in the late 1920s and '30s, particularly after Georges Claude's patent had expired, the production of neon signs developed into a new form of craft. For individually produced signs for shops, hotels and restaurants, special types of writing and patterns were created, and the tubes were blown by mouth and shaped by hand. In the 1930s, around 5,000 glass blowers were working on the production of neon advertisements in the USA.[97] Even if, in the case of Georges Claude, we are dealing with an early global player and an unrivalled effects showman, the triumphant progress of the business contributed to the development of a new craft skill that could not be carried out by machines.

Eddie's Institute

In Manhattan, on the corner of 125th Street and Madison Avenue, there was once the only organized school for neon designers, the Egani Institute. It represented an aesthetic approach that was totally market-oriented. For the founder of the institute, Edward Seise, ornamentation and abstract forms were highly suspect. At Egani (short for Eddie's Glass and Neon Institute) producing neon meant simply shaping letters – no more, no less. Nevertheless, generations of advertising artists were graduates of the Institute.[98]

Anyone unable to attend Eddie's Institute or take up an apprenticeship with a neon craftsman had to educate himself with the aid of technical literature. A variety of relevant manuals appeared on the market in the '30s giving people advice on setting up their own neon workshop. In the United States Samuel Miller and Donald Fink's *Neon Signs: Manufacture – Installation – Maintenance* was available for reference after 1935. In Great Britain there was W. L. Schallreuter's introduction to *Neon Tube Practice*. Competing with him was the manual by a certain S. Gold. In Germany the engineer Paul Möbius published an introduction to the 'manufacture, application and installation' of neon lights.

These manuals, unlike *Claude Neon News*, did not preach the religion of franchise-capitalism and the mythical superman Georges Claude but presented down-to-earth introductions to a new craft. Miller and Fink (who were connected with the electricity industry and therefore not without their own vested interest) itemized what was needed in the way of materials and conditions – for example, a workbench with a fireproof cover, running water, gas supply, blower fan and various burners. With these available, the work could begin. Because, according to Miller and Fink, a neon sign was relatively simple, it could be constructed by 'anyone who has the mechanical ability and intelligence to apply his knowledge'.[99] After thus reassuring their readers, the authors went through the different types of neon advertisements – from the 'swing sign' hanging on a horizontal bar on the front of a building to the vertical 'upright sign'; from the 'outline skeleton sign' running along the corners of a building to rigs on the roofs. The neon sign for a gas service station on a free-standing pillar, called the 'pedestal sign', was introduced, while a 'vestibule sign' could adorn an entrance – in the case of theatre and cinema entrances this was a 'marquee'.[100]

The manuals naturally also described layout principles. Gold, the British manual writer, warned artists that the word 'CAFÉ' arranged vertically would look like incomprehensible Chinese characters to English people viewing it. This was particularly true if the E was given an accent. In general, one should follow the rule that horizontal writing is easier to read than vertical – and that the gaps between vertically placed letters should be made smaller to increase their readability. (Here Gold proclaimed that 'readability' was a word he had just invented.[101]) The German Paul Möbius also warned against placing letters vertically. Surprisingly, given the historical context – his book appeared in 1938 – he recommends 'total freedom in the choice of form'. Möbius only listed modern writing styles and not the Gothic script usually associated with the Third Reich.[102]

The illustrative manuals proved that the production of neon advertisements did not have to be the monopoly of a centrally controlled and global organization (even if Georges Claude would have preferred it to have remained so). On the contrary, it was totally feasible to acquire these techniques through entrepreneurial spirit, practical application and creativity and to try one's hand at becoming a neon artist. The American manual by Miller and Fink reads like a hymn in praise of the republic of independent craftsmen. It was positively worth it, the authors argue, for people to try setting up their own neon workshop; the future of the craft was assured. It was a business that could show a healthy profit with relatively little investment. Its success depended 'largely on the ability of the . . . craftsman to master the processes involved in tubing manufacture and to market the signs on a fair basis'. As the transport of neon tubes was expensive and the shortest possible distance between the workshop and the installation site was always an advantage, a small neon workshop situated handily in or near a medium-sized town would be a promising business model. Miller and Fink prophesied boldly: 'It is very probable . . . that each small town will have its local neon shop.'[103]

Contemporary observers appear to confirm this prospect. As the British journalist J. B. Priestley noted after a journey across the American Southwest in the '30s, driving through small desert towns one could be forgiven for thinking that someone had picked up a bit of Sunset Boulevard in Los Angeles and dropped it down again right there.[104] Right across the American continent, neon-lit cities were spread out, full of life, entertainment and modernity. It was not just the illuminated advertisements themselves, however, that became symbols of commercial success. Their production, too, could be seen as an opportunity to live a creative life independently of the large companies.

The American Piazza

Though by now neon cities had sprung up everywhere, there was still a centre of the neon democracy: Times Square. In the 1930s, from any corner of this mecca of American entertainment, 300 different neon installations could be seen, ranging from tiny writing in a window to a monumental sign installation on the roof of a building.[105] Even the traditional lights between Times Square and Columbus Circle (a journalist counted over 100,000) were not just a shining white any more.[106] By the mid-1930s the 'Great White Way', as the entertainment mile of Broadway was called, had long been turned into 'Rainbow Ravine'.[107]

In New York neon no doubt contributed to a heightening of spectacle. The electric advertisements that had been impressive to start with were developed further from the early 1930s onwards. Advertising installations combined light bulbs, neon tubes and switching mechanisms that simulated movement. New projection technology made it possible to show cartoons on photoelectric cell surfaces, thus reaching a new level in the animation of advertising. This represented the last word in innovation and being up-to-date. By 1928, the *New York Times* was able to announce by using clusters of light bulbs flashing over 261 million times an hour, that Herbert Hoover had beaten Al Smith in the presidential elections.[108] Something that seemed equally spectacular, though politically less relevant, was the advertisement for Pepsodent toothpaste, showing an illuminated showgirl on a swing, swaying back and forth all night long high above 47th Street.[109] More and more spectacular advertisements followed, appealing to all the senses. On 27 September 1933, thanks to an advertisement for A&P Coffee, people on the sidewalk could, for the first time, get the real smell of coffee coming out of an artificially steaming gigantic cup. Due to a production error the steam condensed, causing it to rain on the corner of Broadway and 47th Street on its inauguration day. (The installation was quickly put right.)[110] In March 1936 Wrigley's unveiled what came to be known as a neon aquarium. In the centre there were giant fish, with bubbles rising up from the bottom and advertising messages flashing: 'Steadies the nerves', 'Aids the digestion' and 'The taste lingers'. The installation, designed (naturally) to be the largest of its type in the world, weighed over 110 tons. It was nearly 25 m high and 60 m in length. It had 29,500 light bulbs installed, and over 300 m of neon tubes.[111] A journalist noted that the packet of chewing gum shown was as big as a railway car, one fish as big as a whale. The installation nevertheless aimed to be biologically accurate, with Dorothy Shephard, the designer, having based her design for the neon animal world on creatures from the aquarium in her living room.[112] From 1938 two rose stems 30 m high, each with four flowers, grew and faded, over and over again, on the Studebaker Building on 48th Street, one on either side of the name of Four Roses Whiskey. On the corner of Broadway and 46th Street there appeared a gigantic bottle pouring Bromo-Selzer every fifteen seconds into a 3-m high neon glass. On the same corner people in 1940 were amazed to see for the first time the Wilson Whiskey advertisement showing a whole multimedia apparatus of illuminated fountains and cartoon animations with a neon cocktail being poured anew every seven seconds.[113]

These enormous installations do not appear to have much in common with the writing and symbols produced by simple craftsmen. Nevertheless the most spectacular signs were still recognized as the work of individuals. Douglas Leigh, the most well known of all the neon boffins, achieved notoriety on Broadway for his advertising installations. He came from an obscure town in Alabama and, the story goes, had arrived in New York at the age of 22 with nothing but $9 in his wallet. His life was celebrated as a typical American success story, a testament to the power of individualism and the entrepreneurial spirit even at the height of the Depression. Leigh was everywhere in the New York media and posed for the cameras presenting the latest illuminations and flashing effects on Times Square to Hollywood stars.[114] Every new installation, destined to be the talk of Manhattan, was to be the largest and most spectacular in the world. Take, for example, a whiskey advertisement on Columbus Circle that set off a kinetic spectacle using red, white, gold and green neon extending over more than 1,000 sq. metres. Or the Ballantines advertisement that activated 1,600 light bulbs and around 700 m of neon tubes projecting rings thrown by a clown up into the night above Broadway in a sequence of 57 images. Not to mention illuminated cartoon ducks kissing in an advertisement for Old Gold cigarettes or cartoon mice dancing on fountains blown by whales. Leigh's ideas always seemed to work, making the world of Times Square even more spectacular, more sophisticated and more surreal.[115] His powers of design reached their apogee in 1941 when 'Camel Man', a gigantic portrait of a young man, first blew smoke rings through his open lips on the corner of Broadway and 44th Street. The mechanically produced circles of real steam (not cigarette smoke) wafted through the night air, getting bigger and bigger as they went and stopping people in their tracks. Soon they even floated, metaphorically, over the Hudson River – Douglas Leigh installed similar installations in 22 other American towns.[116] The pause for a smoke lasted for 24 years, with practically no other advertising installation enjoying such a long life.[117]

Times Square was less a traditional public square (except on New Year's Eve or, later on, for the victory celebration at the end of the war) and more an open-air theatre for advertisements. The advertising industry aimed to present the most spectacular shows here as the area was not only a haunt of New Yorkers. Thousands of tourists came here every evening to see the lights.[118] By 1929 a New York agency announced that this part of the city was a 'national advertising medium'. It not only saw a million people a day but these included two million 'wealthy visitors' a month from all over the USA. They would tell the folks way back home all about the spectacular advertisements.[119] The rental for the advertising spaces was based on an exact count of the number of passers-by. It was a known fact that 1,100,000 people were in the area every day. It was also known how they were distributed. In the sales negotiations over the advertising spaces it was accepted that the corner of Seventh Avenue and Broadway was a 'men's corner', with more men than women going past, and that vice versa the corner of Fifth Avenue and 42nd Street had considerably more women than men passers-by.[120]

Seen in this light, the city might at first glance appear to consist of nothing but spectacle and products. To contemporaries, however, neon advertisements seemed to be signs of democratic diversity rather than the effect of centralization. The New York journalist Meyer Berger, on the occasion of the unveiling of the Wrigley neon aquarium, described Times Square as a laboratory of illuminated advertisements. He collected enthusiastic anecdotes rather than looking too closely at the advertising techniques. He pointed out that the advertising companies continually put up public service announcements free of charge (during the First World War these included advertisements for government bonds and the summer of 1934 saw the family-oriented slogan: 'Have You Written to Mother Lately?'). The advertisers would also react to the personal wishes of New Yorkers. A woman had written to the Ford organization because the automobile company's enormous neon sign always started to light up before the sun went down. For that reason her little daughter was never able to see a proper red sunset. According to Meyer Berger, Ford reacted immediately: the switching-on time was changed and the little girl got to see her sunsets.[121]

Anecdotes such as these illustrate the slightly sentimental view with which the already convinced citizens saw the world of neon in the '30s. They regarded the signs, with their tales of fantasy and their messages, as fascinating aspects of New York life.[122] The energy consumed by these lights, coffee smells and smoke rings, and the energy they gave back to the city, were part of the very essence of a metropolis based on the consumption of electricity. As with so many of the neon texts of this period, New York's lights were seen as symbols of democracy, as opportunities not just for big business but also for small business people as well, for traders and craftsmen, to bring their services before a wider public. Because Times Square presented such a successful light show, the global phenomenon of illuminated advertisements was described more and more as typically American. A New York journalist visiting Moscow in 1934 listed, at the start of his travel descriptions, the New World attractions *not* to be found there: after skyscrapers he mentioned in second place neon lights.[123] On the other hand, Meyer Berger made fun of Western Europeans and their cool reaction to city advertising, recounting an anecdote legendary among advertisers in which an English visitor, crossing Times Square after patiently listening to his guide to this world of the light show, finally asked politely: 'Very good, but don't you think they're rather conspicuous?'[124]

Totalitarian Neon

It is tempting to give in to the romanticism of American neon and treat neon lights, with their handmade quality and variety of colours, as symbols of a vibrant democracy, with other, colder, illumination techniques being more typical of a totalitarian dictatorship. The Paris International Exhibition of 1937 provides support for this theory. The Eiffel Tower, a symbol of French democracy, was adorned with neon lights (admittedly the work of the right-wing extremist Georges Claude). More than 10,000 m of fragile glass tubes shone in a network of light charmingly arranged and delighting the public. They were coloured blue, green and pink and mounted to a height of 55 m. This was a work of art in the seductive colours of a Western European metropolis.[125] The German pavilion, by contrast, had the word 'DEUTSCHLAND' above a swastika made up of illuminated tubes developed by the Osram company. They were not filled with neon, however, but coated on the inside with a fluorescent substance activated by ultraviolet rays. They gave off a cold white glow, nothing like the colours of New York's 'Rainbow Ravine'.

Then again, the new fluorescent devices were not a specifically German product. They were being developed at the same time by American companies and by the Dutch corporation Philips.[126] And the Nazis made full use of modern, coloured neon advertising in the early years of their rule. In 1933–4 the Berlin authorities gave instructions for the light in shop windows to be intensified and also for illuminated signs to be set up that should stay on up to midnight. In this way city centres were to be made more lively. In line with a return to certain old German traditions, small shops were encouraged to present their products with illuminated signs. So, soon there were imitations of former guild signs and emblems of neon cakes outside cafés. Osram not only developed the cold white fluorescent tubes promoting the German swastika in Paris but also polychrome tubes producing any desired colour combinations and enlivening city streets even more. In 1937 the Europa-Haus in Berlin presented a frontage dominated by brightly coloured advertisements – such as ones for 'RADEBERGER PILSNER' and 'AUGUSTINERBRÄU' beers, competing with one another for the attention of passers-by.[127] The neon sign of the Nazi newspaper *Die Braune Post* was hailed as an example of successful urban illuminated advertising. The installation measuring 16.5 × 10 m was put up on the Columbus Haus. This had been built by Erich Mendelsohn, who emigrated to England in 1933 (only a few years previously his book of photographs, *Amerika*, had introduced the illuminated advertising of Manhattan to the German public).[128] Elaborate light shows were a feature of Nazi party rallies. The so-called domes of light, as Anne Hoormann shows, communicated 'the modernist technological side of National Socialism along with the anti-modern, regressive elements such as Volk, race, the struggle for survival'.[129] A similar phenomenon is seen in the case of Mussolini's propaganda machine in Italy in the late 1930s. High above the urban squares, illuminated letters were suspended proclaiming, for example, that the 'Empire' had arisen again on 'Rome's hills of destiny'.[130]

Neon was definitely not the monopoly of democrats. Certainly in the public sphere, especially in the German capital Berlin, it was an element of Nazi propaganda. But the new rulers found it more important to bring actual fire back to the city – the natural flame, called 'Party Member Fire' in propaganda material. Rituals were held that were explicitly directed against the Kurfürstendamm, seen as Americanized or 'unGerman', with its electric light shows. The torchlight procession 4 km long that took place on 30 January

1933 and the brutal ritual of the burning of books on 10 May 1933 formed contrasts to the already globalized neon world of the main business avenues.[131] In the end, however, the Second World War relativized every aspect of urban illumination. In May 1940 orders for a 'blackout' were issued in Nazi Germany. It was a temporary switch off at least for illuminated advertising. According to the historian Dirk Reinhardt it was not to be seen again in German streets until liberation by the Allies.[132]

April 1942: Darkness at 'Rainbow Ravine'

The lights of New York City, the American military warned, were visible at night up to 48 km out in the Atlantic. Bombers could make the lights out from well over 300 km away. An order was therefore issued, at the end of April 1942, to plunge the cities on the East Coast into darkness.[133] For the first time since the 'lightless nights' of 1917, when coal shortages forced the electric lights of New York to be switched off, the lights of the night-time metropolis went out. The illuminated clocks on the skyscrapers were turned off. In the offices, hotel rooms and high-rise apartment blocks, a strict blackout was enforced. The amusement park at Coney Island ceased its restless flickering. Also in darkness was the world's highest night-club, the Rainbow Room on the 65th floor of what was then the RCA Building.[134]

On Times Square, the 'Rainbow Ravine' capital of American light shows, the new darkness had a disturbing effect. 'Crowds pass through the comparative gloom of the canyon that is the square and seem puzzled', a reporter from the *New York Times* put it on 30 April 1942.[135] Douglas Leigh complained that the measures would rob 'the most famous street in the world of its glamour'. Nevertheless he had had all sixteen large advertising installations on Times Square turned off willingly like a good patriot.[136] Those responsible in the American military praised New Yorkers for their discipline and right thinking over the question of the blackout. Tourists, though, sometimes turned on the lights in hotel rooms that were not yet subject to the blackout. And night cleaning staff lit up offices in skyscrapers now and again by mistake. But these infringements were not really serious.

Much more difficult to control was the large number of neon signs flashing not just on the big advertising installations of Manhattan but on bars, hotels, cafés, shops and cinemas across the whole New York area. Many of them still shone even after all the other buildings were blacked out and when even the East Coast locomotives were operating without lights. Like no other historical event these initial days of the blackout proved that neon advertisements had become universal sources of light throughout the entire city landscape of the East Coast. Colonel Walter Metcalf, representative for the 'Second Civilian Regional Defense District' and therefore for the conurbation of New York, assessed citizens' preparedness for the blackout as 'excellent'. Nevertheless, disciplining the owners of neon signs proved to be a 'question of public education'. 'Apparently', Metcalf said grimly, 'some people do not understand an order until they get it from a cop.'[137]

In the greater part of his article, the *New York Times* reporter who described the blackout showed a discipline and right thinking of which Colonel Metcalf would have approved. With respect to the neon lights, however, he deviated from the strictly patriotic line on the blackout. His panorama of urban life in the face of the general blackout praised the neon signs in the darkened landscape of New York rather poetically:

> Seen from the 102nd floor of the Empire State Building after 8 o'clock the city's streets were squares of brooding shadow rimmed by sidewalk lamps and by red neon signs that bloomed like poppies.[138]

Like the chemist William Ramsay before him, the journalist was using a choice metaphor borrowed from the natural world and applied to electrically charged tubes. No one was to write in quite that vein ever again in the period after the Second World War.

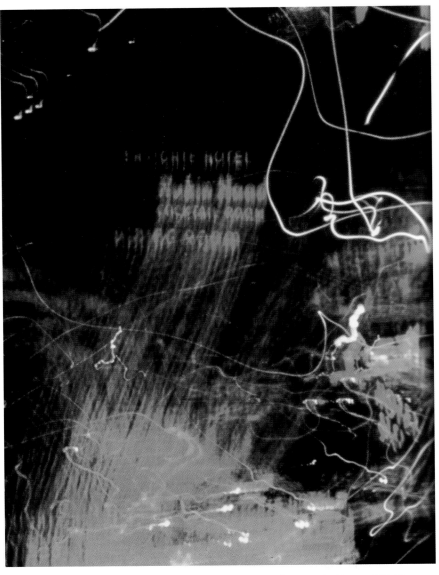

László Moholy-Nagy, *Night-time traffic (Pink, orange, and blue traffic stream)*, Chicago, 1937–46.

3 NEON WILDERNESS

Nelson Algren's War

When leading American writers were called up for military service in the Second World War they were usually given privileged positions editing military journals in the propaganda or entertainment sections of the American army. Not so in the case of Nelson Algren from Chicago. The author of a couple of novels and noted for being left-wing, Algren was enlisted as a regular soldier. His draft papers, however, were stamped mysteriously 'Special Assignment', so perhaps his radical political views were not unknown to the military authorities. Possibly his wartime detail also had something to do with the fact that, as a young man, he had done time in a Texas prison for the attempted theft of a typewriter.

Algren was not to become much of a war hero. His period of service was marked by continual bust-ups with his superiors. He was noted for his lack of discipline, excessive card playing and similar consumption of alcohol. He found the officers' privileges extremely unfair compared to the lot of the regular soldiers. When sent to Germany – he arrived in Düsseldorf in May 1945 – he was surprised by the relative prosperity of the defeated Rhinelanders. When he was stationed in Marseille for three months he went AWOL in the poor quarter of the town, trying his luck on the black market.[1]

Nelson Algren, born Nelson Abraham, never spoke in detail of his role in the struggle against Nazi Germany. In a late essay he portrayed his memories of the war as vague light and sound effects. He described the sky over the forest near Düsseldorf in May 1945, the sound of the ocean near the Bar Atlantique in Marseille. He realized that in the end he felt drawn back to the 'ordinary' moon of home on Milwaukee Avenue in Chicago.[2] It was not wartime experiences that inspired his first book after his return to this city in the Midwest but the neon advertisements of his home town. In the bars of 1945, Algren observed, there were illuminated signs for beers that had not existed before the Second World War. But at the counter the same drinkers were sitting as before. This is the origin of his short-story collection *The Neon Wilderness*, published two years after the end of the war.[3]

2.1 Billion Lux in Chicago

Chicago was the right place to be writing a book about light effects. Here social differences always stood out in contrasting light and shade. When Algren wrote *The Neon Wilderness*, some city neighbourhoods were still lit by old-fashioned gas lights, while in other neighbourhoods the electric lighting was in a deplorable state. Along the affluent streets, however, extravagant floods of light showed off the modern architecture and the giant business centres.[4] Even half a century before, when Chicago was just growing into a city, these sharp contrasts had characterized the urban landscape. The World's Fair of 1893 opened here during a severe economic crisis, celebrating the 400th anniversary of the discovery of America one year late.[5] This exhibition dramatized the newly developed electric light in a way never known before, the press describing the glowing light show as the 'most marvellous of the marvels of our age'.[6] The novelist Theodore Dreiser lauded the nightscape as a 'Garden of the Gods'. Thousands of dots of electric light seemed to the writer to be a silken thread 'spun out of flaming silver and molten gold'.[7] At the same time, 1890s Chicago was marked by unrest among workers and by extreme poverty. As the exhibition opened, various factories closed down as a result of the financial panic of 1893. The silken dots of light shone out in a city of chronic unemployment.[8]

When a new international exhibition took place in Chicago in 1933–4, again during a gloomy economic crisis, neon tubes played a decisive role in the spectacle of light. This time the 100th anniversary of the founding of the city was held under the slogan, the 'Century of Progress'. The main idea behind the design of the exhibition was the fantasy of a 'magic city' bathed in a 'gigantic pool of light'. The buildings were made, less magically, of the cheapest of materials: asbestos cement, tin and planks of wood, generously painted in different colours. The architects of the exhibition pavilions largely dispensed with windows (who needed daylight anyway?), allowing the surfaces to take over. Coloured light lit up coloured pavilions. Seventeen spotlights created a play of light imitating the aurora borealis. The outside lighting alone amounted to 2.1 billion lux.[9] More than 20,000 m of neon tubes were used altogether – glowing in two dozen different colours.[10] Altogether, the event, the advertising literature proclaimed, would let loose 'the largest flood of coloured light ever produced by any city'.[11]

It goes without saying that Nelson Algren was not carried away by such superlatives. In March 1935, six months after the success of this colourful spectacle had ebbed somewhat, his first book *Somebody in Boots* was published. The novel accompanies the underclass of drifters wandering across the United States. It tells of violence and despair, ending its panorama of poverty in the Chicago of the World's Fair period. Algren contrasted the immaculate neon shows, described in the novel as a 'zigzag riot of fakery', with the experiences of the homeless, prostitutes and hobos.[12] Against the background of the light shows and the equally glowing patriotic speeches given at the exhibition site, in *Somebody in Boots* Algren criticized the large-scale poverty extending to all communities in the city. He pointed to the 'ten thousand children who don't have enough to eat'.[13] He showed prostitutes and beggars trying desperately, and without success, to benefit from the exhibition. In his novel, these American outcasts are camped out right at the entrance to the exhibition site. A neon sign in the national colours of red, white and blue shines out above their heads, with the promise: 'A CENTURY OF PROGRESS BIGGER AND BETTER THAN EVER'.[14] The novel's attitude to this is given relatively unambiguously by the chapter's epigraph. It expresses the idea of overcoming a society based on class, of bringing about the free development of all people – and it comes from *The Communist Manifesto*.[15]

'Like Living Flame'

For Nelson Algren, working on *The Neon Wilderness*, it was important to be as near as possible to his marginalized characters. After his return from Europe he rented a couple of simple rooms in a slum where Polish immigrants lived. He collected impressions by sitting at the counters of the downmarket bars. He spent hours sweating in Turkish baths and eavesdropping on the conversations of the underworld characters who frequented them. And he went back again and again to police stations where small-time crooks were being 'booked'. There he recorded their justifications, explanations and excuses. Just as the regulars in the bars interested him, he was attracted by the repeat offenders. His stories were to reflect the long-term and seemingly unchangeable life cycles of the urban underclass. He described a closed world.[16]

Now Nelson Algren was no longer concerned with the sharp contrast between staged light effects and real-life experiences. At the centre of his work was the poetic but nevertheless precise description of city neighbourhoods where the light of neon tubes lit up the lives of the characters: places where jukeboxes constantly pumped out their songs on the evening air – and where poverty and marginality did not exist in a vacuum, but in communities linked to the rich popular culture of their time. Algren began *The Neon Wilderness* with a quotation from a poem by David Wolff in which the image of a 'night with argon peaks' dramatically illustrates the terrors of a dark urban vision.[17] As with argon in Wolff's poem, neon serves Algren as a dramatic metaphor underlining the struggle for survival in the urban jungle of Chicago. Algren's stories use naked light bulbs as metaphors of isolation and despair. Neon, in contrast, represents the public space of the street and the bar, the possibility of community in this hard world.

The term 'neon wilderness' was used by Nelson Algren in the very first story of his narrative cycle. 'The Captain Has Bad Dreams' describes the rituals in a police station, witnessed on many occasions by the author. The story records an almost uninterrupted series of short confessions and obvious lies from small-time crooks. The figure of the police sergeant interviews the men and gives cynically critical advice ('Why don't you take a good belt of cocaine and jump out a twenty-story window?'). But this misanthropy is only superficial. The sergeant is in fact transformed into showing sympathy: 'His life was no longer measured by the days of the week, but only by the monotonous monotones of ragged men offering threadbare lies.'

In his dreams, the sergeant observes the world of these men – the neon wilderness. He sees them as blind men hanging around the columns of the elevated trains, 'where a calamitous yellow light filtered downward all night long'. His dream is described in now dark, now fluorescent, terms and the men pass him by in an endless line, their faces 'half averted, forever smiling uneasily as though sharing some secret and comforting knowledge of evil which he could never know'. The police officer occupied every day with these men's confessions only realizes in his dreams how little he knows of their world of poverty, small-time criminality and drug abuse. These human beings live 'in an unpossessed twilight land, a neon wilderness whose shores the Captain sometimes envisaged dimly'. His curiosity about these existences is continually frustrated: 'in sleep he sought that shore forever, always drawing nearer . . . yet never, somehow, attaining those long, low sands'. The neon wilderness is impenetrable.

It is entirely plausible to see Algren in the figure of the sergeant, the author having intentionally turned his attention, out of literary curiosity, to the fate of such marginalized city dwellers. Algren also analysed the status of the urban underclass and tried to come to terms with the inseparable gulf between the intellectual observer on the one hand and the slum dwellers caught in an eternal struggle for existence on the other. Even if Algren himself had a semi-criminal background following his theft of a typewriter, he was in the end describing the neon wilderness as an outsider. He, too, was torn between cynicism and empathy.[18]

Unlike his uniformed central character, however, Algren did not just investigate the neon wilderness at the police station. *The Neon Wilderness* has historical depth and a breadth of vision. We get to know about more than the Chicago of the 1940s, more than the automated rhythms of city life. We are plunged into the backgrounds, the tragedies and rare triumphs revealed by the life stories of urban dwellers. Algren tells of boxers and hookers, soldiers and gamblers. He did not limit himself to dry-as-dust case studies but endeavoured – not always successfully – to flesh out the journalistic side with the ways in which these characters saw themselves, their dreams, their version of heroism and virtue. For example, in 'No Man's Laughter', the Second World War becomes a hell of a break for a small-time crook from Chicago. The car thief Gino Bomagino, a much-ridiculed figure on the city streets, becomes a bomber pilot in the war and sacrifices his life in an absurd act of bravery in the skies above Alaska. Because light always plays a key role for Algren, the flame engulfing the aeroplane lends a dramatic dimension to this seemingly insignificant life.

Algren's empathetic writing, however, is more at home with neon and less with the sky above Alaska. This is illustrated especially by 'Design for Departure', a programmatic story from this collection about the fate of a woman marked by extreme sadness. The central character, Mary, has a birthmark on her face, is raised by two alcoholics, becomes a prostitute in the hands of a conman and finally falls victim to heroin. 'Design for Departure' relates her life in a cheap hotel where day and night are totally given over to the rhythm of the city. This is defined by the daily rental and the finer details of the rental conditions ('No Extra Person in Any Room over Six Hours'), by the city noises pouring in, by the drugs that make Mary's life bearable and, like flashing advertisements, become part of the story ('Veronal. Allonal. Luminal. Veronal'). But the most impressive thing remains 'the ceaseless, night-fuming neon that moved like living flame, all night, up and down the fire escape'.

Neon tubes and the jukebox – these two urban technologies were linked together via Algren's depiction of them from Mary's perspective. Like a 'blood-red shadow', the neon light 'passed and repassed, without cessation from dusk to dawn', and then suddenly stops when the jukebox is turned off at four in the morning. Like the light the jukebox, too, seems to be in control of people. The customers sing along with the machine 'till the human voices sounded mechanical, and the juke sang in half-human tones'. The visitors to the bar turn into semi-machines. But technology also turns into human form. In her increasing state of confusion Mary sees the jukebox as a lover singing just for her and for whom she feels pity.

In *Somebody in Boots* Nelson Algren had still been playing rather crudely with the contrast between the real life of the underclass and what he saw as the neon lies of the World's Fair spectacle. In *The Neon Wilderness* he observed Chicago with a more sensitive feel for the relationships between light, sound and human fate. People interact with technology – the jukebox, neon light. But it is not always coldness and anonymity that mechanical sound and electric flickering have to offer. In the environment shaped by the jukebox and by neon, his characters come together. And in the detailed and poetic representation of that environment Algren was able to develop a new perspective on urban culture, its nightmares and its possibilities. The fact that Mary, in her confusion, willingly and according to plan finds a way out of her room, flashing in the red neon light, via a heroin overdose, is on the one hand a tragedy. On the other, it is proof that this woman gets what she wants – and this happens to be suicide – because she can interpret the neon city. The city of the poor becomes a poetic environment in *The Neon Wilderness* – and its inhabitants are actors, not merely victims.

Moholy-Nagy on the Corner of Randolph and State

While Nelson Algren was on his way to Düsseldorf as a frustrated GI, at the same time collecting material for *The Neon Wilderness*, László Moholy-Nagy, an émigré from Berlin, was engaging with a fictive Chicago of quite a different sort. Along with his fellow countryman and colleague, the pioneer light artist György Kepes, while working for the Allies he came up with the idea of creating a network of lights that would exactly reproduce the light pattern of the city of Chicago on Lake Michigan. In the event of air attacks by Japanese or German bombers the city would be blacked out. The carpet of lights above the lake would cause the enemy squadrons to drop their bombs into the water.[19] Moholy-Nagy and Kepes in this way created a city without a body, made up entirely of light. Algren, by contrast, imagined a Chicago of the people, a Chicago the reality of which there was no escaping – except possibly via an overdose.

But, like Nelson Algren, Moholy-Nagy also experienced a certain amount of fascination with the real city. He spent a whole evening, for instance, on the corner where Randolph Street and State Street meet, standing for a long time amid the traffic and photographing the spotlights, the street lights and the neon advertisements on the hotels, restaurants and nightclubs of the area. A police officer ordered him to move on. But Moholy-Nagy stayed where he was, letting the cars drive towards him and continuing to take photographs that recorded the visual chaos of the cityscape on colour slides. Arriving back home, his wife remembered later, he looked like a ghost. But, he stated, he had brought home 'one of the most beautiful set of slides I have ever seen' from this street corner.[20]

Moholy-Nagy had arrived in the city in 1937. Unlike Nelson Algren, who saw himself as part of the urban underclass, he was on the one hand already an established artist, on the other he was new to the USA. Algren had lived in Chicago since the age of three. Moholy-Nagy was a cosmopolitan and an exile. Having grown up in Hungary before spending a long time working at the Bauhaus, he then emigrated from Germany to the Netherlands and then on to Great Britain before he was enticed to go to Chicago by a position at the 'New Bauhaus'. Now he found himself in a city that represented the powerhouse of architectural innovation, at the same time as being riven by extreme social differences. His interest in the lights of the city had been aroused as early as the 1920s (and he had also taken similar pictures in the main streets of Berlin to those at the corner of Randolph and State, though these were still in black and white).[21] His script of 1921–2 for a never-to-be-produced experimental film called *Dynamism of the City* dealt with the

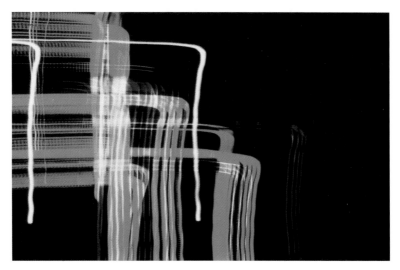

László Moholy-Nagy, *Neon signs, Chicago, 1939*.

bewildering array of illuminated signs of the urban environment. He had always insisted that architects, artists and other creative people had to be involved more intensively and more innovatively with the luminous city. He himself had dreamed up the idea of an 'advertising cannon' – a spotlight projecting writing and images on to the night sky. As an artist, he had a somewhat ambivalent relationship with the commercial nature of advertising, without, however, being able to turn his back on the technology and the creative possibilities presented by it.[22] During his time in London he had participated in the design of Simpson's department store, which, as one of the most innovative buildings of its time, had neon lights covered by shades built into the shop front.[23]

The streets of Chicago and the possibilities offered by colour photography gave Moholy-Nagy the opportunity, amid the urban environment, to abandon any link to materiality. At night, on the corner of Randolph and State, he created images that were as frenetic as the city itself; just as intangible, just as chaotic. Chicago has become almost abstract in the slides that he produced on his nocturnal wanderings, although the neon signs along the street anchor the intoxicated images in time and space. The 'EASTGATE

HOTEL', the 'Robin Hood', one 'COCKTAIL ROOM' and a 'DINING ROOM' are revealed in this panorama. What remains invisible, however, are the people frequenting these bars, restaurants and hotels. The photographer was only looking at the light.[24]

The 'Rusty Heart'

Moholy-Nagy and Algren were experiencing the same city. One, a modern artist through and through, saw urban space as a canvas for experimenting with visual effects. The other was only interested in the light as it illuminated his underprivileged characters. The elaborate visions of the avant-garde were always alien to Algren. He identified entirely with the interests of the subculture that he focused on in his writing. So he became mad about boxing and a devoted punter on the horses and was at home in all the low-life bars.[25]

The Neon Wilderness aimed for urban realism. Thus, Algren positioned himself in the mainstream of Chicago writers. Right at the start of the century Upton Sinclair, chronicler of the slaughter houses and slums, had identified city literature as the almost documentary recording of social injustice. Algren's Chicago contemporaries, writers like James T. Farrell and Richard Wright, went in for a critical and minutely detailed engagement with the industrial city. This form of urban narrative, however poetic it may seem to be in the case of Algren, was always closely allied to journalism, even more to sociological study – such as that being carried out at the University of Chicago's influential Institute of Sociology. Such writers sought a close knowledge and understanding of the industrial city.[26] They, as much as the sociologists, were intent on researching the almost village-like structures of immigrant neighbourhoods.[27] They were less interested in carrying out stylistic experiments in text of the kind in which Moholy-Nagy was engaging via colour photography. Algren, for example, characterized his own writing as a form of emotionalized reportage. When writing about prisoners, he said: 'you have to know how many bars there are in a jail cell'.[28] To him, a writer has achieved quite a lot if, in the course of his life, he had managed to tell the story of a single street.[29]

Algren's literary career started in the 1930s and '40s, when politicized and true-to-life narrative works were appreciated as never before in American cultural history. His second novel, *Never Come Morning*, was published in 1942. It was controversial both with the critics and the general reader but proved to be a success.[30] Immediately after the end of the war Algren was therefore hailed as the great hope for American fiction. A reviewer on the *New York Times* was impressed by *The Neon Wilderness* as a portrait of an existentially challenged world. He singled out the light metaphor, describing Algren's Chicago as a 'sunless place of whispering, tangible shadows'.[31]

In the city itself Algren was now recognized as *the* local writer. People came to hear him lecture and he was invited to give an interview that was broadcast via the new medium of television. In February 1947 he received a visit from Simone de Beauvoir, an admirer of his writing. He showed her the most run-down bars and the most interesting homeless shelters. She began an affair with him – thus turning a mildly successful novelist into a figure on the international intellectual scene.[32] The first National Book Award, soon to become one of the most prestigious distinctions in American literature, was given to Algren for his novel *The Man with the Golden Arm* (1949), which continued the slum perspective employed in *The Neon Wilderness*, developing it into a gripping character study.

Two things, however, soon took a turn for the worse: Chicago's industrial base and Nelson Algren's reputation. Between 1947 and 1982 the city lost almost 60 per cent of its factory jobs in a process of massive deindustrialization.[33] A world metropolis of the industrial age turned into just another regional city. Like so many American cities Chicago was drawn into a crisis marked by a decline in infrastructure, a flight of the middle class into the suburbs and communal corruption.[34] Nelson Algren appears to have seen this process coming very early on. The city dwellers described by him as gathered round jukeboxes and under neon advertisements may well have formed functioning communities but they were largely divorced from economic success and meaningful professional activities. The city of Chicago, Algren observed, was nothing but a sort of crossroads where people only stopped for as long as they did not have any better options.[35] In an essay published in 1951, *Chicago: City on the Make*, he made a comparison between the Pottawatomies, the former inhabitants of the land around the Great Lakes, and the similarly doomed tribe made up of his lower-class central characters, whose home was in the city with the 'rusty heart'.[36] Algren's heroes were still living in their isolated, rundown neighbourhoods, in the light of the 'neon flowers, bleeding all night long'. But in fact, according to Algren, the city had long been marked by the pale shadow of modern light sources, by the grey of managers and their behind-the-scenes speculations.[37] Loving Chicago, he concluded, was like loving a woman with a broken nose.[38]

Even if Algren had a definite feel for the tragedy of deindustrialization, his reputation as a writer suffered a decline similar to that of the neon wilderness with which he so closely identified. This was because the literary world of the 1950s was also undergoing something of a transformation. Politically motivated realism was quickly losing its privileged position. Algren was seen as yesterday's fashion. The leading literary critics, many of whom had an academic background, considered his left-wing radicalism to be an old-fashioned attitude from before the war and his naturalistic representation of poverty even as a relic from the turn of the century. Leslie Fiedler called Algren the 'bard of the stumblebum'. In *Time* magazine the reviewer of *A Walk on the Wild Side* (1956) criticized the clichés in Algren's writing: his hookers always had 'a heart of gold' and his homeless always more humanity than actual working people.[39] Algren's poetic identification with the marginalized reminded a generation of intellectuals of the sentimentality of a drunk.[40] And Chicago itself – far from the American East Coast and given a literary scene dominated as never before by New York – was seen as a relatively uninteresting part of the world. The writer Richard Wright played a special role by reason of his status as an African American 'ghetto author'. Algren, on the other hand, the writer of the white working-class, drunks and the homeless, appeared to have misread the signs of the times.

Even at home in Illinois, Algren's distinctive literary identification with poverty, and with all those jukeboxes and neon flowers, looked like a relic from the past.[41] In the decades after the war the ethnic make-up of the inner-city areas of Chicago had been completely transformed. The mainly Eastern European immigrants, so often the heroes (and antiheroes) of Algren's prose, moved to the suburbs. African American and Hispanic immigrants took over the neighbourhoods. The writer did not mean much to them (and vice versa; these new inhabitants of Chicago only appear as marginal figures in Algren's fiction). After the writer's death, a section of Evergreen Street was renamed Algren Street. A little later, however, Hispanic voters who had never heard of the writer called for the renaming to be reversed. They got their way.[42]

It's Not a Wonderful Life

When George Bailey, an otherwise happy family man and generous head of a cooperative bank, is faced with the biggest crisis of his life he wishes he had never been born. And he has his wish fulfilled. He wanders through the small American town of Bedford Falls, where he has spent the whole of his life. And he realizes, now that his life has been erased from human history, nothing is as it was. The formerly peaceful place with its village-like street has changed into an urban jungle made up of illuminated advertisements. George's wife, never having met him in this new reality, is a stereotypical old maid; a vivacious old acquaintance is a prostitute; his friends Bert and Ernie are no longer easy-going small-town heroes but narrow-minded, frustrated characters. Initially incredulous at his removal from the known universe, then shocked at the dramatic consequences, George charges panic-stricken through the neon wilderness that has long ceased to be called Bedford Falls but has become Pottersville. It has itself turned into an advertising sign, named after a hard-nosed businessman – a figure symbolizing faceless capitalism and the embodiment, just as much as the flashing neon, of the pitilessness of a George Bailey-less town.

Still from *It's a Wonderful Life* (dir. Frank Capra, 1946).

This is the opening of *It's a Wonderful Life* from 1946, a film by the successful American director Frank Capra and one of the most popular schmaltzy comedies in cinema history. The Pottersville section of the film, however, is anything but schmaltzy and far from comic. Admittedly in the end – inevitably – the film comes to a tear-jerking happy ending when Bailey ends the nightmare of never having been George Bailey and comes back to life just when the community of Bedford Falls has collectively solved his financial crisis. The film, however, shows just how closely linked both visions of America – functioning community or soulless capitalism – are and how little it takes to change the vision of communal solidarity into a nightmare. Capra's thin veil of sentimentality and populist optimism is shockingly cast aside in Pottersville.[43] En passant we see the metaphorical future of the glowing lights. In Hollywood films of the early '30s, neon had symbolized glitz and glamour. Films like *Gold Diggers of 1933* or *Dames* showed women bathing in neon tubs, playing on neon grand pianos, admiring themselves in neon mirrors.[44] Just as light installations transformed the glamorous film theatres into spectacular entertainment palaces, likewise the films themselves used the new, attractive, streamlined technology. But this was now a thing of the past.

George Bailey's wandering through the flickering night refers naturally to the classics of film noir, those dark visions of the American city that continually focused on the dissolution of identity. In these films neon signs always indicated the secrets of the street. Elisabeth Bronfen reads film noir as the genre of 'dark modernism', going beyond the everyday into the nocturnal, opening a space for reflection and recounting narratives that only take place in secret.[45] Thus the neon sequence in *It's a Wonderful Life* reveals the idea, hidden beneath the surface, of the rapacious, brutal city. It is true that Frank Capra was no genre director – and this, his masterpiece of schmaltz, is no film noir either. Capra belonged to a mainstream cinema churning out optimistic narratives that told of the power and energy of American democracy. In this sort of cinema, neon had by 1946 already lost its innocence, the glowing lights going the same way as the traditional workaday city and Algren's left-wing inspired realism – all heading in the direction of a positively darker future. Now neon, as in Pottersville, stood for gloom and decay.

Neon: The Decline

By the late 1940s neon was beginning to give a rather sad impression, not just at the movies. The design of the signs now often lacked inspiration. Business owners and hoteliers left them in a bad state for far too long before repairing them. Broken signs stayed broken. Those who installed new lights soon chose ones made of artificial material, as they were bigger, cheaper and brighter. After the Second World War a 'New Look' took off in neon just as in fashion. Elaborate outdoor signs of a new, large-scale kind were made of plastic or plexiglass and now only used neon as a fluorescent material that was visible indirectly. As advertising customers with the most capital were the first to go in for these new designs in artificial materials, classical signs displaying neon tubes soon took on a cheap-looking quality, appearing old-fashioned and becoming associated with small-scale establishments on the slide.[46] When

nothing but chaos (a 'hodgepodge'), the journalist pronounced; the district was living by 'shopworn debauchery', the people in rags and 'leaden-eyed' – and the blood of a man sprawling on the ground shone in the neon light. As if to show off his erudition in the context of these observations, the reporter quoted at the end from T. S. Eliot's poem 'The Hollow Men' ('This is the way the world ends . . . not with a bang but a whimper').[51] Quite differently to Algren, who always tried to feel at home in the slum, this literary-minded reporter presents a neon area of town as being totally alien to the world of the narrator – and of the reader.

This journalistic view of such neighbourhoods is typical of the fate of neon light from the late 1940s on. This is particularly true of Los Angeles, where the first neon advertisement in the United States, the Packard sign in orange and blue, had caused traffic jams as early as 1923.[52] In the exclusive suburb of Bel Air, for example, any erection of neon signs was prohibited.[53] Neon now served as a dividing line between well-adjusted and dysfunctional neighbourhoods, between the abandoned underclass and the middle class that was rapidly becoming suburban.[54]

Just as lacking in empathy as the journalist from the *Los Angeles Times* was the crime writer John D. MacDonald, who specialized in this new literary area. His novel *The Neon Jungle* (1953), clearly inspired by Algren, only touches on social conditions in passing, being mainly focused on the excitement, toughness and blatant sexuality arising from downtown city areas with their flashing lights. The novel describes a neighbourhood in a nameless American metropolis as a 'raddled and lusty woman' who has reached 'the weary end of middle age'. The area is 'still colorful' – but then only because neon is in evidence in its narrow streets: 'A fizzing and sputter and crackle of BAR GRILL LOUNGE INN and ROOM APTS HOTEL and POOL BILLIARDS BOWLING and TRIPLE FEATURE GIRLS BALLROOM CLUB FLOOR SHOW'. There were 'always a few dead letters' but, the novel jokes heavily, none more spectacular than the night the Essex Tavern lost its first two letters.

Like Algren, MacDonald was coming to terms with the post-industrial world. The narrator sees 'empty mills with broken windows,

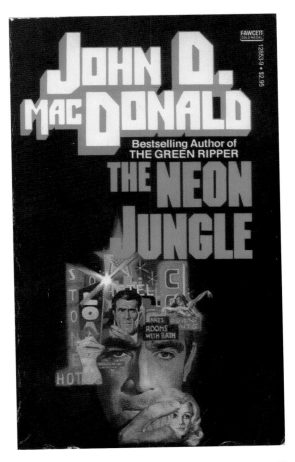

Cover of John D. MacDonald's *The Neon Jungle* (1953).

like eyes that accuse'. Also like Algren, this writer identified himself as being in opposition to what was seen as elite high culture. Here in the neon jungle, the narrator emphasizes, people don't go in for 'self-conscious reading of Proust in satined dressing rooms'.[55] Such a stance is unlikely to produce very cultivated prose and more likely to give a thrilling glimpse into a world of violence, family tragedy and the 'Varaki Quality Market' – a family-owned market and crime spot where neon burns day and night. Unlike Algren's writing, MacDonald's excursion into the neon wilderness does not lead to a literature aiming to change the world (or one's neighbour-hood). Rather, it reinforces the myth of the 'tough guy'. In the world of neon there is more and more of a focus on the masculinity of its heroes.[56] For Algren, a woman lit by neon light was still a heroine – however sentimentally she was portrayed. For MacDonald, any of his female characters venturing into the glow and flicker of the neon lights was taking a terrible risk.

Between 1950 and 1964 John D. MacDonald wrote 34 books. It is therefore not really surprising that *The Neon Jungle* comes across as rather formulaic.[57] (A 'regular guy' soldier rescues a woman with a past from the urban chaos. The soldier is killed in the Korean War. The woman with the past needs to find another hero pronto.) As a record of the history of neon, however, *The Neon Jungle* is very revealing about a new attitude towards the American city and its problem areas. These are viewed with a detached cynicism as the haunts of the abandoned, the violent, the hopeless, those without a voice. The trashy-looking colours of the neon lights, the mechanical buzzing, the faulty equipment – all seem to represent the exact metaphorical equivalent to these people. In such novels, the neon city that is shaking things up – a place that had once brought Americans of various ethnic backgrounds together and had redefined sexual roles – became a neon jungle. It was where women went bad and men showed off their courage. Family men, on the other hand, could only fantasize about such things from the safety of the suburbs.

The Man with the Golden Arm

Even if the neon ghetto was becoming more and more isolated, Nelson Algren once more staged a comeback in the mid-1950s. Otto Preminger, one of the leading Hollywood directors, planned to film Algren's novel, *The Man with the Golden Arm*. Frank Sinatra, unquestioned star of the period, took the role of the main character, Frankie Machine. As in *The Neon Wilderness*, in this novel Algren had taken as a setting one of the most ordinary city neighbourhoods in Chicago. Neon signs are shown flashing constantly (even if they are used ironically: beer advertisements, for instance, seem to the desperate hero to be signs of God's existence).[58]

Algren's book tells the story of how Frankie Machine struggles to achieve an independent life beneath these lights.

Preminger's film project started very promisingly. Nelson Algren was called to Hollywood to work on the script. The studio put him up at the luxurious Beverley Hills Hotel and looked forward to a period of productive cooperation between Preminger, the European émigré, and Algren, the man from Chicago. The writer found fault with his accommodation – the 'pretzel-shaped swimming pool and a fountain blowing pink water, in a room with a sterilized television set'. However, he found a solution straightaway, renting a room in a dosshouse in the neon ghetto of Skid Row, the very area that the *Los Angeles Times* called 'Bum's Heaven' and 'Wino's Valhalla'. From his hotel room there Algren could see a neon sign advertising 'GOOD BOOZE' and was sure that he could do some excellent work on the film script in this spot.[59]

The result, however, was a non-starter. Preminger thought the notorious outsider Algren was not competent to write dialogues or set scenes. Algren thought that the privileged Preminger was not competent to turn his book into a film. Among other things the director had asked him how he had got to know such 'animals' as the characters of his book.[60] After only two days there was a rift. The writer's Hollywood career was over.

The plot of *The Man with the Golden Arm* was considerably altered after Algren's departure. Gone was the fact that Algren's hero Frankie Machine (alias Majcinek) is a war veteran and that his drug problem arises from morphine treatment during his time as a soldier. Frankie becomes a junkie pure and simple, his background being dropped as of no interest. The radically dark ending of Algren's novel saw Frankie killing his dealer and hanging himself. This was rewritten for the superstar Sinatra. What now happens is that Frankie's wife, whom he no longer finds very attractive, first kills his drug dealer and then herself. This has the further advantage that Frankie can go off with his new romance, played by Kim Novak. And the book's specific urban context turned out to be as important to Preminger as being faithful to the plot: the plan to shoot the film in Chicago was dropped for financial reasons and the director had the neon wilderness completely rebuilt in the studio.[61] All in all, a modern city novel in which drug addiction was just one problem among others turned into a film about a junkie focusing entirely on Frankie's state of dependence.

As a result there is almost nothing to see of the magic qualities of Algren's neon in Preminger's *The Man with the Golden Arm*. As in MacDonald's *The Neon Jungle* the neon advertisements only convey the message that the neighbourhood is low class and a hangover from a bygone age. Flickering signs flash the prospect of 'GIRLS GIRLS GIRLS'. Other signs indicate 'HOT DOGS', 'CHILI', 'BEER', or, as evidence of poverty, a 'BUDGET PLAN' and 'MONEY TO LOAN'. But all these calls fall by the wayside. The only important presence is the drug dealer's – and he doesn't advertise his services with a flashing sign. Even if the film takes on Frankie's vision of the future, for example his dream of having a professional career as a musician playing the drums, he has always got to get out of this place.[62] Neon does not act as a temptation, neither in the negative sense of satisfying an addiction nor in the positive sense of enabling self-improvement. Unlike Frank Capra in *It's a Wonderful Life* Otto Preminger did not even allow any disturbing dystopia to emerge from the flashing signs. This was typical of the city visions produced by the American cinema after film noir, neon having already lost even the power to cause nightmares.[63]

Critics behind Frosted Glass

By 1960 a book like *The Neon Wilderness* already seemd somewhat old-fashioned. Once upon a time neon had been an inspiration for committed urban fictions. It had blazed a trail for a new perspective on the urban underclass and had given rise to a kind of literature describing the relationship between music, light and urban poverty with poetry and empathy. Now it seemed this 'neon wilderness' signified nothing but an unambiguous image of a bygone age. The neutral look of buildings associated with the International Style, intentionally lacking in ornamentation and using glass and steel, became the new idiom for city architecture. At the same time the urban planners who made room for the motor car in the 1950s turned the neon ghettos bordering urban centres into building sites for freeways, junctions and parking lots. The fascinating network of the neon period unravelled.[64] In the new downtown areas there was little left to see of Algren's claustrophobia – the lights of the tubes and the sounds of the jukebox, automated and rhythmic, dominating lives. As the writer's experiences in Hollywood showed, mainstream American popular culture also gave his fictions a wide berth and he lived to see his view of the world dramatically losing credibility, even in literary circles.

When *The Neon Wilderness* was republished in 1960, Algren took advantage of the opportunity to take his revenge, at least on his intellectual East Coast critics. His introduction to this edition praises Walt Whitman, the nineteenth-century poet of fraternity and solidarity, for being a passionately egalitarian writer who also dedicated his poems to the poorest, most marginalized sections of American society. This passion, according to Algren, had once been an inspiration for American literature. But now these writers had vanished. They had been replaced by new powers in the land, 'armed with blueprints to which the novel and the short story would have to conform'. Algren coined names for these new masters of literature. Leslie Fiedler, who had been particularly critical of him, he called 'Leslie Fleacure'; Lionel Trilling, 'Lionel Thrillingly'; Norman Podhoretz, 'Justin Poodlespitz'. Fleacure, Thrillingly and Poodlespitz were responsible for imposing the pervasive idea of an American literature that was 'untouched by life in America'. The typical representative of this new generation, Algren stated, was always shielded from 'rough weather . . . from nursery to campus to the day his name is printed beside his daddy's on a frost-glass office door'.[65]

Faced with this sophisticated establishment, Algren's literature stood for empathy, showing sympathy for the fate of a 'woman doing hard time in brothel or jail, of the youth forced to a choice of informing or going up himself'.[66] As always, it is via the glow of a neon tube that Algren sought to identify himself as an opponent of the elite and a true friend of ordinary people. On the one hand, the 'payola jungle' is taking over – everywhere are to be found 'apartments with wall-to-wall carpeting where a hidden hi-fi is playing softly'. On the other, in Algren's carpetless zone the 'night-burning neon' was still shining out. There the writer and his characters, for good or evil, were continually being illuminated, plunged into darkness, then lit up again by the indiscriminately glowing and flickering lights of the city.

Nelson Algren ended his day of reckoning with the literature of his time by penning a really bitter comment. *The Neon Wilderness* could, he said, be read in every European city in translation. But in Chicago, the very place that these stories are about, they were not even given shelf-room in the library.[67] Consequently he did not end his life in the city with the rusty heart and the broken nose but far away from the neon wilderness and separated from the nearest metropolis by a belt of rapidly growing middle-class suburbs – in the small coastal town of Sag Harbor, Long Island, New York.[68]

4 LAS VEGAS: CITY OF LIGHTS

Little Dave at the Desert Inn

Dave Hickey first went to Las Vegas when he was a child in the 1950s. One hot afternoon he was sitting with his family in the darkened kitchen of a pink-coloured bungalow. Dave's father and Shelton, the owner of the house, were drinking beer and listening to Billie Holiday's 'Gloomy Sunday'. Over and over again Shelton told his visitors how great it was that he could just throw his saxophone into the trunk of his Pontiac and go and perform at the Desert Inn. He was employed as a resident musician there, in a casino topped by three neon cactuses – green, yellow and blue – sticking up in the air, the owner's name Wilbur Clark shining in flowing red letters and, of course, the name 'DESERT INN', glowing in white light.[1]

It was the period when neon was in decline in all the other American cities, beginning at the end of the 1940s. Prosperous hotels and restaurants were replacing the thin, fragile glass tubes with large-scale plastic installations. Neon was becoming the trademark of establishments that were having problems. Along the great American interstate highways, Route 66 for instance, handmade neon advertisements had once been tailored by skilful producers to suit individual motels in specific locations. Now they were gradually giving way to the mass-produced plastic logos of the motel chains spreading throughout the U. S. and looking all the same everywhere, whether you were in New Mexico or Maine.[2]

Las Vegas was different, though. The use of coloured tubes had been raised up into a fine art – a riot of light, way out in the desert. The neon of the hotels, casinos and restaurants set the city

Hacienda Resort Hotel and Casino, Las Vegas, Nevada.

of hedonism ablaze like nowhere else in the America of the '50s. In 1951 Fremont Street was to become home to a 15-m-high neon cowboy with the nickname 'Vegas Vic', waving at the visitors and inviting them into the Pioneer Club where his boots were placed. A gigantic horseshoe made of neon and light bulbs advertised the Horseshoe Hotel and Casino. The Apache Hotel in the same building boasted the neon outline of a proud Native American. The Golden Nugget Gambling Hall had a large illuminated sign, 16 by

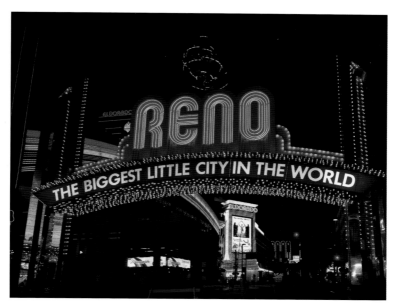

The landmark Reno Arch, Nevada.

16 m, with flashing lights towering above it. In the middle of it was a flashing neon gold nugget, 4 m in diameter, sending out beams of light over a metre long. In 1957 the Mint Casino launched its whole frontage into space, like a pink and white rocket, topped by a neon flashing star.

As in Times Square, the sequencing of the light sources simulated constant movement and transformed Las Vegas into an edgy, dynamic urban environment.[3] Over the years, the illumination of the hotels and casinos became ever more intense until, in the end, the buildings themselves seemed to be shining, flashing, flickering – one great mass of light alongside another, the structures themselves hidden behind the visual effects, one quickly followed by another.

When the new casinos stopped being located on Fremont Street, in the city centre, and established themselves on the Strip, the great highway towards Los Angeles, this gave a new impetus to innovation. On the 'Champagne Tower' of the Flamingo Casino, built in 1953, white bubbles made of light bulbs sparkled. On the Stardust a plastic planet shone, with neon tubes and light bulbs creating a cloud of stars and shooting starlight up into make-believe space.[4] The light effects did not just adorn existing buildings. They themselves served as three-dimensional sculptures, becoming architecture or at night becoming free of any relation to actual constructions. On the Strip, signs and frontages stopped shining out close beside their nearest flashing rivals. Instead they stood alone, projecting their glow up into the desert sky.

Even young Dave recognized the beauty of Las Vegas. In the company of the proud saxophonist he saw the 'million lights' adorning the Desert Inn. He observed the elegantly dressed guests, the shining turquoise swimming pool. He listened to the sound of the roulette wheels and to the music. And he could see his father's growing irritation, envying his friend Shelton's secure job in the neon metropolis.[5] Because that was another advantage of the entertainment city in the desert. This was the only place where jazz musicians did not have to worry every day about their next engagement. In the south of Nevada a city had arisen where show business was king. The usual class distinctions did not hold sway any more. Musicians belonged to the establishment.[6]

As if to emulate Shelton, outdo his father and be close to this glamorous neon world, Dave Hickey returned to Las Vegas decades later with a permanent job – albeit not as a saxophonist. Hickey had in the meantime become one of the most noted art critics in the U.S., taking up a professorship in art history at the University of Nevada. In 1997, when he was well established there, he noted down his childhood reminiscences in the passionate essay 'A Home in the Neon'. He lauded his new home town as an 'ardent explosion of lights in the heart of the pitch-black desert'.[7] In Las Vegas, Hickey stated, the setting sun behind the black mountains leaves hardly any impression, whereas the neon light 'glitters with a reckless and undeniable specificity'. He preferred the 'honest fakery of the neon' to the 'fake honesty of the sunset'.[8]

By the time young Dave had become that great essayist, Las Vegas, the former home of neon, had long reinvented itself. In the interim the casinos of the city had largely gone in for non-neon imitations and replicas of Paris, New York and Venice. In came pirate battles and water fountains and, in the words of the Americanist Laura Bieger, the 'orchestration of "genuine" high culture'.[9] To make way for these new palaces, mainly reflecting European culture, the most popular hotel and gaming complexes of the all-American neon era were eventually demolished.[10] 'Today it looks like Disneyland', a gaming industry big shot complains at the end of this era in Martin Scorsese's *Casino* (1995).[11]

At the same time Las Vegas was growing so rapidly in the late twentieth century that the impressively illuminated theme town was turning into an industrial centre and a city with millions of inhabitants. The only difference was that entertainment was the key industry and not slaughterhouses as in Chicago or automobile manufacture as in Detroit – 'the city's move to the norm', as the historian Hal Rothman summed it up in 2003.[12] At the same time Rothman warned of the toughness of life in this 'normal' Las Vegas, where the constant presence of gambling and pornography proved the old saying that this was a wonderful place if you didn't have any weaknesses.[13] The largest city in Nevada, a state with a notoriously underdeveloped welfare system, may have once been famous for its neon and is now known for the constant threat of rapid social decline.[14] Significantly it is not a charming hedonist that haunts the pages of the most widely read contemporary novel about Las Vegas but a self-destructive drunk. In John O'Brien's *Leaving Las Vegas*, true to the Algren tradition of stories about losers, he is accompanied by a prostitute with a golden heart. Neon is not a glowing presence in this Las Vegas story.[15]

But for Dave Hickey the city remained, even at the end of the twentieth century, a powerful metaphor charged with wonderful associations. Here there were no cultural and social hierarchies – anyone could be a winner, no matter where he came from (the essayist did not say very much about losing).[16] The 'home of neon' represented the best of capitalism: freedom to choose, democracy, the possibility of reinventing yourself. As in Nelson Algren's Chicago, Hickey's Las Vegas is shown as a place where you could be free from the pressures of the cultural elite. It was just that the left-wing oriented humanism of Algren had not made it to the desert.

From Connecticut to Nevada

In the late summer of 1968, notorious for its student uprisings, thirteen students enrolled at Yale University in New Haven, Connecticut, for a research seminar offering a trip to Las Vegas. Nine of them were studying architecture, two urban planning and two graphic design. Three professors were running the event. Beforehand the students, divided into small groups, spent three weeks in the university library in New Haven working on pre-arranged topics. Then the group travelled to the West Coast and spent four days in LA visiting, among other things, the artist Ed Ruscha's studio and Disneyland. Finally the sixteen researchers left California for Southern Nevada and their actual destination, Las Vegas. They stayed there for ten days – free board and lodging – at the newly renovated Stardust Casino. They were supplied with vehicles free of charge by the local car rental firms. Once, the visitors flew over the Strip in a helicopter. As one of the accompanying professors had been given an invitation to the official opening of the Circus Circus Casino, the whole group ended up attending this gala event. The students showed up in party clothes they had bought in the second-hand store run by the Salvation Army in Las Vegas and which they had painted in keeping with the local neon look using fluorescent colours.[17] The group went to town on the task of recording the Las Vegas aesthetic, producing 3,000 m of film material and 5,000 transparencies in the city.[18]

A certain Vaughan Cannon offered his local knowledge to the group. He wasn't just any old tour guide. In his day job Cannon worked for the Young Electric Sign Company (YESCO), perhaps the most important neon firm in the history of architecture. YESCO's founder, Thomas Young, had arrived in Las Vegas in 1932 seeking to extend his advertising business, based in Utah, over the border into Nevada. He had found a sleepy little town where at this time there were only a few fairly inconspicuous neon signs advertising a number of bars, a hotel and a cigar shop. YESCO changed all this – and profited handsomely from the explosive growth of the city. As a result of the Hoover Dam being built in the immediate neighbourhood of Las Vegas, and of Nevada's liberal, gambling-friendly legislation, the place became an entertainment capital in next to no time. And YESCO designed the lights for it. The firm put the artistic design of the facades of the hotels and casinos on a professional footing, creating animated patterns using light bulbs and coloured neon lights. Whereas, in the 1930s, self-educated advertising artists had been in charge of the illumination of Las Vegas, Thomas Young's company gradually started taking on a new generation of designers, some of them with Hollywood experience as scenery designers or cartoon film artists. They turned neon signs into something more than mere billboards stuck on to a building. Through their manipulation of spectacle, flashing lights and glowing tubes covered entire external walls, eventually bringing their effects right out into the street – as at the newly designed Boulder Club in 1947.[19]

The visitors had travelled all the way from New Haven, Connecticut to Nevada to witness these spectacular installations. The seminar guided by YESCO's Vaughan Cannon was called 'Learning from Las Vegas, or Form Analysis as Design Research'. The professors included the architects Denise Scott Brown, Robert Venturi and Steven Izenour.[20] Their book *Learning from Las Vegas* arising out of this trip was published in 1972, and was to become one of the most widely read architecture texts of the late twentieth century. No other piece of writing, according to Martino Stierli, has influenced discussions on architecture and the city to such an extent.[21] This text played a key role in the reappraisal of the urban landscape all over the world, highlighting as it did architecture focused on the street and the kind of spectacular ornamentation that was frequently seen as being vulgar.

Prior to *Learning from Las Vegas* it had been fashionable to pour scorn on roadside advertising. In his widely read polemic *God's Own Junkyard* (1964), the German-born architect Peter Blake described the way the American landscape had developed as the destruction of civilization. While her husband Lyndon was stepping up U.S. involvement in Vietnam, Lady Bird Johnson, the First Lady, devoted herself to work on the 'Highway Beautification Act', which in 1965 declared war on 'neon, junk and ruined landscape'. Among other things, this law resulted in a number of junkyards being hidden behind screens.[22] The authors of *Learning from Las Vegas* simply turned this debate about vulgarity on its head and declared the neon period in Nevada to be a key episode in the history of art. They saw the host of signs and lights not as a tasteless eyesore, but as the obvious expression of the new forms of mobility and perception of their day. For them, 'the intensity of light on the Strip as well as the tempo of its movement is greater to accommodate the greater spaces, greater speeds, and greater impacts that our technology permits and our sensibilities respond to.'[23] They compared Las Vegas first to Versailles, then to Rome. Just as pilgrims to the Italian capital went from church to church, in the same way a gambler in Las Vegas could move from one casino to another. In both cities, public and private space were similarly subject to 'violent juxtapositions'.[24] The design of neon advertising involved an extremely subtle creative process. There was therefore a pressing but worthwhile need to engage with the design, the vocabulary and the range of styles employed by the creators of the signs. To underline this necessity, the three *Learning* authors compared the company employing their guide Vaughan Cannon to the painting 'factory' of Rubens.[25]

Learning from Las Vegas was less provocative than such statements might suggest. The authors were reacting to a widely perceived crisis in the building of American cities in the second half of the twentieth century. They were confronting the forces that, in Nelson Algren's Chicago, for example, had turned the once close neighbourhoods of a city on a human scale into a no-man's-land torn apart by the motor car.[26] The authors identified with Las Vegas in a bid to encourage the architects of their time to develop a more respectful relationship with popular culture. The neon sign at the Flamingo should be the spur to a 'new architecture' for a pluralistic society, bringing an end to the tyranny of what they saw as the architecture 'lacking in symbols' associated with modernity. It was the very seriousness of the followers of the Bauhaus school that they were attacking. They called for an ironic attitude to buildings, particularly as regards ornamentation; something that would reunite architecture with the popular and end its elitism.[27] They were not calling for neon signs on the Champs-Elysées. They were simply after a new modesty in architecture, a new sensitivity for 'the tastes and values of other people'.[28]

Anyone who reads *Learning from Las Vegas* carefully, nevertheless notices that this enthusiasm for Las Vegas only lasts as long as the city meets the expectations of these visitors, newly hooked on all the aspects of pop culture. Denise Scott Brown observed in a new edition of the text in 1977 that the 'delicate and intense' neon towers that had been so admired by the trippers from Connecticut had been replaced by 'bland, white, plastic, rear-illuminated message boards'.[29] Just at the moment when the theorists of architecture started to sing the praises of the fantasy nature of neon light, Las Vegas had already started out in another direction.

The 'Totally Neonized Society'

Hymns of praise to Las Vegas were the expression of an extremely laid-back attitude towards what some cultural critics considered to be superficial trash. They sprang from a simple faith in popular taste and architecture not often associated with established intellectuals.[30] Becoming an aficionado of the glowing lights was, for the authors of *Learning from Las Vegas*, synonymous with breaking away from the cultural elite and finding new creative forms and new narratives in what was widely looked down upon as being trivial. And they were far from being the only ones whose ideas were turning towards the bright lights of Nevada. For design historian Alan Hess, for instance, they were signs of the vitality of everyday architecture, 'an outdoor museum of American popular culture', that had absorbed and highlighted the energy, the readiness to experiment and the inspiration of its environment.[31] Other admirers pointed to the rivalry between the oldest neon company YESCO and its competitors, quick off the mark when it came to competing for every new major order from the casinos. The newcomers' light sculptures served as advertisements both for the gaming palaces and for their own individual creativity. So, for example, it was not a case of anonymous flickering lights in the desert but the light effects

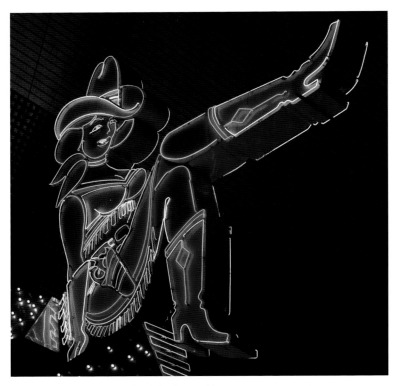

'Vegas Vickie', neon sign for the club Glitter Gulch, Fremont Street Experience, Las Vegas, Nevada.

of the Riviera that were seen in the work of Marge Williams. Likewise, those of the Silver Slipper were recognizable as the work of Jack Larsen; the frontage of the Stardust as the work of Kermit Wayne.[32] Charles Barnard, designer of the giant illuminated cowgirl 'Vegas Vickie', called the work of this generation of advertising artists 'heroic' – products of the individualism typical of the American West.[33]

But there are also less heroic stories to be told about the neon era. One of these could start with the fact that the most sensational visual spectacles Las Vegas had to offer in the 1950s were not the work of creative designers but of those who were planning for a nuclear holocaust. More than 100 underground atomic tests were carried out in the Nevada desert, at a test site only about 95 km from the city. While bombs were exploding within visible distance, in Las Vegas 'atomic cocktails' were being mixed and dancing girls dressed in an 'atomic look' went through their stage routines. In 1953 a 'Miss North Las Vegas Atomic Bomb Contest' was held to find the beauty most deserving of this title.[34] Girls in bikinis posed with Geiger counters. 'Miss Atomic Blast' appeared in nothing but an imitation atomic cloud made of cotton wool.[35] The well-known (at least locally) stripper Lili St Cyr arranged her wedding to coincide exactly with an atomic test.[36] Whenever a test was due, people drank the night away, getting together in the small hours to turn their eyes towards the south, past the neon advertisements, into the glow of the atom bomb of that day. The pianist at the Desert Inn, saxophonist Shelton's colleague, had composed the 'Atom-Bomb Bounce' – Boogie Woogie music providing the sound track for these atomic nights.[37] Critical observers of Las Vegas find this continual flirtation with the bomb typical of the superficiality of the gambling capital, of its cynical, relentless self-marketing. The literary critic Ken Cooper read Las Vegas of the '50s as a metaphor for an atomic world from which there was no escape: 'a microcosm of atomic roulette'.[38]

It was not only the atomic cloud that gave rise to this different perception of Las Vegas. Just at the time when young Dave Hickey was standing transfixed by the Desert Inn, there were other visitors who were less easily impressed. The journalists Katharine Best and Katharine Hillyer, for example, on a visit to Nevada in the early '50s, thought the city 'a totally neonized society'.[39] In an account written by them and published in 1955 as *Las Vegas: Playtown USA* they did not focus on the multiplicity of lights but on the totalitarian nature of this cityscape marked by hedonism. This included the fact that all aspects of life in Las Vegas were subject to racial segregation. Best and Hillyer did not notice particular light effects on the casino towers. They were more interested in another spectacle: persons unknown had erected two burning crosses in the style of the Ku Klux Klan close to where 120 African Americans were living. The two authors used their book to undermine the advertising techniques of the casino owners. They asked tourists in Las

Vegas to pass their time in Nevada doing nothing but horse-riding, hiking in the desert and playing badminton on 'imported grass'; not spending a penny on gambling and thus outsmarting the bosses of what they perceived as neon totalitarianism.[40]

Other critically inclined journalists investigated the many links between organized crime and the gaming industry in Las Vegas. Their reports also displayed little enthusiasm for Southern Nevada's glowing tubes. In *The Green Felt Jungle*, for example, published in 1963, investigative reporters Ed Reid and Ovid Demaris, after two years' research into the underworld of Las Vegas, called the neon city a 'grotesque Disneyland'.[41] (Elsewhere Ed Reid referred to the city as a 'gigantic television set with 20 channels, all of them broadcasting full-color spectaculars at the same time'.[42]) They were less interested in the exteriors of the casinos than in the interior mechanics of the gambling businesses. They were not describing what they saw in terms of creative advertising but as indicators of the relationship between architectural details and the maximization of profit. They noted that there were no chairs or sofas in the casinos (except, of course, at the roulette tables). There were no clocks, likewise, and no windows or doors that might allow for a glimpse of the sun or the moon and thus give some idea of real time. Reid and Demaris did not allow themselves to be distracted. They ignored the flickering lights and focused on the 'true story of Las Vegas'.[43]

Later, cultural historians often agreed with the early critics of Las Vegas. The fact that the frontage of the Stardust Casino installed in 1958 covered an area 70 m wide and was lit by more than 2,000 m of neon tubes and 1,000 light bulbs; that the tower of light at the Lucky, built shortly afterwards, soared 50 m up into the air; that the pylon at the Dunes was made up of 5,000 m of neon tubes and 7,200 light bulbs, reaching 60 m up into the sky, costing half a million dollars and consuming 624,684 watts of electricity; and that, in 1968, the Stardust went on to erect a tower of light yet another 2 m higher, with a lift in the supporting column, and 25 m wider, with a 30-m-high cloud of stardust made of neon lights and light bulbs?[44] To critical observers, all these superlatives, outbidding one another, appeared to be part and parcel of the soulless

A ground crewman controls the tether cable while erecting a sign at the Stardust Resort and Casino, Las Vegas, late 1960s.

self-marketing of a gambling empire. For the technology historian David Nye, for instance, the light shows of Las Vegas – unlike the 'miracles' of the Industrial Revolution – produced nothing but spectacle. The achievements of technology witnessed in railways, skyscrapers, bridges and even the floods of light in the modern city seem sublime in other places. In Southern Nevada, Nye claims, they merely serve to encourage irrationality and the narcissism of the gaming table.[45] Following in the footsteps of the investigative journalists Reid and Demaris, the historian John A. Jakle points to the actual function of the spectacular light effects: only in such dramatically lit surroundings could visitors be induced to forget

Sign for the Stardust Resort and Casino, Las Vegas.

the natural rhythms of life and devote themselves entirely to gambling.[46] For the French philosopher Bruce Bégout, Las Vegas is, in the end, 'Zeropolis', the city of nothing. It makes a mockery of reality, according to Bégout, turning reality, the human community and the concepts of culture and civilization into a 'grotesque farce'.[47] Bégout reads the neon light show as a typical aspect of this farce. Behind its flashing lights, the incessant repetition of effects and the bright colours turning people in the street the same blue, green or violet as the lights, there is a total absence of meaning. Apart, that is, from the insistently flashing demand that one fall for the fiction constructed by the city, believe in it, allow oneself to be mesmerized by it.[48] A neon figure like 'Vegas Vickie', Charles Barnard's flashing neon cowgirl, becomes for Bégout an icon of 'robotic eroticism'. She is a figure of myth exuding 'boundless cruelty', a 'celestial and mechanical whore'.[49]

The positions are clearly defined. The authors of *Learning from Las Vegas*, like the essayist Dave Hickey, felt at home in the city's lack of authenticity. They applauded its effects and its superficiality, played the role of happy hedonists and lovers of personal freedom and looked upon capitalism with its shining neon opportunities for competition as the best of all possible democratic systems. Critics such as Bruce Bégout, on the other hand, expected more from the city. Neon seemed like a nightmare to them. Las Vegas, Bégout writes, is like a neon tube which 'without any concern for history . . . pulps all human events into an electromechanical swill of parody which leaves absolutely nothing in one piece'. The city turns everything real into a joke.[50] For the Marxist urbanist Mike Davis, the situation is even more dramatic: the gambling metropolis, using up water and energy, polluting its whole environment, seems to him a nightmare vision of the future of our planet. 'No other city in the American West seems to be as driven by occult forces' and so ignorant in relation to social and natural pressures. It is therefore, for Davis, completely understandable that in Stephen King's horror novel, *The Stand*, the central character, apparently even unpopular with Marxists, chooses to set up his headquarters in Las Vegas: the devil himself.[51]

Take Aim at the Machine: New Journalists in Las Vegas

The neon lights of Las Vegas not only gave rise to extremely positive and extremely negative reactions in the late twentieth century. They also inspired some considerably more nuanced accounts. For the 'New Journalists', American reporters with literary ambitions in the late 1960s and early '70s, the neon city in the desert became an intellectually challenging subject. For writers such as Tom Wolfe, Hunter S. Thompson, Joan Didion and John Gregory Dunne, the place like no other represented postmodernity. This was where popular culture was at, seeming as it did to blur all social and cultural distinctions.[52] Las Vegas was spectacular, as spectacular as the period of the Vietnam War, the hippy counter culture and experimenting with drugs – a period in which, as Todd Gitlin wrote, 'reality appears illusory and illusions take on lives of their own'.[53] The desert city built on fictions was therefore the perfect place to develop new forms of essay and reportage, texts that challenged the boring seriousness and alleged neutrality of mainstream journalism. The new reporters quite consciously went out in search of the glow and the flicker, so as to exploit the sources of this energy.

Admittedly it is questionable how consciously aware writer Hunter S. Thompson was of the neon city. When he set out for Las Vegas from Los Angeles in spring 1971, along with his friend, the lawyer Oscar Acosta, the pair had loaded into their car generous quantities of mescalin, LSD and cocaine in addition to a large number of other drugs – as Thompson wrote, 'a whole galaxy of multi-colored uppers, downers, screamers, laughers'.[54] A variety of these substances were consumed during the journey across California and Nevada. Thompson's piece on Las Vegas does not therefore fulfil his actual journalistic brief at the time (which was to write an article for the magazine *Sports Illustrated* on a motorcycle race taking place in the gambling capital). Instead, it turns into a meditation on the interaction of drugs and Las Vegas. Arriving at the hotel, the reporter notices 'a gigantic neon sign outside the window'. Not only does it block the view of the mountains, it also really gets on his nerves. The narrator sees 'millions of colored balls running around a very complicated track, strange symbols & filigree'. He hears the noisy buzzing of the installation and in a panic warns his friend of the 'machine in the sky . . . some kind of electric snake coming straight at us'. (The attorney advises him to 'shoot it'; the reporter replies: 'Not yet . . . I want to study its habits.'[55]) After a visit to the Circus Circus (Saturday evening in this casino, Thompson informs us, is what the world would be like 'if the Nazis had won the war'), the text steps up the feeling of paranoia. The gigantic clown outside the gaming centre – a colossal tower of light on the Strip – takes on a life of its own, becoming a 'vicious nazi drunkard', 70 m high, appearing in the middle of the night outside the hotel and shouting 'Woodstock über alles!' It doesn't matter whether you are talking about neon installations or any other items from the paraphernalia of modernity (such as the 600 pieces of transparent Neutrogena soap supplied on request to the two guests by the chambermaid); either way, in Las Vegas it is all too much. Thus *Fear and Loathing*'s narrator has to conclude that the city is no place for psychedelic drugs: 'Reality itself is too twisted.'[56]

Hunter S. Thompson's contemporary John Gregory Dunne, a scriptwriter and novelist, arrived on a visit to the irritating flashing lights a bit later. What he was carrying by way of baggage was not a ridiculously large amount of drugs but a nervous breakdown he had had shortly before and was hoping to recover from in Southern Nevada.[57] What he was after was seeing new people, hearing new stories and finding himself in the alien cityscape.[58] He was arriving in the city at a moment when he felt like a man who had been bypassed by time. Unlike his fellow countrymen who were ignorant of history, he still knew the difference between 'VE Day' (the day of the Allied victory in Europe) and 'VJ Day' (the end of the war against Japan). And at the wheel of his car he was not singing the recent hit 'Light My Fire' by The Doors but, in Latin, a medieval Gregorian chant.[59] It is no great surprise, then, to learn that Dunne did not feel very much at home in Southern Nevada. Instead of checking in to one of the glittering palaces on the Strip, he stayed at the Royal Polynesian motel, where empty peanut butter jars were used as glasses and 'aging showgirls' were swimming in the pool.[60] The neon of Las Vegas did nothing for him. The towers reaching up into the sky seemed to him to be 'over-loaded utility poles'. He called the casinos 'celestial hamburger stands and gimcrackery fairy palaces'.[61] His eye was caught, not by the light shows of the city, but by the grotesque bodies of the inhabitants. First the narrator observes his landlady's artificial leg, then he encounters a prostitute with only one breast, and then in the topless bars of the city he notices the sagging breasts and the skin 'crosshatched with veins and maternity stretch marks'. Finally, in the bars on Fremont Street, he sees bikers weighing 300 lb as well as 'women whose features had long since been swallowed by their jowls', both groups having the same 'slack fatty tissues nourished exclusively by a diet of cornflakes and Dr Pepper'.[62] If Thompson's travel report is a little over the top and paranoid, Dunne produces an autobiographical sketch brimming with exhaustion, alienation and a modernist disgust at the stupidity and ugliness of everyday life. Las Vegas is an 'idiot Disneyland'. Only at night

Old motels and historic neon art: Las Vegas, Nevada, 2007.

Directions in Las Vegas, Nevada, 2007.

is everything different. Then Las Vegas is 'an idiot Disneyland with lights'.[63]

On Joan Didion's visit to Las Vegas, unlike her husband John Gregory Dunne she was less interested in breasts and sagging jowls than in identifying how the city fitted into American culture in the late '60s. The signs that Didion noticed were the ones shining out over the wedding chapels in the city. 'ONE MOMENT PLEASE – WEDDING' the words outside said while ceremonies were taking place as on a conveyor belt. (The journalist saw another chapel with the advertising slogan: 'Sincere and Dignified Since 1954'.[64]) Didion observed a pregnant bride, her husband and her family celebrating the instant wedding just finished with shrimp cocktails and steak in a restaurant on the Strip. She noted the colour of the champagne (pink) and listened as the bride wept, declaring amidst the tears that everything had been just as beautiful as she had 'hoped and dreamed'.[65] For Didion, a reporter based in Los Angeles, this world of neon chapels, pink-coloured sparkling wine and pregnant brides was a scene from the past, a complete contrast to the rapidly changing life of metropolitan America. Las Vegas made such an impression, in fact, that in a novel published a few years later, *Play It as It Lays*, Didion created a sort of counter figure to these conveyor-belt brides: the actress Maria Wyeth, experiencing Las Vegas in a state of profound personal crisis and encountering this world of banality with extreme sensitivity. Maria is so thin-skinned that she can feel the 'waves of voices' just like 'colours and the power of light'. She imagines herself blindfold confronted with the neon advertisements of the Thunderbird or the Flamingo and being able to sense through her skin which casino she is standing in front of.[66] Her sensitivity, however, is accompanied by a traumatic feeling of isolation. In her fragility Maria drifts through Las Vegas, leaving it behind without so much as a trace. Her presence is observed but not registered.

Unlike her husband, Didion managed to develop a perspective on the city that avoided the voyeurism of male visitors to Las Vegas. Like Dunne, however, who seemed to be celebrating his detachment from the 'idiot Disneyland with lights', Didion also gave the impression of being superior to the spectacle of pop culture. It is not the brides in the neon chapels that Didion identified with. Her real heroine is the hypersensitive Maria, who is as ethereal as light itself.

At the start of the twenty-first century, the historian Hal Rothman looked back at the literary history of his city. He decided that travel pieces such as those by Dunne, Didion and Thompson said next to nothing about Las Vegas but a great deal about the neuroses of their authors.[67] Then again, the travelling reporters were after something totally different from an accurate portrait of the neon city. Hunter S. Thompson's work provides the most powerful example. Here, far from the metropolitan centres and right in the heart of popular culture, a writer's relationship with American culture could be revealed for what it was. So Thompson's Las Vegas journey led to a creative breakthrough. He was carried away by his writing, setting out in a new direction that produced the fantasy *Fear and Loathing in Las Vegas*, which has become a classic work of contemporary literature.[68] It is possible that in the writing of the 'New Journalists' there was only room for one extreme

Treasure in the Neon Museum's 'boneyard' in Las Vegas, Nevada, c. 1980–2006.

form of expression. The flashing signs of Las Vegas dim next to Thompson's manic prose.

'Hospital-fruit-basket Orange': Tom Wolfe

Tom Wolfe, the most celebrated New Journalist, had visited the city in the early 1960s, following which he wrote 'Las Vegas (What?) Las Vegas (Can't Hear You! Too Noisy) Las Vegas!!!', an essay that would be difficult to match for its excitement about the capital of neon. Wolfe did not see the glow and the flicker either through a drug-induced haze like Thompson or through the distorting mirror of an idiots' Disneyland like Dunne. He observed the city with genuine enthusiasm for the new forms and effects developed by Nevada designers. Wolfe made up a whole host of terms to sum up the forms of the signs: 'Boomerang Modern, Palette Curvilinear, Flash Gordon Ming-Alert Spiral, McDonald's Hamburger Parabola, Mint Casino Elliptical, Miami Beach Kidney'.[69] He described their colours with the words 'tangerine, broiling magenta, livid pink, incarnadine, fuchsia demure, Congo ruby, methyl green, viridine, aquamarine, phenosafranine, incandescent orange, scarlet-fever purple, cynic blue, tesselated bronze, hospital-fruit-basket orange'.[70] He was clearly enthusiastic about the shows the signs put on, the sophisticated flowing champagne at the Flamingo, the tremendous plans for what would be the next gigantic tower of light.

Unlike his fellow reporters, Wolfe was also interested in the creators of these pulsating effects, the advertising artists of the city. Thus he described Vaughan Cannon, later the *Learning from Las Vegas* group's guide, admiringly as 'one of those tall, blond Westerners, the builders of places like Las Vegas and Los Angeles, whose eyes seem to have been bleached by the sun'. The reporter was full of enthusiasm when Hermon Boernge (a colleague of the tall blond cowboy), asked about a particular artistic effect several storeys high, first answered 'I don't know' and then swiftly added: 'It's a sort of nose effect. Call it a nose.'[71] Neon designers like Boernge and Cannon, Wolfe said, were totally pragmatic. They didn't even have terms for the forms they created, working on the enormous lighting projects of this totally new city unthinkingly and untheoretically. This made them into heroes in Wolfe's eyes.

The admiration shown by Wolfe towards the neon city was not, however, as innocent as it might seem. In the end this writer, as much as Vaughan Cannon and his fellow designers, saw himself as a go-getting salesman for the new forms and styles – an innovator, a prophet. This was not perhaps for the whole Western city of light but for a new type of journalism in the 1960s directed against the boring seriousness of conventional reportage. His motivation was to sell his own 'new journalism' and to provoke the literary scene. So, for example, in one satirical piece he described the editors of the *New Yorker*, that most influential intellectual magazine, as mummified bodies chiefly spending their time exchanging notes.[72] Wolfe launched his almost manic style against this bureaucratic establishment. In a piece about the racing driver Junior Johnson he described the noise of the racing car as 'Ggghhzzzzzzz-hhhhhhgggggggzzzzzzzzzeeeeong! – gawdam!'. In his report from Las Vegas, the first sentence repeats one and the same word ('hernia')

57 times, imitating the monotony of the croupier's calls.[73] Wolfe's use of language took its cue from the flashing of neon, the onomatopoeia of comics, cinematographic effects – anything that wasn't dusty, hackneyed and uptight. He saw himself as a pragmatic, experimental designer of a new idiom beyond the ken of a stuffy intellectual elite. Just like the improvisational neon designers, he presented himself as a man of action writing from the gut (the fact that he had a PhD from the elite university of Yale was largely glossed over).

Tom Wolfe was not, however, particularly enthusiastic about the people under the neon light. When, for example, he came across pensioners having a pleasant evening in the casinos, he summed them up as people in 'those last years, before the tissue deteriorates and the cores of the cerebral cortex hang in the skull like a clump of dried seaweed'. The aged ladies had 'that fleshy, humped-over shape across the back of the shoulders' and their torsos 'hunched up into fat little loaves supported by bony, atrophied leg stems sticking up into their hummocky hips'.[74] The last stop on his tour of the neon world led the traveller to Las Vegas's psychiatric services, where he did not notice illuminated signs but rather the convulsive movements of the patients – for example an 'old babe' who in a totally institutionalized fashion continually moved her hand back and forth, pulling the handle of an imaginary slot machine.[75] The contrast between the exquisite flashing of the lights elsewhere in Las Vegas and the grotesquely moving bodies on the psychiatric ward is striking. Wolfe considered neon to be extremely decorative and ideologically perfect. But those lit by neon did not count as attractive in his eyes.

Nelson Algren had at one time sought out the neon district of Chicago to show his solidarity with ordinary people. In his stories and essays he identified profoundly with the rusting, teeming city. He walked the same streets as László Moholy-Nagy, who had brought with him to the Illinois of the post-war period an enthusiasm for the metropolis typical of the avant-garde of the 1920s. Now, two decades later, a good 2,700 km further west, the *flâneurs* of Las Vegas were not into urban utopias. Wolfe, Didion, Dunne and Thompson, and Dave Hickey after them, exploited Las Vegas as a metaphorically powerful stage on which their own egos and their relationship with popular culture could be dramatically highlighted. Simply by being so egocentric, the New Journalists of the 1960s and '70s are highly representative of visitors to the urban space in Southern Nevada that promoted not togetherness and urban tradition, but radical individualism and ignorance of the past. Tom Wolfe, the most daring exponent of glow-and-flicker writing, was particularly well placed to embody this. When the reporter, spellbound by the lights of Nevada, came to sum up the artistic traditions of the twentieth century, he finally even attacked that exile who, two decades before, just as fascinated as Wolfe himself, had photographed the neon of Chicago by night – shortly before his life was brought to an end at only 49 by leukaemia. The greatest fan of Las Vegas had no time for the artist, though. 'The hell with Moholy-Nagy,' Tom Wolfe wrote, 'if anybody ever heard of him.'[76]

5 GREEN FINGERS

The Waterfall on Broadway

Louis Faurer wandered through Manhattan almost every day, his walks taking him to Times Square. The 'hypnotic dusk light' attracted him, he said later. His whole life during this period, between 1946 and 1950, was devoted entirely to taking photographs at night in this vicinity and then developing them in the darkroom belonging to his friend and colleague Robert Frank.[1]

Although a fashion photographer for magazines such as *Harper's Bazaar* and *Flair*, Faurer took these photos on his own account and they were of an entirely personal nature. Unlike László Moholy-Nagy walking through Chicago, Louis Faurer did not focus on the abstract play of light but on the people out and about in Times Square. He photographed those passing by: loners, couples, families and flower and match sellers. These subjects included a cinema ticket-lady in her ticket booth surrounded by enormous letters advertising the film 'GOONA GOONA LAND OF LOVE' and a sophisticated cigar smoker in front of an entrance stairway with a sign inviting one to 'DANCE WITH BEAUTIFUL GIRLS'. Faurer's aim was to get closer to the people in Times Square and capture their 'enduring spirit . . . bathed by such piercing white light'.[2] Like Moholy-Nagy, however, he also experimented with photographic techniques. At the start of an evening he set the aperture, focus and speed on his camera and then did not alter them at all, even when it grew darker and the lights appeared to be shining brighter. In this way nothing was lost of the atmosphere. He made his way through the crowds as if in a trance.[3]

Louis Faurer, *Bus No. 7, New York City, 1950*, photograph.

Faurer wandered through streets that had for some time returned to being a test lab for the advertising industry once the blackout of the war years was over. Douglas Leigh, the whiz-kid of the lit advertising spectacular, unveiled one of his most enormous installations in 1948. In place of Wrigley's flashing neon aquarium between 44th and 45th Street, Leigh set up a 40-m-wide waterfall, high above Broadway. On both sides of the cascade and above the neon signs 'CLOTHES for MEN' and 'APPAREL for WOMEN' a male and female statue posed for a clothes store. At first the two of them were naked. Later, supposedly after protests from prudish passers-by, both figures were clothed in togas made of neon lights.[4] A Budweiser advertisement set up in 1952 on the junction of Broadway and 49th Street brought to life an eagle made of neon lights that switched in precise sequence, so that the bird appeared to take flight over the wide roof of the building. A prancing, 20-m-high model made of light demonstrated that Miss Youth Form, the aristocrat of briefs, stayed right where it was supposed to stay.[5] On 44th Street, the cartoon character Lulu appeared in pastel-coloured neon, swung back and forth on a trapeze, turned somersaults and finally slid down a giant handkerchief – until an equally giant hand grabbed her with the animated slogan: 'SOFT! STRONG! POPS UP! KLEENEX'. If Douglas Leigh had had his way, Times Square would have been even more fantastic. He would have liked to produce whole apartment blocks in the shape of advertised products: a glass of orange juice as big as a building, for example, or a building in the shape of a perfume bottle that would spray passers-by with clouds of scent.[6] But the most innovative light effects were of a more abstract nature. From 1952, at the north end of Times Square, there was an advertisement for Canada Club whisky which put on a light show that experimented with flashing lights and colours in a strikingly non-figurative way.[7]

Louis Faurer went in for wild collage in his photographs. They were ambiguous, sometimes unfocused.[8] They played with light streaming from innumerable lamps and tubes on to the film- and theatre-goers and dramatically highlighting faces and movement. A picture from 1949, shot on Broadway, shows five young, laughing women in a car. To the left of them, the sign 'GOTHAM' is lit up; on the right, behind them, are Pepsi-Cola installations; in front of them, reflected in the hood, are the advertisements they are driving towards. Using this rather jumbled outward appearance Faurer sought and found precise pictorial expression for the amazement of the young women. At other times the juxtaposition of lights and passers-by seems instead to create mini-dramas of urban disorientation. For instance, a father and a son look transfixed, but in different directions, at the signs flooding them with light. A whole family have stopped on a sidewalk as if blinded by the effects. Faurer also captured intimate moments (a woman rearranging her companion's dishevelled hair on his clearly visible bald patch; cigarette smoke coming out of a pedestrian's mouth blending with the haze of the lights). Another time he went for a little distance rather than intimacy – photographing Times Square as a passenger on a moving number 7 bus. But the bus's windows are like human eyes and the picture, as so often in the case of Faurer, comes across as a reflection of city experience itself. Whether on a bus or in the street, the photographer was not in search of a higher viewpoint, an analytical position. He focused almost entirely on individual particularities, seeing himself as a humanist who documented the world of neon like a twentieth-century village photographer. In this way he could spontaneously follow the moods of the city, the play of light and shade, faces, bodies, illuminated signs. What was on show here, as before the war, was democracy enjoying itself by night. Still.

Graz, 1953: 'Advertising Comes from Nothing'

Alois Hergouth, the eleventh child of a mason, returned to Graz, Austria, in autumn 1945 aged twenty, after being a prisoner of war. He started to study ethnology, linguistics and the history of religion and also began writing: his first pieces of journalism and poetry, which were published in daily papers in the capital of Steiermark or broadcast on Graz Radio. In 1947 he interrupted his studies for six years to devote himself to literature. In 1953 his first collection of poems was published – a slim volume in the series 'Steiermark Authors', which offered young regional writers a first chance at publication. Hergouth chose the title *Neon und Psyche*.[9]

Few post-war European authors took neon lights as the main subject of their writing. It was certainly a surprise to find it in the work of this young Austrian, as Hergouth tended to go in for more timeless images: 'Abendlied einer Amsel' (A Blackbird's Serenade) and 'Geplätscher des Brunnens' (Murmur of the Fountain); and timeless combinations of images, such as: '*Schneeblume weiss / Mohnblume rot, / und ein blauer Regen über den Wiesen*' (Snow-flower white / poppy red, / and a blue rain over the meadows). Hergouth's poems aim at conveying universal truths. They are not usually historically specific. Even poems such as 'Soldatengrab' (Soldier's Grave) deal with the atmosphere of the post-war period using traditional imagery:

Das Ross
hat den Reiter verloren,
und irrt, und

klappert mit glänzenden Hufen.
Wohin?

The horse
has lost its rider,
and is wandering and
clip-clopping its shining hooves.
Where to?

However, some of the poems in *Neon und Psyche* deviate from this claim to timelessness. They situate Hergouth's poetry in the modern world. Often they adopt the standard European criticism of commerce and popular culture. Hergouth's poem 'Illustrierte Zeitung' (Illustrated Newspaper), for example, paints the 'Chief editor / of the great worldwide illustrated magazines' as a devil-like character exploiting any 'filmstar in a negligee' and churning out 'page after page of murder, mayhem and munitions'. This satanic figure was out for 'illusions', preferring 'paper flowers' to real ones, and his cheap fictions held out the prospect of 'heaven on earth'. In 'Geschäftsstrasse bei Nacht' (Downtown Street at Night), the poetic voice observing a city comes to the conclusion that 'advertising comes from nothing'. The street lights suggest associations: '*Fiebernder Nebelstaub dreht sich / wie Seidenschatten aus Nacht und Synkopen Parfüm*' (Feverish haze spins perfume / like silk shadows out of the night and feelings of faintness). In a verse describing the desolation of the present there appears the verbless sentence: '*Der blasse, betrunkene Mond vor der Bar*' (The pale, drunken moon at the bar). This is a repeated motif in Hergouth's poetry, the interaction of natural light and neon advertising – producing a sense of hopelessness with violent undertones. '*Nachts hängen / grüne Finger ins Nichts, / und glitzernde Neonschlangen greifen den Mond an*' (At night / green fingers hang into nothingness, / and glittering neon snakes attack the moon) is how the poem 'Illusion' puts it. The ironic 'Hymne an Hawaii' (Hymn to Hawaii) sees illuminated tubes as '*melancholisches Schlinggewächs / unter den Sternen des Broadway*' (melancholy creepers / under the stars of

Broadway), describing the Pacific Island idyll conjured up by advertising as a '*Reklametrick für Likör und Rouge*' (advertising gimmick for liquor and rouge). The poem 'Grossstadtreklame' (City Advertisement) imagines future funerals being staged as '*Weihrauch mit Neon und künstlicher Trauer*' (incense with neon and artificial grieving). *Neon und Psyche* tends to present urban advertising as a programming of people's sensibilities. '*Wir bieten Erbauung*' (We Offer Uplift), is what the flashing tubes say, according to the poet, as well as '*Wir bieten Romantik*' (We Offer Romance) and '*Wir bieten Moral*' (We Offer Morality).[10]

Alois Hergouth aimed his criticism at the totalitarian quality of advertising lights – just like Theodor Adorno, who used neon as a metaphor for the culture industry as a whole and Siegfried Kracauer, who once described the power of light on the office workers of the 1920s. For Kracauer, the power of light turns '*Glanz*' (glamour) into '*Gehalt*' (substance) and '*Zerstreuung*' (distraction) into '*Rausch*' (stupor), but then: 'If the waiter switches it off, though, the eight-hour day shines in again.'[11] Like these modernist intellectuals the poet from Graz described the invasion of people's sensibilities by neon. He was concerned both with the prescriptive programming of the light sequencing and with the way in which the psyches of the target audience were being conditioned by the installations. According to Adorno, art opposes the omnipresent neon brightness with darkness.[12] And so, too, the young Alois Hergouth considered himself to be a poet of depth who devoted himself more to the dark side than the 'glittering neon snakes' – and saw little of substance in the urban wilderness.

Neon und Psyche is not only concerned with local or European neon advertising but continually refers to Broadway, to Hawaii, to the worldwide fantasies reaching Steiermark in Austria after the war via the cinema and the press. Hergouth was more than just a provincial observer. No doubt his critical engagement with the world of advertising and mass culture was a kind of initiation ritual for a poet starting out on his career and embarking on a record of his times.

He quite correctly identified the metaphorical potential of neon snakes. This was good timing as the neon tube was soon to become the unequivocal symbol of the red-light district. Hergouth's poems saw this coming. Thus the observer sees a '*Liebespaar / noch erhitzt und ein wenig erregt*' (A couple of lovers / still stimulated and a bit excited) at the sight of the 'neon snakes' in the city. The 'worldwide illustrated magazine of mass culture' published by the Devil himself shows 'the filmstar' with 'more than exciting breasts'. The poem 'Grossstadtreklame' imagines 'night clubs . . . particularly exciting', along with 'nylon-covered legs' and 'heart machines / all non-stop'. *Neon und Psyche* put over the message that the 'green fingers' made of light no longer extended just into nothingness. They were reaching out for the bodies of the passers-by.

Lolita in the Light

While Alois Hergouth was working on *Neon und Psyche*, another European writer, an émigré to the United States, went hunting butter-flies with his wife. They bequeathed the insects caught to the most prestigious scientific institutions, such as the Zoology Museum of the University of Harvard or the Cornell University collection. Their summer hunting expeditions took them all over America. They stopped in Telluride, Colorado, in Afton, Wyoming, and in Ashland, Oregon. In the evening, and when the weather was too awful for the hunt, the writer devoted his time to a novel recording the im-pressions gained on these trips. This novel featured a couple going on treks across the USA in the 1950s. He made his central character a man the same age as himself, but he gave him a partner on the road who was considerably younger than the author's real wife.[13]

In 1955 Vladimir Nabokov, the butterfly hunter, was to describe, in the novel that became *Lolita*, the light of the glowing tubes in as detached a manner as Alois Hergouth. The novel observes every-day American life with great amusement, ignoring neon at first. The narrator Humbert Humbert – lover, seducer and violator of twelve-year-old Dolores 'Lolita' Haze – refers to such advertisements just once in passing while chauffeuring his child-wife back and forth across the u. s. Only after losing Lolita are the shining letters and signs forced to his attention. In deep despair Humbert is driving through a small town at night 'somewhere in Appalachia' where 'sherry-red letters of light' are visible, a

> large thermometer with the name of a laxative quietly dwelt on the front of a drugstore . . . the outline of a restaurant sign, a large coffee pot, kept bursting, every full second or so, into emerald life, and every time it went out, pink letters saying Fine Foods relayed it, but the pot could still be made out as a latent shadow teasing the eye before its next emerald resurrection.

The neon lights, Nabokov writes, pulsate in a slower rhythm than Humbert's heart. The novel constructs a tight connection between the sometimes ridiculous, sometimes monstrous and sometimes fascinating narrator and the spectacular lights going on and off. In the flashing of the neon lights he begins to weep, 'drunk on the impossible past'.[14] It doesn't take long for the paedophile also to remember the moments after sex with the twelve-year-old in which he felt 'shame and despair', in which he had embraced his Lolita 'at the peak of this human, agonized selfless tenderness' – albeit only until his 'lust would swell again', the child would sigh 'oh, *no*' and the reader can only presume that Humbert passes over in silence the violation that followed. All this takes place 'in the neon light coming from the paved court through the slits in the blind'.[15] But this scene of sexual violence is not accompanied by enticing letters, signs, symbols – the intertextual collage of thermometers, restaurant marquees and coffee pots. It represents the cold hardness of Humbert Humbert; it also symbolizes the anonymity of a world that allows space to a Humbert Humbert.

The Invention of the 25-Cent Peepshow

As Hergouth and Nabokov predicted, escalating desires transformed the history of neon light. And there is no better place to observe this process than in Times Square. Proudly soaring neon eagles, aquariums of illuminated fish, Lulu turning somersaults on the paper handkerchief – these charmingly pulsating symbols now gave way to another repertoire of images. The centre of the neon universe, once bathed in democratic optimism, was being increasingly taken over by pornography and prostitution.

In the late 1970s the lighting designer Rudi Stern traced the transformation of Times Square back to the decline of the production of neon as a craft. The new advertising techniques, Stern complains, went in for plastic in a big way, thus sounding a death knell for the sophistication of the glowing lights. Stern insisted, full of nostalgia, that once upon a time families had wandered across Times Square enjoying the 'electric street theater'. This was now a thing of the past.[16]

Possibly, however, it was not plastic that ruined Times Square. Gradually this spectacular showcase for inventive advertising art degenerated into a positively demonic distorting mirror of urban life. The blame for this should largely be put on the rise in prostitution, drug dealing and pornography. This was in evidence everywhere in America but was particularly extreme in Times Square, the American piazza.[17] Even before the war the neighbourhood had been known as an area for drug dealing, a centre for the sex industry and the place to get 'adult books'.[18] In the post-war years it became increasingly noted for male prostitution in particular. In the mid-1960s the arrival of heroin further boosted criminality in that part of the city. In 1966 the first 25-cent peepshow was opened, giving rise to a spate of such businesses.[19] By the mid-1970s the majority of cinemas in Times Square were devoted entirely to pornographic films. Entrepreneurs on the make opened topless shoeshine booths as well as intimate peepshow joints, sometimes doing away with the glass screen between the clients and performers and thus providing extra services.[20] You didn't get the smell of coffee wafting over the pavement but the sound of porno films being broadcast on to the street from the cinemas to attract customers.[21] Gone were Douglas Leigh's dreams of buildings looking like a glass of orange juice and architecture imitating perfume bottles. The smell was that of a new neon wilderness.

'At the Foot of the Pricks'

A bit further north of the rapidly changing Times Square, Langston Hughes had helped to kick off the Harlem Renaissance back in the 1920s. This was the first black literary and artistic avant-garde to be appreciated also by white audiences. In this period Harlem became a centre for African American culture. Combining literary experimentation with jazz rhythms, Hughes was to become one of the most popular writers of his generation. And identification with the city was to remain part of his artistic project, even after the Second World War. He was delighted, he stated, that God had not just created trees but had permitted men to make neon signs as well.[22] In his poem 'Juke Box Love Song' the poetic voice promises a 'sweet brown Harlem girl' that he would weave her a crown of neon signs.[23] In 'Neon Signs' Hughes lists the advertisements of the leading jazz clubs – from 'WONDER BAR' to 'MANDALAY' and 'SHALIMAR' – and he combines them with references to such musical giants as Thelonius Monk and to times when the alienating light blends with the offbeat jazz: 'where a broken glass / in the early bright / smears re-bop sound'.[24] Unlike young Alois Hergouth in Austria, Langston Hughes didn't dream of overcoming what was seen as trivial in popular culture. Instead it was a key factor in his writing, a kind of poetry best described by the term 'be-bop modernism'.[25] Neon lights in these texts turn into hip, sophisticated fragments. They shine as brightly as the language in Hughes's most vigorous texts; they are as evocative as jazz and just as disjointed, rhythmic, flashing.

Hughes's mainly white colleagues, the Beat Generation poets, were to develop a wholly different view of New York's neon in the '50s. They neither thanked God for electric advertisements nor wove wreaths out of glass tubes for their loved ones.[26] But they were all very interested in Times Square. This was where, according to the poet Allen Ginsberg, there was a 'huge room' waiting to be experienced, 'lit in brilliant fashion by neon glare and filled with slot machines, open day and night'. This is where 'apocalyptic hipsters' met, said Ginsberg. He introduced these very figures in his long, epoch-making poem 'Howl', as a new generation on the edge of madness. It was not the aesthetic aspect of neon signs that attracted the latest American avant-garde but prostitution, drug dealing and small-time crime.[27] Neon pointed the way towards a world of the marginal and the rejected – that is, towards those sub-cultures that the Beat poets were particularly fascinated by.[28] The glow itself appeared to be magnetic: Ginsberg talked of the 'undersea light' of Times Square. This was intensified and made hallucinatory by certain mind-expanding drugs – just the thing for these poets, who were not always models of sobriety.[29]

The most common literary reactions, however, were provoked by the blatant sexuality of the neighbourhood. 'On Times Square all these dirty old men' is how a chapter begins in Jack Kerouac's novel *Visions of Cody*, from the early 1950s. The writing here takes the sexual marketplace as its starting point for further journeys across the American continent following on from his successful novel *On the Road* (before tanking up for the first time Kerouac goes in for a long, drawn-out meditation on pornography and masturbation).[30] In *Neon Poems*, a volume of poetry by the Beat poet Charles Plymell, the poem 'In NYC' reacts to the erotic energy on Times Square. New York stands up in 'night erection', 'voyeur steam' is given off and the poet encounters 'genital flesh hungry / on 6th AVE, or 3rd or 5th', and sees the city as an 'ecstatic asshole sucked like steaming clams'. Times Square is a surreal part of the world, where perception is assaulted by the neon light, 'grinning poison inside a spinning head'.[31] Unlike Langston Hughes's association of the neon signs of Harlem with a liberating urban culture, the flashing lights of the Beat poets are linked to a harder, more sexualized world.

This new, provocative neon literature culminates in the books written by male prostitutes about Times Square. These introduced their readers, on the one hand, to the somewhat darker sides of the urban wilderness. In 1963 John Rechy's novel *City of Night* compared partly casual, partly aggressive sexual contacts to the very similar qualities of neon advertising. A 'great hungry sign' screams the word 'FASCINATION', writes Rechy, who sees the sign 'groping

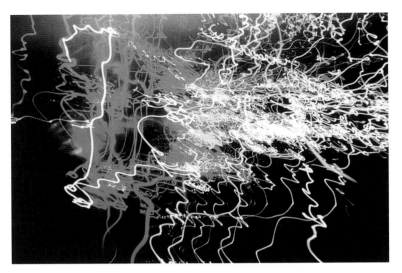

László Moholy-Nagy, *Auto headlights, Chicago, 1939–46*, paper print on glass.

luridly at the darkness' and describes how 'the world of that street bursts like a rocket into a shattered phosphorescent world'. The narrator experiences this unreal part of the world and prostitutes himself, while all the time despising the neighbourhood as much as those cruising its streets.[32] On the other hand, male prostitution produced a positive identification with the 'city of night'. Prostitution turned the shining lights into a key metaphor. In *Néons*, the novel published in 1987 by the French writer Denis Belloc, a rent boy called Denis, hanging out in Manhattan, describes the skyscrapers of New York as 'huuuge pricks'. He locates Times Square 'at the foot of the pricks' – for Denis, 'something exists here, there's life'. He enjoys the 'hustling and fucking' and calls Times Square the place where he wants to die, 'nameless, against some filthy wall covered with graffiti'.[33] For Belloc's heroes, at home in the neon areas of Paris, trading their own bodies is an obvious choice anyway. The lights, whether in New York or on the Seine, make it possible to live an autonomous life ('in the neon light of the boulevard and the sharp stink of the pissoirs I'm all alone: the absence wearing makeup'[34]). Real despair only overcomes him when a client tries to reclaim him and won't let him go back to the streets. In the end the rent boy becomes an artist recounting his own story by painting pictures of bodies drifting through the night.[35] As in the case of Langston Hughes, the neon poet of another age, dreams of freedom and creativity are illuminated by neon light even at the end of the twentieth century. But now it was sex, not jazz, that the flashing lights were providing the accompaniment for.

'A Bath of Acid Neon'

In 1979 Jane Dickson moved to Times Square. At first she only went to the area because of a job, then she set up her studio there, and then that was where she started a family. As part of the artists' collective COLAB, Dickson organized the 'Times Square Show' in 1980, an exhibition that deliberately sought to put an area of ill repute in the spotlight of artistic creation. Dickson went to a local striptease club to draw the strippers and came across all sorts of male clients, who treated a young woman with a sketch pad as an obvious sex object. But Jane Dickson was captivated by the lights in the neighbourhood – even though, unlike Denis Belloc's central character, she came from a world of privilege (she had studied at Harvard).

In fact, what characterizes the paintings that Jane Dickson did on Times Square in the early 1980s is detachment. There is no longer anything like Louis Faurer's improvised photographs of gawping, foot-loose city folk out on the town. Dickson's pictures are of bodies, not faces; silhouettes rather than clearly defined characters. The blurring of Faurer's photographs, however, has its equivalent in Dickson's paintings. One moment using oil pastels on a flat canvas, another moment on sandpaper, they are aimed less at technical perfection than at intensity of atmosphere. Dickson's pictures freeze the street theatre of the neon world. The area around Times Square comes over in her work as desolate, with human figures looking almost ridiculously small. Edward Hopper, Jane Dickson's forerunner in the representation of urban loneliness, still allowed his characters some individuality. This artist's figures, by comparison, are lost in the 'city of night'.

Jane Dickson, *White-haired Girl*, 1983, oilstick on canvas.

Jane Dickson insisted that her lifeless-seeming representation of the area arose directly out of her observations on Times Square. The vibrant space for interaction between light effects and passers-by had become a kind of waiting room by the 1980s. The drug scene and the prostitutes did not attract keen *flâneurs*, according to Dickson, but mainly clients and hustlers. 'I was interested in looking at people who were hanging out and just waiting', the artist said, 'waiting to turn a trick, or pick up a trick, sell drugs, or whatever.'[36] This is what the art critic Gary Indiana saw as the main quality of these paintings – their illustration of 'the terrible monotony' produced by the urban sex and narcotics industry. These were not the shining lights of an American Champs-Elysées but a neighbourhood that had become extremely violent as a result of the dealing in hard drugs, and in which the deafening silence could also be scary. Just as Vladimir Nabokov transformed the neon advertisements in *Lolita* into a harmless flood of neon light, in a similar way Dickson's art focused more on the vicious, menacing quality of Times Square than on its flashing light effects. Gary Indiana's 1989 essay talks of a world plunged into 'a bath of acid neon'.[37]

Prescribed Units of Light

Night paintings and rent-boy novels, Beat poems and *flâneurs'* photographs were more than just individual reactions to the neon city. They blended together, telling collective stories about Times Square. They played a key role in the 1970s and '80s when the area was up for a makeover (and for marketing real estate). There were controversial debates about the future of Times Square in which the cultural significance of the neon wilderness took centre stage. This was the moment when the romanticized image of the 'Great White Way' and 'Rainbow Ravine' upstaged everything that had made Times Square into a centre for erotic pastimes, even during the supposedly innocent '30s. According to this narrative, Douglas Leigh's fantastic visions seemed to be the inspirational dreams of a grown-up boy, the advertising whiz-kid who had transformed the American piazza into a laboratory for the play of light and colour.

And also, especially when there was talk of potential real-estate investors, it involved what was now a 'rundown' neighbourhood whose problems had to be described in terms of a cancer. Without an operation to remove it, the gloomy prediction ran, the sex industry of Times Square would spread out all over Manhattan.[38]

And it was operated on. Beginning in the 1990s, multinational companies started to alter the character of Times Square with their strongly family-friendly principles. As a result of police activity and strict new regulations, all SRBS ('sex-related businesses') in the area were closed down.[39] Getting rid of the 'pederasts, prostitutes and pimps' and bringing back the 'bright lights' – this was, according to the city planners, the aim of the makeover.[40] What disappeared from the neon wilderness of Times Square was therefore not the neon, but the wilderness. After 1987, 'ZR 81-732', the 'Times Square Zoning Amendment', had prescribed the number of LUTS ('Light Units in Times Square') that could be installed on new buildings. This requirement to be lit up was – not surprisingly – enthusiastically welcomed by anyone associated with the open-air advertising industry.[41] Critics such as the urbanist M. Christine Boyer were afraid, however, that an urban centre which had been unique in terms of the energy of its cultural innovation would turn into a ghetto of old-style neon signs. To be sure, in 'Rainbow Ravine' the illuminated advertisements had been subject to programming, but not the actions and reactions of the passers-by. Now the piazza was being transformed into a shopping mall where all activities would be controlled. The Walt Disney Company, according to Boyer, had turned Times Square into a theme park called 'New York Land'.[42]

To the American novelist Samuel Delany, the disappearing sex clubs, toilets and porno cinemas of the neon city were not cancerous growths of the urban landscape. They were forums of multicultural, civilized interactions based on mutual respect. In an essay published in 1999 Delany characterized the desexualization of the area as a dramatic campaign of disciplining.[43] He pointed out that eight out of ten sexual contacts in this part of the world had taken place voluntarily and without payment. It was only literary works such as those by rent-boy author John Rechy that had made prostitution a centre of attention for readers.[44] Delany particularly approved of porno cinemas and the variety of sexual options provided by their darkness (and the author was completely open about revealing his own variety of experiences in these places). Here, he writes, in the physical contact between men of different ethnicities and different social classes, there had been encounters that are central for the 'vision of a democratic city', for cosmopolitan life – a sort of matrix of democracy.[45] It is not networking among equals that in the end makes a city but chatting in the supermarket queue, a discussion with a stranger in a bar and likewise, the author insisted, contact between two men watching one another masturbate in a public toilet. For Delany this interaction was valuable as an urban experience: two strangers meeting who may, or may not, follow up with a conversation.[46]

Attractive Dystopia: Blade Runner

The neon wilderness, whether in New York, Chicago or Las Vegas, was always characterized by close contacts between different strata of society. It often took on an erotic quality. And it was based on a kind of intensification of urban life that was controlled by the self-image of different, competing companies rather than simply by the advertising strategies of large corporations. It was thanks to this coexistence and rivalry under the glow and flicker that the city of the twentieth century had become a wilderness in the first place. All this was difficult to interpret and something that was characterized in literature in particular as an aesthetic challenge. Now it was being gradually replaced by the more predictable, commercially pre-programmed and tightly controlled 'dreams' of entertainment typical of postmodernism.

There was a lot of nostalgia for the disappearing 'intensified' city – and not just in New York. When the film director Ridley Scott was planning his latest project in California in the early 1980s, he immersed himself in images of the big city in history, looking at Hogarth's street scenes from eighteenth-century London, photographs of busy markets in New York's East Side and pictures of the flashing

Still from *Blade Runner* (dir. Ridley Scott, 1982).

lights of Times Square. This research was to produce a film whose perspective would be simultaneously 40 years into the future of the city and 40 years back into the past.[47] *Blade Runner* (1982), Scott's science-fiction classic, was filmed in the Warner Brothers studio in Hollywood using the usual 'New York Street'.[48] That was where the gangster films of the 1930s had been shot in their day – the early neon era.[49]

Blade Runner opens up a whole series of collective anxieties and issues. Scott's vision of the future plays both with the possibilities of genetic engineering and with the locale of a teeming, unreal city totally dominated by advertising messages.[50] The film is particularly popular with theorists of postmodernity, possibly because it seems to prove that the differences between cloned copies and human beings are in the end negligable.[51]

Neon tubes, so often for critics the symbol of empty effects, are introduced by Scott less as a futuristic decorative element than as a symbol for the traditional city. In *Blade Runner* the grand commercial projects of 2019, for example, are communicated on giant overhead screens – not on hand-bent, flowing illuminated signs. The old-style neon advertisements symbolize an imperfect, authentic urban life that has survived despite genetic manipulation and the colonization of the universe. The (malfunctioning) neon advertisement for Schlitz beer advertises a beverage first sold in 1856 by a German immigrant in Milwaukee, Wisconsin.[52] The illuminated advertisement for the Hotel 'YUKON' goes back to the time of the gold rush long ago. The Budweiser advertising and the Pan

Am advertisement embody good old American brands (admittedly the prophecy in *Blade Runner* comes unstuck as Pan Am went bust as early as 1991). *Blade Runner* situates neon in film history: in film noir, the classic genre of the big city by night.[53] Even the clone with whom Detective Deckard, played by Harrison Ford, has an affair looks remarkably like the cool cinema heroines of the 1940s. But the film goes even further back: in Deckard's living room you find a grand piano and sepia-coloured family photographs reminiscent of earlier centuries, underlining his own humanity in a world populated by clones. The neon advertisements have a rather similar metaphorical function.

In addition, *Blade Runner* desexualizes the urban wilderness. Ridley Scott was evoking a Times Square without bringing in prostitution, porno cinemas and mutually masturbating *flâneurs*.[54] Perhaps this is the reason for this dystopian film becoming so unexpectedly popular with intellectuals, who are professionally more involved with the head than the body. For example, the Californian writer on film, Scott Bukatman, comments enthusiastically about the untidy, heterogeneous city presented in *Blade Runner* – the 'delirious chaos' of this metropolis that, despite all the gloom, inspires in people a feeling of liberation.[55] And the architectural theorist Norman M. Klein remembers a series of public lectures in Los Angeles in 1990 in which three of the five invited urban planners expressed their hope that LA would one day look like the cityscapes of *Blade Runner*.

The Bodies of Bangkok

As the Canadian literary critic Timothy Yu shows, the aesthetic of *Blade Runner* is not wholly innocent. The vision of the big city projected by the film imagines the Los Angeles of the future as a metropolis divided up according to an ethnic hierarchy: Asians living on the street (the owners of the nostalgic neon advertisements), Deckard living above them (his apartment being located on the 97th floor) and, dominating everybody, the 700-storey pyramid belonging to the Tyrell Corporation. The film is supposed to show

Neon in Tokyo's commercial districts, in *Lost in Translation* (dir. Sofia Coppola, 2003).

a multi-ethnic city. The fans of *Blade Runner* feel at home there. But Timothy Yu suspects rather that Ridley Scott's darkly attractive vision of a postmodern future was fed by orientalist fantasies and anxieties. For him 'The future is Asian' motif in *Blade Runner* has a positively 'obsessive' quality.[56]

In fact a general Western love of the shining Asian city is difficult to miss – above all among lovers of neon. In the 1990s Rudi Stern celebrated Far Eastern cities as an example to the world as regards the colour and sophistication of their neon advertisements.[57] His colleague in Vienna, Dusty Sprengnagel, agreed with him, raving about the classic neon designs of Hong Kong, their abundance and what were often, for Western eyes, undecipherable signs.[58] In 'Nocturne with Neon Lights', a short story published in 1985 by the English writer Frank Tuohy, the reader accompanies an English businessman on a walk across Tokyo. The attractive neon advertisements suggest to him the possibility (that in the end goes hopelessly wrong) of cheating on his rather boring British wife by having an affair with a Japanese woman. In *Foreign Neon*, a collection of poems from 1991 by the American writer Daniel Halpern, a man feeling simultaneously comfortable and trapped in winter domesticity hankers after 'other locations, long flights / to high contrast cities / lit up at night in foreign neon'.[59] Early on in the twenty-first century, German photographer Peter Bialobrzeski produced a series of photos called *Neontigers*, in which Asian cities bathed in light are to the European eye both enchanting and alienating. In Sofia Coppola's film drama *Lost in Translation* (2003), the neon world of the Far Eastern city becomes a completely incomprehensible environment through which the American characters seem to be drifting, losing any connection to the actuality of their life.[60]

Earlier Western writers had caricatured the Far East as backward and imitative. That was the origin, as the cultural theorist Homay King shows, of the dreamlike worlds full of illegible signs, giving the impression of being fantastic, bodiless, dematerialized.[61] At the start of the twenty-first century, fictions based in the big city returned to the state of being that had fascinated intellectuals back in the 1920s – those neon street advertisements that escaped reality so that all of life was nothing but a glow and a flicker. The neon world of Asia promised a new, dematerialized city, a revival of urban fiction for the Moholy-Nagys of the present day.

However, there are other ways of telling stories about Asian lights. The Korean-American poet Suji Kwock Kim, for instance, in a long poem about the cityscape of Seoul, imagines a passer-by wandering beneath the city lights who, though 'drunk on neon', can still make out the effects of war and poverty.[62] The Taiwanese sociologist Pei-Chia Lan takes up social scientist Lauren Langman's term 'neon cage' in a study of cosmetic salesgirls in Taiwan. This examines the control mechanisms, body-politics and concepts of desire that condition the work of these women permanently exposed to bright lights.[63] A poignant perspective on the material circumstances behind the shining surface is provided by the Vietnamese-American poet Mong-Lan in 'BANGKOK [neon lights]'. The text starts like an ode ('O the orchids of Bangkok'), praises in an increasingly ironic tone the seductions, the decadence, the freedom of the city and then soon touches on the social background behind the erotic fiction – describing, for example, village girls dancing topless like 'embarrassed sardines'. Going into the nearest neon bar, the poem shares with us the spectacle of small birds being inserted into the 'cunts' of the dancers as well as table tennis balls and various other objects. The observer sees 'needles and needles being pulled out of cunts, / a whole string of sharp needles' and finally 'a whole string / of razors being pulled out'.[64] Mong-Lan's ode exposes by the use of cool irony. She does not respond to the promise of the neon lights with any moral lessons but with an increasingly sober bar for bar, dance for dance, object for object account. Perhaps this is because the perverse rituals stand in such sharp contrast to the beauty of the lights. The lumious spectacles are only made possible by the contortions of real bodies.

Ineffective and Innocent: The Flickering GDR

What began after the Second World War with Louis Faurer, trance-like and foot-loose in the city, ends with a hangover. Neon dreams of a glittering, fairy-tale world are quickly brought down to earth with a bump. And the fans of glowing neon lights are reminded that soft lights and not-so-sweet commerce go together well.

However, there is one short-lived nation whose neon story is different. The example of the German Democratic Republic, socialist East Germany, points towards a sort of middle way between the lightness of light and the weight of reality. It all began, albeit quite predictably, with the production of propaganda symbols. Immediately after the Second World War 22,000 m of glowing red tubes were needed in a hurry to provide Soviet stars for the command posts of the USSR military authorities. Added to these were the plain illuminated signs promoting the state, such as 'DER SOZIALISMUS SIEGT' (Victory to Socialism) – for example the one put up in Pirnaischer Platz in Dresden on 1 May 1968. But in general GDR neon comes across as pretty tame commercial design. In those days, attractive images of widespread consumption shone down from fragile tubes on to East German citizens. On Leipzig's Karl Liebknecht-Strasse, for example, a family of four ate neon soup care of the VEB (People's Collective Enterprise) of Feinkost-Leipzig. A pet shop on Karl-Marx-Allee in Berlin advertised itself by using illuminated tropical fish and animated bubbles. In Lange Strasse in Rostock a sophisticated, flowing advertisement announced the fact that the artificial fibre Dederon was 'the thread of total reliability' (the name Dederon, rather less elegantly, derived from the German name for the GDR – 'DDR' – with 'on' added). On Strausberger Platz in Berlin a neon bear played ball with a girl to promote the 'Haus des Kindes' children's centre. In Leipzig's Prager Strasse a blue neon boy held up a book, advertising the local giant book store with the words 'mehr / lesen / wissen / können' (read / know / learn / more). Not far away in Katharinenstrasse the black-and-white mascot of the 'Pinguin Milchbar' (Penguin Milk Bar) was shown standing in front of icebergs waiting for the end of the Cold War.

What we are talking about here are partial illuminations using laboriously assembled installations in a country otherwise devoid

Dederon advertisement, Lange Strasse, Rostock, photograph, 1960s.

123

A state-owned HD (Handelsorganisation, or Trading Organization) department store in the GDR. The neon arrow's text reads '*Ihre Einkaufsstätte*' ('Your Place to Shop').

of light effects. GDR advertising artists carried out their work despite political restrictions, lack of materials and lousy technology. In the West, new-style advertising slogans were produced within minutes using cutting-edge machines. GDR technicians had to saw laboriously by hand. Their job was hampered by economic problems and those issuing the orders were often inefficient. The illuminated advertising for Lipsiator beer, for instance, was turned down by the acting director of the VEB state-owned beverage cooperative on the grounds that the 'promotion of "Lipsiator" to increase demand' was 'totally incompatible with the possibilities of catering for the demand'. The sophisticated advertising for Margon mineral water, in which sparkling bubbles consisting of white rings of light fizzed in a neon glass, was for a product that was often unobtainable in the Communist part of Germany.[65]

Despite this tendency towards inefficiency, GDR artists were responsible for some remarkable illuminations in East German towns. Neon was applied artistically without the aid of any Western technology. In fact, advertisement producers managed to create a democratic version of the form in the towns of the GDR without recourse to the negative sides of capitalism. The innovation with

124

which they played with lights and text using highly original and fluid forms was more a display of individual creativity than of the mass programming of a totalitarian regime.

This argument is well illustrated by an anecdote from the early Cold War era, the authenticity of which can be vouched for by Frank Müller, a producer of neon signs from Saxony. Walter Ulbricht, party leader and head of state in the 1950s and '60s, was visiting Dresden. A neon sign decorating the Pionierpalast Walter Ulbricht, the 'pioneer palace' bearing his name, was missing a letter. So as he was driving by, the venerable leader saw a sign saying 'alter Ulbricht' – 'old Ulbricht' – instead of 'Walter Ulbricht'. An embarrassing matter, so the damage was repaired. Immediately afterwards other letters went missing. The next day Ulbricht read as he passed by: 'Pionier-palast Walter bricht' (Pioneer Palace Walter throws up). Whereupon, Frank Müller tells us, the whole installation had to be taken down. An order was issued 'that, in future, illuminated advertising instal-lations' were to be 'lit up in such a way that there can be no changes to the wording that distort the meaning'.[66] This was how subversive GDR neon could be.

Dan Flavin, *the diagonal of May 25, 1963 (to Constantin Brancusi)*, 1963, yellow fluorescent light.

6 ART FROM TUBES

Sick Apricots, Baroque Rockets

The artist who called himself Billy Apple got some extremely bad press in December 1968. He had recently discovered neon as a material (its glow seemed to him the 'purest, hippest colour in the world'), exhibiting his electric sculptures made with illuminated tubes in the foyer of the Pepsi-Cola Building in New York City. But the prominent journalist Tom Wolfe, despite being a neon enthusiast and a fan of pop culture, had nothing but scorn and ridicule for him. Apple's installations reminded the writer of a 'sick apricot'. The colours were 'curiously pallid', the shapes 'limp', the tubes tended to flicker. There was nothing innovative about this art. On the contrary, it reminded the journalist of neon signs for the run-down drinking joints of the 1930s. To see more interesting neon, according to Tom Wolfe, you only had to go a few blocks to any crossroads on the West Side of Manhattan or drive along Route 22 in New Jersey. There every drive-in, every cafeteria, every bar displayed better neon signs. He felt embarrassed for Billy Apple.[1]

The scope of Tom Wolfe's argument was wider than just New Jersey, taking in the American West and going beyond Las Vegas as far as the Pacific coast. There, in southwest California, lived his personal hero and a kind of anti-Apple – an advertising artist called Melvin Zeitvogel. This man had designed a neon sign for Buick cars in San Diego that by Tom Wolfe's reckoning made not just New York's sick apricots, but the whole art of his day, seem completely old-fashioned and naive. 'Each letter of BUICK' in Zeitvogel's advertisement was 'on a baroque rocket'. The light shot up into the sky orange, yellow, red, exploding in the 'crazed atomic nucleus at the top'. The installation was altogether 'insane', 'marvelous', Wolfe enthused. This was art that was driven only by market competition, art for the public, for millions of Americans in their '327-horsepower family car dreamboat fantasy creations'. Like the neon designers of Las Vegas, Melvin Zeitvogel, a modest man in his mid-50s, besides not seeing himself as an artist also found it difficult to put his creative intentions into words. As a result, the articulate journalist applauded this not quite so articulate Mr Zeitvogel as a shining example and used his eulogistic essay to pour scorn on the whole 'New York status sphere'. At the same time he rubbished the magazine *Artforum*, the Bauhaus, Ludwig Mies van der Rohe and Le Corbusier, 'all lyrical users of neon' along with their 'very personal sense of color' – and last but not least, poor Billy Apple.[2]

Speedee's Dismissal

Tom Wolfe described the light artists of his generation as other-worldly poets and the commercial advertising artists as pragmatic, reality-oriented geniuses. But in fact the artists dismissed by Wolfe were highly aware of urban light effects. And neon advertising was in a much worse state than Wolfe's paean to Melvin Zeitvogel suggested. The gadget freak from Southern California had created his Buick masterpiece in the late 1950s, an era that was far more kindly disposed towards his craft. In the American city of the late '60s, though, these aesthetic tubes now disappeared for good from the face of the city, ousted by plastic. At most they survived in the red-light districts. (The most spectacular neon architecture in New York in that period was, for example, installed at the Pussycat Lounge and Cinema – a giant peepshow.[3]) Even in Las Vegas, a new era was beginning. Caesar's Palace opened there in 1966, the first big casino to largely do without flashing lights. The new fashion was theme architecture, designing things in imitation of a place or a period. Pillars, fountains and life-size artificial centurions seemed more typical of Caesar's era than obviously post-Roman neon light shows.[4] Zeitvogel's medium, celebrated by Wolfe for being so incredibly dynamic, was in danger of being forgotten – and with it his particular materials, plus the knowhow and tricks of the glass-maker's trade. The Egani Institute, New York's traditional neon school, closed it doors in 1971 for ever.[5]

By the 1960s the most original, most creative neon advertisements were relics of a bygone era. Ever since 1947 giant, illuminated drops had been splashing into the Los Angeles night from the tap of the Clayton firm of plumbers. Since 1950 the red neon dog above Larry's hot-dog store in Burbank had been nodding between two yellow illuminated pieces of bun. Almost as old was San Diego's Pied Piper, complete with rats – the neon sign for the vermin removal company named after him.[6] Impressive dragons spat out neon fire over the entrances to Chinese restaurants all the way from New York's Chinatown to Ogden, Utah. These, too, were creatures of the 1950s.[7] 'Coffee Shop Modern' – the flamboyant light architecture of snack bars, restaurants and bowling alleys – had once spawned cafeterias in the shape of aeroplanes and cake shops installed underneath giant neon windmill sails. Now these gave way to new, less conspicuous styles of building. 'We're trying to get away from the old flashy coffee shop look with its bright, flashy colors, large neon signs and bright interior lighting', the owner of a fast-food restaurant in Denver put it.[8] The first branches of what was later to become a very successful chain of snack bars, set up in Southern California in the early 1950s, had been built with an elaborate neon design. A chef called Speedee, animated by light effects, strolled past elegantly flowing yellow arches made of glass. But his career came to an end only a few years later. And from then on, instead of glass tubes filled with neon, plastic modules surrounded the McDonald's hamburger grills.[9]

Speedee's dismissal is very typical of the disappearance of hand-made work from American cities. The decline of the neon city was part of the widespread deindustrialization and suburbanization that had also altered Nelson Algren's Chicago. The term 'American city' was to become an anachronism in the late twentieth century, as it no longer corresponded to the actuality; by 1970 more than half of the American population was living in suburbs. Even as a business centre, the inner city was on the wane. 'Downtown', the home of reliable, traditional department stores and restaurants, once upon a time the trendsetter for the American city, was rapidly losing its importance and its attraction.[10] Even in New York, the most densely populated of all the cities, large-scale urban planning measures were destroying narrow old streets and bringing an end to the architectural jumble. The urban wilderness was replaced by freeways with high-speed traffic. The view was dominated by the glass and concrete towers of the now flourishing service industries. Advertising was no longer just colourful and straightforward but aimed at the 'soft sell', developing brand loyalty through the use of indirect, often ironic, campaigns.[11] Flashing signs seemed old-fashioned by comparison. The city of hand-crafted objects and materials was replaced by a more abstract Manhattan.

New York artists of this period nevertheless consciously sought out the signs and the lights of the old city. They valued the traditional small workshops producing tools and materials for assembling pieces. They went to neighbourhoods where objects were still prized.[12] Dave Hickey's judgement on the art of the 1960s was that the physical object ruled.[13] And the illuminated tube grew in status. The artist Larry Rivers, a former professional jazz saxophonist, called neon 'the most simple and strong form of illustration' – because night acted as its canvas, because it told stories, because it conveyed joy, celebration, 'circus qualities'.[14] The artist Chryssa, who was brought up in Athens, started work on a sculpture in New York in 1964 – more than 3 m high and made of neon, steel, aluminium and Plexiglas – entitled *Gates to Times Square*. According to Chryssa, the area had been providing her with intellectual stimulation for decades; it was a 'Garden of Light'. She was now responding to the flashing aesthetic challenge.[15] The artist Stephen Antonakos, like Chryssa born in Greece, considered the glow of the tubes to be the most important source of inspiration for his work. He had been incorporating all manner of objects into his sculptures, working with cushions, dolls, buttons, umbrellas, light bulbs. He experienced a revelation one night, though, when he was walking home from his

New York studio. He saw an advertisement for a restaurant shining down from way above him. 'What a color!' he said. Since then he had been hooked on neon.[16]

The art historian Andrea Domesle has shown that the light artists of this period added a bodily dimension to writing. As in artistically executed medieval manuscripts, letters and words displayed a form of representation that was almost sensual.[17] But it was not just the writing that fascinated artists. William Christenberry, for instance, working in Washington, DC, collected old advertising signs and neon advertisements out in the country in Alabama and used them as part of his sculptures and photographs. Robert Rauschenberg preferred to photograph the signs by daylight because only then could you see the interplay of light and material, the network of changing lines, shadows and materials.[18] The artist Keith Sonnier was taken with the neon lights in Louisiana: 'Coming back from a dance and driving over this flat land and, all of a sudden, seeing these waves of light going up and down in this thick fog.' This sight produced in Sonnier the strongest religious experience.[19] (Decades later the American actually designed a light installation for a place of worship – albeit in Steyr/Upper Austria, in the parish church of St Franziskus.[20])

In European cities in the 1960s, too, the energy of neon tubes was being felt. To the Italian artist Mario Merz, who had experienced the student revolts in Paris in May 1968, lit-up neon seemed the perfect symbol of a vibrant counter culture. At the same time the commercially rather dated technology fitted in with the Arte Povera he had dedicated himself to: an approach to art that used apparently worthless materials. Merz combined neon tubes formed into sets with what were at first sight totally incompatible materials. The question 'che fare', the Italian translation of Lenin's famous 'What is to be done?' blazed at the viewer from a metal pot filled with wax. The statement of a North Vietnamese general was written up in neon lights on an igloo. Interpreters of art have focused on the difference between the 'hot' wax material and the seemingly cold light in these sculptures.[21] For Merz, however, the neon lights represented very much the warm, organic power of language, the heated debates that led to the utopian experiments of the student revolts.[22]

This new enthusiasm for neon was the result of the so-called 'New Sculpture' movement of the 1960s. Artists experimented with all sorts of materials that they came across – lead, felt, foam, rubber, latex. Often, what they were after was making the sculpture itself into an improvised, ephemeral object. The aim was to ditch respect for the material and the art of sculpture.[23] Out of this process the aesthetic, hand-crafted technique of neon lighting was also re-discovered, and now – this is the paradox – it was treated with great respect and care. Through cooperation between neon designers and architects, projects came about in the 1970s that helped the tubes associated with urban decay to stage a comeback. The spectrum ranged from the neon hair of a dummy in a window display at Bloomingdale's New York department store to colourfully glowing decoration on the fronts of office blocks in Atlanta, Norfolk and Miami.[24] The architects Venturi and Rauch installed a light tube several metres long above the altar of a Catholic church in Philadelphia (the parish, however, had it taken down again seven months later). On the West Coast the artist Larry Albright bought his own neon advertising workshop to experiment with installations.[25] In the circle around Rudi Stern's New York gallery Let There Be Neon, artists designed guitars, tables, beds and chairs using the material.[26] Stern himself described the anonymous glass makers in the neon workshops as the true artists of the American city.[27] In 1952 the artist Lucio Fontana had praised the neon tube on the grounds that it could 'liberate art from the shackles of the material'.[28] For many artists of the 1960s, however, the glow and the flicker of the tube became an emblem of the true city, of craft and of visible and tangible materiality.

Salvation through the Tube: Dan Flavin

When Dan Flavin gave a lecture on his artistic work at Brooklyn Museum Art School in 1964 it was hard for him to find any kind words for his family. He called his father 'remotely male' and his mother 'a stupid, fleshy tyrant of a woman'. Uncle Artie, who had taught Dan to draw, was described by the artist as fat and red-faced – and he made fun of the way Artie had in those days wanted to show him how to draw ponds using a lot of small crescent shapes.

Flavin's talk was not particularly kind to himself either. At the age of 32 he was 'overweight and underprivileged', besides which he was 'a Caucasian in a Negro year'. He looked back at a largely depressing life. Going to a Catholic school had given him a narrow horizon, the seminary a meaningless experience. During his military service in Korea he had practised drawing by using a fellow soldier who went permanently unwashed as model, brought to an end by a superior officer after a few weeks (he found it immoral, a soldier drawing another with a naked torso). Even on his return to New York Flavin's relationship with art did not prove any more fruitful. He filled his studio with all sorts of materials that he collected on walks along the Manhattan waterfront. He experimented with ink, charcoal, oil, watercolours. But art seemed to him to be a 'tragic practice'.[29] Then, when he saw a Russian icon of the Novgorod School in the Metropolitan Museum, he felt moved by a 'magical, presiding presence' like that which he was seeking in his art. His own works in comparison seemed to him 'dumb, anonymous and inglorious'.[30] In an attempt to get his works to shine, at least artistically, he began to experiment with electric light, installing light bulbs around square shapes. While working as a museum attendant, first at the Museum of Modern Art, then at the Natural History Museum, he made notes for similar future projects, filling the pockets of his uniform with them. A superior, though, told him off: 'Flavin, we don't pay you to be an artist.'

Neon tubes rescued Dan Flavin from simply drifting. On 25 May 1963 he fixed a yellow fluorescent tube more than 2 m long diagonally on to a bare wall. This was the moment when he realized he had found his material.[31] For 33 years, right up until his death, Flavin was to assemble fluorescent tubes. He was fascinated by the way light altered space, the way a straight line, the simplest con- ceivable shape, created a play of light, shadow and space. This was 'better than sculpture', Flavin said.[32] He called his first fluorescent tube piece *the diagonal of personal ecstasy*. As this soon seemed too personal to him, he changed the title. Then the piece was called *the diagonal of May 25, 1963 (to Constantin Brancusi)*.[33] Flavin was not to quit this habit in a hurry, being fond of dedicating his tubes to artists such as Brancusi, Jasper Johns, Piet Mondrian, Henri Matisse, Barnett Newman, Donald Judd and Ad Reinhardt. In this way he made sure that his glowing tubes were seen as belonging to the highest level of late modern art.

The critic David Bourdon was reminded by an early exhibition of Flavin's not so much of Mondrian or Matisse, but of the window display of a fluorescent lighting store right opposite a Greek fast-food restaurant on 47th Street. In 1964, in the *Village Voice*, he voiced his opinion that Flavin's tubes were only art because they were exhibited in the context of art.[34] He was not the only one to have a problem with Flavin's oeuvre. Hilton Kramer also noted, in the *New York Times*, that this man 'was no artist'. Kramer was irritated that he had 'even been given space in an art gallery'.[35]

Despite, or because of, these strong reactions Flavin became one of the leading light artists of the late twentieth century. Three decades after the diagonal breakthrough of 25 May 1963, one of Hilton Kramer's successors in the influential fine arts section of the *New York Times* declared that Flavin's fluorescent tubes, then on display in the Dia Center for the Arts, represented the only possibility for finding inner peace in New York City.[36] The experts of the early twenty-first century did not compare them with electrical goods stores but with the art treasures steeped in tradition that Flavin himself had so admired. They compared the illumination of his tubes to the glow of gilt on medieval paintings. They insisted (for example, the art historian Hal Foster) that Flavin's light was more intense than that of Neo-Impressionist painting.[37] Considering the artist's autobiographical statements and his dissatisfaction with his own background, viewers may conclude that the long, narrow, fluorescent tube, in all its very everyday elegance, brought about his own personal salvation. The man who had once written that there were no 'cosmic cosmetics' in his work, that his fluorescent tubes would 'never inflame for a God', was, on his deathbed, still directing the installation of a work by him in the church of Santa Maria di Annunciata in Milan. Shortly before, he had done the Christmas lights for another temple, but this time to shopping: the top New York boutique of the fashion designer Calvin Klein.[38]

As Attractive as a Tongue Sandwich: Lili Lakich

Unlike Dan Flavin, Lili Lakich never became world-famous. But then she could look back on her childhood with considerably more satisfaction, particularly the year 1953. This was when her father came back from the Korean War and bought a brand-new, bright blue Chrysler. In this the family travelled the U.S. visiting friends and relations from Florida to California. The Lakichs had a particular love of the attractions on the side of the highway, such as sales booths looking like Native American wigwams, hamburgers or teapots – the very buildings that *Learning from Las Vegas* was to introduce to the architecture debate two decades later. Nine-year-old Lili was especially fascinated when Dad's Chrysler was cruising across the American landscape at night. The neon on the motels and restaurants was lit up. 'It was then', she wrote later, 'that the darkness would come alive with brightly colored images of cowboys twirling lassoes atop rearing palominos, sinuous Indians shooting bows and arrows, or huge trucks in the sky with their wheels of light spinning.' Lili was disappointed when, in 1956, her father was transferred to a military base in Germany and there were no longer any attractions on the side of the road but museums, cathedrals and castles instead.[39] But as an adult, back in the New World, she went on neon trips again – for example, to poor neighbourhoods in Mexico City. Here she found a church where neon crowns were lit up on statues of the Virgin Mary, glowing tubes were wound round the figures of Jesus and the words 'Providencia' and 'Ave Maria' shone out in glass letters.[40] This confirmed her conviction that this light had 'spiritual qualities'.[41]

Like Dan Flavin, Lili Lakich was also in search of her own artistic form of expression in mid-1960s New York. She was hooked on electric light, too. She combined painted metal with light bulbs, thus producing sculptural portraits. But, unlike Flavin, she did not draw her inspiration from a confrontation with the canonized works of art history. Lakich loved pop music just as much as light effects. Her first light sculpture, *Self-portrait with Tears* of 1966, was a direct response to 'Cry Me a River', the song by Julie London. A work from 1972 entitled *Don't Jump Up and Down on My Toes, You Loved Me Once, You Know* quoted a number by the 1960s singer Melanie. The model for the neon animation of the piece was the advertisement for The Speak 39, a bar in Hollywood where stars and abstract patterns lit up in totally unpredictable sequences. Many a time Lakich had looked at the front of this place and had ended up by designing equally astonishing sequences for her artwork.[42] She had a light sculpture of a female torso made by the neon shop that also worked for Pink Pussycat Theaters, a chain of porno film cinemas (the neon craftsmen, however, rejected it on the grounds that, as Jehovah's Witnesses, they could not be involved in producing what appeared to them to be Lakich's morally objectionable work). The artist herself worked as a neon designer, for example designing the tubes for the trailer of the Hollywood film *Victor and Victoria* and a light installation – almost 100 sq. metres in size, made up of flashing flamingos, flowers and leaves – for the dance floor of a discotheque in Dallas.[43]

Light artists like Flavin were interested in new definitions of objects and space. Lakich, on the other hand, was driven by enthusiasm for the craft of neon. She had chosen the medium in the first place because it bore no relation to art. She was interested in the stigma of the coloured tubes, the fact that they reminded her of 'sleazy bars, shoe repair shops and cheap motels'.[44] Lakich was fighting on the side of neon. For her it was actually significant that glass makers could not be trained any more, now that such schools had been closed down. It annoyed her that in Paris, the birthplace of neon advertising, you could only get eight different colours of neon tube in the 1970s. She was particularly irritated that what had once been American urban centres lit up in vibrant colours were now 'dark, dismal and fearful' as neon became a thing of the past.[45]

Lili Lakich, *Don't Jump Up and Down on My Toes, You Loved Me Once, You Know*, 1972, mixed media.

Lakich's art, however, was also becoming a thing of the past. At least she never became a big name on the established art scene, as opposed to the subculture comprising fans of neon advertising, glass makers and folks nostalgic for neon. In 1985 she noted that, after twenty years of artistic activity, she had never managed to win a single art competition. The Whitney Museum had called her works 'wonderfully ferocious', but she had never been invited to a world-famous biennial. Her least personal sculpture – showing a female torso installed underneath the motel sign 'VACANCY / NO VACANCY' – was occasionally displayed in explicitly feminist art exhibitions. As regards her other works, however, the sculptress was denied recognition by the art world. On one occasion a critic had written about her: 'Lili Lakich's neon sculptures are like tongue sandwiches. Either you like them, or you don't.' To be compared to a tongue sandwich, according to the artist, was something she would rather have been spared.[46]

It was particularly tragic for Lili Lakich that her contemporary Dan Flavin, for many the greatest 'neon artist' of all time, was not a neon artist at all. Flavin did not work either with neon or with other noble gases and certainly not with artistically hand-crafted glass. (Tiffany Bell, a former assistant to the artist, remembers how Flavin liked to correct those of his contemporaries who referred to his works as 'neons'.[47]) In his studio you found regular machine-made fluorescent tubes coated on the inside. These were very much the standard objects of American consumer culture, like the soup cans and packets of washing powder that Andy Warhol had made use of. And they were just as uniform. This was exactly what made fluorescent tubes attractive for Flavin. At the same time, the man who got his material from the tube factory occupied a position in the highest strata of fine art. While Lakich lovingly devoted herself to a down-to-earth craft of neon, the leading assembler of fluorescent tubes identified himself with the most important artists of the twentieth century. It is true that he occasionally recognized the aesthetics of the everyday – thus the interior of a Chinese restaurant in Brooklyn, for instance, could be the source of his inspiration to use the colour combination pink and yellow.[48] But what interested

Flavin was the greatest possible sophistication – an 'aristocracy of taste' as Dave Hickey described it.[49] The reduced glow of his tubes had nothing in common with the fantastic light shows that nine-year-old Lili had admired through the window of that bright blue Chrysler, nor with the emotional works that she produced as an adult woman. Nor had it anything in common with the passion that inspired Lakich to found the Museum of Neon Art in Los Angeles in 1981. It was neither admiration for glass makers nor enthusiasm for creative flashing light sequences that had made a light artist of Flavin.[50] Art was not work for him, nor was it craft. He lived by the motto: 'Art is thought'.[51] He was, in this way, no friend of neon.

Bars, Bodies, Wittgenstein: Bruce Nauman

A neon figure is hanged, his enormous penis erect in death. The word 'RAW' flashes out in red, becoming 'WAR' in orange. Five men made of light are marching, their arms and legs sticking up in the air, along with their sex organs. A clown puts out his hand in greeting, another one refuses to take it. The word 'EAT' appears in yellow, becoming 'DEATH' in blue. A green and a pink-coloured figure look at one another and hit each other in the face. In a flashing list, one neon statement after another appears, phrases like: 'LIVE AND DIE' and 'DIE AND DIE', 'SHIT AND DIE', 'PISS AND DIE', 'SLEEP AND DIE', 'LOVE AND DIE', 'HATE AND DIE' and their opposites: 'SHIT AND LIVE', 'PISS AND LIVE', 'EAT AND LIVE'. A yellow and a greyish silhouette stand face to face and stick their forefingers into each other's eyes. The words 'RUN FROM FEAR' appear in yellow and underneath is lit up: 'FUN FROM REAR'. One body bends over another, takes the neon penis into its mouth, stands up again.

In the case of the American artist Bruce Nauman, the originator of all these works, the material neon appears to be creating nothing but vitality. His light installations continually remind one of the straightforward messages and directness of popular culture. They use the simplest vocabulary of the English language and refer to

Bruce Nauman, *Raw War*, 1970, neon.

the most basic bodily functions. Coming out of the period between the late 1960s and the mid-1980s, like Lili Lakich's pop sculptures they reflect everyday America of the late twentieth century. Those like *Raw War* appear to comment on the Vietnam War; those like *Run From Fear / Fun From Rear* on the blatant sexual atmosphere in urban red-light districts; and those like the crude clowns with their prominent penises in the 1980s, on the collective anxieties about the then new AIDS epidemic. For the curator Joseph Ketner, Nauman's neon caricatures are moral artworks that are as aggressive as human beings themselves.[52] At the same time they tap into the positive energy of popular culture. One of Nauman's neons, for example, owes its existence to the song 'Sweet Substitute' by the jazz star Jelly Roll Morton.[53] Unlike Dan Flavin, who was all about light and space and highly intellectual comments on modern art, Nauman's tubes appear to originate in the neon tradition based on the material and the physical body.

Like the artists who were turned on to the dated material neon in the streets of New York, Bruce Nauman discovered the tubes of noble gas in the 1960s, when they were more associated with the rundown city than with expertly orchestrated light shows. Nauman's first studio, on the border of the Mission District in San Francisco, had been a grocery store. It was situated on a street where various bars and stores used this already rather dated form of advertising. Nauman rigged up one of his first neon signs in the window of his studio.[54] It was in the form of a spiral making the statement: 'The true artist helps the world by revealing mystic truths.' Like all the other signs in the vicinity, the device was intended to be just like any illuminated sign advertising beer.[55] Nauman thus became part of the world of the Mission District. He did not see his light installations as sculptures but as 'signs', just as a bar or shop owner would.[56]

On close analysis, this description has something overly populist about it. The artist Bruce Nauman does not really belong to that group of enthusiasts like Lili Lakich who revived neon as a craft and developed it as a kind of visual pop music. The light sculptures form a relatively small section of Nauman's multifaceted oeuvre, which comprises video, sculpture, performance and photography. Besides, the artist did not make any of the neon signs himself but had the work put together by craftsmen.[57] (For an exhibition in Baltimore in 1982 the exhibits were done by the local Claude Neon branch.[58]) It was not Nauman's aim to create particularly decorative lights. He was after a neutral, anonymous form of expression – 'an art that would kind of disappear', as Nauman put it, 'that was supposed to not quite look like art'.[59]

Bruce Nauman did not arrive at this invisible art via an involvement with impressive advertising craft products but because, more generally, he was investigating the function of language itself. In his studio in the Mission District he was at this time less concerned with beer ads than with postmodern authors such as Vladimir Nabokov, whose relation to reality was not totally innocent and who were more concerned with highly artificial, self-referential language games.[60] Nauman discovered Wittgenstein's *Philosophical Investigations*, in which the philosopher demonstrated how things could and should be questioned and how to pursue arguments up to the point where their meaning or meaninglessness is clear for all to see.[61] Reading this was what introduced Nauman to neon: because these tubes illuminated words and in so doing tested their meaning. (Catherine Nichols sees Nauman as an artist who investigates the places where language starts to fail as a means of communication.[62]) A neon sign claiming that the artist is helping the world 'by revealing mystic truths': this seems either extremely naive or extremely ironic. But it represents an attempt to establish a claim in Wittgenstein's sense and to pursue the thought to the end. The illuminated statement is both, according to Nauman in an interview, a 'silly idea' and also something that he believed at that time. 'It's true and it's not true at the same time', he said later. 'It depends on how you interpret it and how seriously you take yourself.'[63] To get at the meaning, a statement had first to be put up in lights.

From this perspective Nauman's light art seems to resemble less Lili Lakich's flashing sculptures and more conceptual art with its intellectual ambitions developed in neon tubes. The New York artist Joseph Kosuth, for instance, also saw his installations as a development of philosophy. He was also more interested in Wittgenstein than in the details of lighting technology. Neon was for him the ideal neutral material. The glass tubes were smooth. They made possible the simplest way of writing. Thus they were ideal for linguistic mind-games.[64] Kosuth's piece *Five Words in Red Neon*, created in 1965, highlights reductiveness, the statement referring to nothing but itself.[65] Like Dan Flavin, who actually sought to create 'non-art'[66] but very much liked to quote other artists and artworks, neon art also became an in-joke in the case of Kosuth. In a work from 1965, for instance, numbers lit up in five lines from 'ONE TWO THREE FOUR FIVE' up to 'TWENTY-ONE TWENTY-TWO TWENTY-THREE TWENTY-FOUR TWENTY-FIVE' – the resulting installation, *Five Fives*, was dedicated to the artist Donald Judd.[67] Kosuth used his art, as he wrote in 1988, as a 'test of the cultural code'.[68] The artist did not, however, look for this code in everyday life but in the work of other artists or in European high culture in general. His neon works underline, comment on, edit and annotate texts by Wittgenstein, Sigmund Freud and Robert Musil.[69] The intensified city experienced by the body, the neon wilderness, plays no role at all in Kosuth's art.

Bruce Nauman's thought processes about using light are a bit closer to actual neon worlds than Kosuth's. Nauman thought of language itself as everyday material and as being just as tangible and physical as any other materials found in the city. The materiality of writing becomes abundantly clear in his installations. The neon objects make their construction plain for all to see. Cables and transformers are visible to any observer. The switching gear is clearly programmed. The obvious word games of the language installations are graphically illustrated by the often equally straightforward patterns of language. The physical quality – of words, of technology – is ever present.

One of the first neon works by Nauman was based on drawings he had made of his body shape. This interest in the fragile liveliness of the corporeal was to remain central to the artists's work.[70] Nauman's oeuvre represents an art of the body, seen against the background of the horrors of the twentieth century.[71] Because the testing of fragile liveliness and its limits remained a permanent challenge for Bruce Nauman, neon, being fragile and lively, provided the ideal material. You could bend it and shape it just like human limbs. In 1979 the artist moved from California to a farm in New Mexico (since then he has been automatically referred to as a 'cowboy' among conceptual artists[72]). His light sculptures, however, evoke the demand for attention that is typical of the city, that peculiar urban mixture of intimacy and violence, physical fascination and panic, anxiety and sex. The motto 'RUN FROM FEAR / FUN FROM REAR' Nauman encountered in the cityscape of Southern California. These words, however, had not been shaped by a neon craftsman but by another type of urban artist. An anonymous graffiti author had left them on a bridge in Pasadena.[73]

Tracey Emin and the 'Golden Mile'

In 1898, when William Ramsay discovered the noble gas neon, a historic innovation was being unveiled 120 km away in Margate. This small town in Kent was the first seaside resort to offer its visitors deckchairs. Eight years before it had introduced donkey rides as an amusement – another first. In the 1970s and '80s, however, when Tracey Emin was growing up in the resort, Margate was not known either for its seating arrangements or its donkeys – nor either for the fact that J.M.W. Turner had painted impressive seascapes here in the 1830s (he had called the local views the 'loveliest skies' in the whole of Europe).[74] Margate in the late twentieth century was famous for its 'Golden Mile', a seedy British version of the Strip in Las Vegas, a rather rundown promenade dominated by neon lights with rows of nightclubs, bars and cafés.

In the meantime Tracey Emin had moved to London, becoming in the 1990s one of the leading exponents of Britart. This is when she took up neon as a material. And she reckoned to have been influenced in this by Margate's 'Golden Mile'. Neon is 'sexy', she said. 'It's spangly, it's pulsating. It's out there, it's vibrant.'[75] She had practically 'grown up with neon'; it had always 'had a wonderful influence' on her.[76]

Tracey Emin showed another side of Margate's Golden Mile in her 1995 film *Why I Never Became a Dancer*, in which super-8 movie images of the resort's signage – for 'MARIO'S', 'BURTON', 'TIVOLI', 'GRAB CITY' – reveal intimate memories of her youth. Off-screen Emin talks about Margate's cafés and bars, 'lunchtime discos' and her sexual awakening as a thirteen-year-old. She describes her promiscuity, her enthusiasm for sex as a cheap pleasure that she was able to indulge in anywhere in the town – on the beach, in the parks, in the hotels. At the age of fifteen she was any man's. Then she discovered dancing. *Why I Never Became a Dancer* relates the day when young Tracey took part in a dancing competition, convinced she'd embark on a new career. The young men in the audience, many of them former sexual partners, shouted out 'Slag, Slag, Slag' and submitted her to communal humiliation. In the second part of the film, however, we see the grown-up Tracey Emin dancing on her own, full of joy and self-confidence. She moves to the disco classic 'You Make Me Feel (Mighty Real)' and dedicates this sequence to the very same young men of Margate.[77]

Lili Lakich had not managed to be successful in the art business of the 1960s and '70s with her emotionally charged neon sculptures. Tracey Emin made it in the 1990s – though not at first using illuminated tubes but provocative performances and installations, films and drawings. By the end of the twentieth century the art business was open to performance and confessional art and therefore to the sort of emotionality that had once been the subject of ridicule, turning Lili Lakich's works into 'tongue sandwiches'. Emin's most well-known artworks – the tent with the names of all those she had ever slept with sewn into it and her unmade bed – confronted the public with total autobiographical openness. Her oeuvre also includes an uncompromising 'curriculum vitae' relating how she was raped in an alley in Margate at the age of fourteen.[78]

Emin's neon pieces, starting in the late 1990s, are equally personal. As with Bruce Nauman, these are extremely simple installations; words up on the wall. Their shape, however, imitates Emin's handwriting, which makes them seem much more intimate than Nauman's neutral letters. On the level of content, Emin's neon statements,

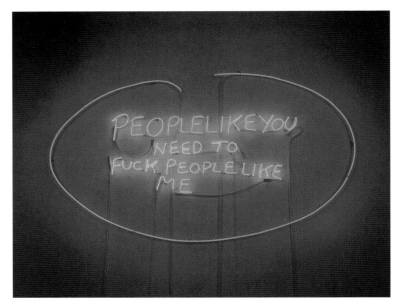

Tracey Emin, *People like you need to fuck people like me*, 2002, neon.

sometimes in block letters, sometimes in joined-up letters, reveal painful and humiliating experiences involving sexuality and powerful emotions. 'MY CUNT IS WET WITH FEAR' is one of the signs. Another quotes the statement 'FUCK OFF AND DIE YOU SLAG', yet another 'PEOPLE LIKE YOU / NEED TO / FUCK PEOPLE LIKE / ME'. The lines 'Good Smile / Great Come' refer to the promising sides of sexuality. Pink tubes form the outline of a female bottom and suggest further associations for the title *Give It to Me Like a Man, I'll Take It Like A Man*. A *Love Poem for* CF from 1997, written with neon, describes the feeling of being 'About to be smashed / into a thousand million / Pieces'. Words inside a white illuminated heart remind a lover 'You Forgot to Kiss my Soul'; others come across as a note of self-therapy: 'Fantastic To Feel Beautiful Again'.

Unlike the philosophical Bruce Nauman, Tracey Emin is always concerned with how language works in tandem with her own experiences. She is not in the business of illustrating Wittgenstein. Nevertheless, Emin's light installations also involve metaphorical interaction between powerful but fragile neon tubes and texts about

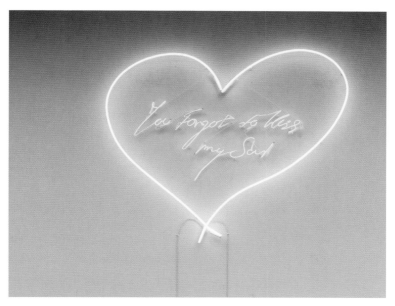

Tracey Emin, *You Forgot to Kiss my Soul*, 2001, neon, montage.

the artist's sexual energy and vulnerability.[79] At the same time Emin's recourse to flashing lights fits in with her strategy of always making her unconventional background, which was hardly conducive to fine art, into the subject of her art in as challenging a way as possible. Perhaps living up to her 'Mad Tracey from Margate' persona – a nickname she gave herself – Emin made a now infamous drunken appearance on a televised debate about contemporary art.[80] The 'Golden Mile' is where she was at home. Associating neon tubes with the lights of Margate, Emin revealed not just a jumble of youthful reminiscences but the concrete social context of her life.[81]

The critical view of Emin's oeuvre focuses on the artist's position in relation to post-feminism. Emin's rather unpolitical, glamour-friendly stance and the similarity of her work to the medium of pornography comes across to a lot of observers as problematic, to others as an innovative stance in relation to the gender constructions shaping the art world. When Emin sewed statements like 'YOU CRUEL HEARTLESS BITCH' and 'I HATE WOMEN LIKE YOU' into pink-coloured quilts, she very definitely stepped aside from any gender clichés.[82] In a similar way Emin took on neon, that symbol of sexual commerce, in order to express her own views on sexuality and to throw light on the world of her own past.[83]

Hostile observers might classify her installations more as illuminated advertisements for the Emin brand of art than as sophisticated prose works in light. The media critic Anne Hoormann has shown in this context that contemporary light art is often installed as background decor in spaces of consumption. Art from tubes illuminates shopping malls and company headquarters – just as torches and lamps decorated the frontages of the buildings of the powerful in the Baroque era.[84] In urban centres those who have a professional interest in marketing the city brand will be light art's biggest supporters. Lights have always made cities more attractive – and light art could be taken simply as the newest gimmick developed in this process.[85] This argument sees the light artists of the twenty-first century as producers of advertising – Melvin Zeitvogels of their time, but with much dimmer tubes.

Tracey Emin did turn her illuminated artworks into advertising signs. In spring 2010 the artist returned to her home town. She appeared in front of the Margate Pier and Harbour Company building, now adorned with a pink-coloured neon installation featuring Emin's characteristic handwriting and the words: 'I've never stopped loving you.' Emin made use of the PR event to advertise not just her own artwork, not just Margate, but also the Turner Centre – housed in a new art museum for the resort costing millions. 'Wherever art goes, so does commerce!', the artist assured her audience. She promised potential tourists that Margate was the best place for a 'dirty weekend'.

Even if the audience in front of the Margate Pier and Harbour Company building was witnessing the light artist in the act of unashamed marketing, on this occasion Emin was beating the drum, not for one of the centres of the global art and culture industry, but for a tatty old town worthy of the attentions of a Nelson Algren. Margate, only 90 minutes away from London, was seen at the start of the twenty-first century as a place without a future. The local news was all about violent crime. The remains of two teenagers were found in the house of a serial killer; murder, knifings and muggings were part and parcel of everyday life. There weren't any tourists to speak of any more. One out of every five inhabitants was on welfare, giving the town the nickname 'Benefits-on-sea'. On a visit in spring 2009, a reporter from the London *Times* saw only amusement arcades that had gone bust, shut-up shop fronts, gangs of youths hanging around in the town. She met a young mother who didn't exactly share Emin's enthusiasm for the much-vaunted future art museum. The 'Turner Centre' was 'the biggest load of f***ing rubbish', a complete waste of money given the fact that most of the fifteen-year-olds in Margate were illiterate; 'they couldn't give a stuff', was the woman's view.[86]

What Margate has gained from Emin having been there is not very clear. But of course you could read her pink 'I Never Stopped Loving You' as very much an attempt to return her art, marked as it is by the glaring lights of Margate and now so immensely successful, to its place of origin. And to include the town in benefiting from her own rise to fame. The most successful era for neon light once gave rise to Nelson Algren's *Neon Wilderness* and thus a literary work that was more interested in the particular reality of life for impoverished city dwellers than in the fascinating urban surface of the big city stage. The illuminated art of the twenty-first century also inspires artworks based more on the 'rusty heart' of the urban environment than on its glossy surface. Taking hold of the microphone to give a speech on that spring day, with the audience eager before her and her glowing pink declaration of love to crisis-ridden Margate overhead, Tracey Emin burst into tears. Then she made a heartfelt plea for the lights of the 'Golden Mile', now in darkness, to be lit up again. The audience seemed very excited.[87]

City lights (Neon-Gai), Tokyo.

7 LISTENING TO NEON

More Than a Buzz

Neon buzzes. That is its music. Let's leave it at that. The neon expert Dusty Sprengnagel, for one, describes what happens with your ears when you pass by neon signs in the tropical humidity of the Bangkok night. Rain falls on the badly insulated cables of the neon equipment. The passer-by, out and about in the night of the colourfully lit South Asian city, can make out a buzzing sound like that of insects. This, according to Dusty Sprengnagel, is a unique experience.[1]

Neon music, in a stricter meaning of the term, comes, for example, from Atsuhiro Ito's 'noisecore' band, Optrum. Ito brings fluorescent tubes on to the stage. He amplifies their buzzing electronically, modulates it and makes the tubes flicker optically as well as acoustically – an instrument he has named Optron. This is done to the accompaniment of a drum played punk-style.[2] If neon has anything to do with music beyond this, then it must be found in such places as the former Emerald City Disco in Cherry Hill, New Jersey. Visitors to this place at the end of the 1970s danced against the backdrop of a wall with twenty channels of neon switching on and off in sequence and beneath neon chandeliers and neon rockets on the ceiling, all under the direction of a 'light musician' operating a 'bio-electric' keyboard. There were up to 2,000 people dancing to the flashing lights. The designer Robert Lobi, a former musician, said: 'We have created a stage on which everyone can be a star.'[3]

Actually, whether in Bangkok, Thailand, or Cherry Hill, New Jersey, the story of neon light is the story of visual perception. It's what caught the eye of *flâneurs* in the big cities of the 1920s and

'30s, Nelson Algren's eye in 1940s Chicago, roving eyes in Las Vegas and Times Square and light artists at the end of the twentieth century. Glowing neon writing comes somewhere between text and image – in other words, at the heart of visual culture.

But let's not forget there are thousands of neon songs. Neon as a leitmotif for lyrics and neon as a part of band names, not to mention the titles of albums and songs from all over the place. From Canada, where the band Arcade Fire, with their album *Neon Bible*, recently had one of the biggest successes in the genre of alternative rock.[4] From Australia, where the group Silverchair, on their 1999 album *Neon Ballroom*, revelled in a hard, sometimes melodramatic, style of rock.[5] From the beaches of northeastern Brazil, home of the singer-guitarist Tico da Costa with his number 'Paixao Neon'.[6] And from a place a long way further to the northeast – West Berlin, where at the end of the 1970s a band was formed around the sisters Inga and Annette Humpe with the name Neonbabies (one of their first numbers, 'Spass muss sein', or 'You Gotta Have Fun', was a quote from the neon sign over an amusement arcade).[7]

The responses to the use of this metaphor vary enormously. At the start of the twenty-first century the American songwriter John Mayer used the metaphor of neon as a 'light-motif' for a tender song about an enigmatic girl ('Neon').[8] And the flashing lights also inspired creators of music to be more outspoken in expressing their emotions – for example, the electronic combo Neon Stereo & Marcie brought out an EP entitled 'F*ck Me Baby'.[9] Both serious and popuar music have taken their cue from the noble gas. The composer Judith Lang Zaimont's album *Neon Rhythm* (she claims that her work has been the subject of twelve PhD dissertations) was for flute, viola, cello, piano, clarinet and oboe.[10] By contrast, the track 'Neon Music' by DJ Big Ali is a classic example of music to dance to, getting everyone up on to their feet. The accompanying video predictably shows scantily dressed females doing likewise, albeit not grooving with neon sign writing but, in the tradition of Dan Flavin, with regular, possibly phallic, fluorescent tubes.[11]

Just as in literature, neon in the context of music is an immensely ambiguous metaphor. Making an exhaustive list of neon pieces is like trying to make a catalogue of love songs or songs about the night. The term seems to sum up all the joys and sorrows of urban life. The word's shortness makes it attractive. Songwriters familiar with Greek possibly appreciate the suggestion of 'the new'. Those interested in wide-ranging sexual activity celebrate its metaphorical association with areas of the city where such activities are found. Whatever the motivation: the songs and pieces of music inspired by neon lights reflect the aural chronology of the most important transformations of the glow and the flicker in the twentieth and early twenty-first centuries. Their rhythms, melodies and lyrics evoke the vibrant metropolis of modernity as well as fears about the city in the post-war decades. Added to these are associations with moral decay as well as reactions to technology, ranging from cool to paranoid, over the period. With neon as the soundtrack we are once again navigating our way through the story of the illuminated tube.

Down in the Depths of the 90th Floor

In 1936 the worst economic crisis in American history was entering its seventh year. Neon advertisements were attractive, sophisticated and popular as never before. Cole Porter, the child of the creator of a financial empire in the Midwest – and like Tom Wolfe a fan of neon and a graduate of the elite university of Yale – wrote his number 'Down in the Depths' in only a few days.[12] Featured in the musical *Red, Hot, and Blue!*, it is one of Porter's most melancholy songs. For the historian Morris Dickstein, the success of the ballad is proof of the power of popular culture in this period.[13] Those who first listened to Porter's song, Americans going through the Depression, were able to identify totally with the equally depressed 'I' of the piece. However, 'Down in the Depths' does not mention financial troubles or the depths of the social crisis at all. Quite the opposite is true. The singer occupies a penthouse high above Manhattan, on the 90th floor, free to enjoy every comfort. It's just that love escapes him and so, both as a consequence and paradoxically, he feels 'down in the depths on the 90th floor'. Below him he can see 'a million neon rainbows' – ridiculing him by illustrating the enjoyment of life being experienced by all those down there who, unlike him, are not lovesick.[14]

In Porter's number, neon does not yet represent a metaphor for decline or depression. The millions of neon rainbows symbolize the bright, flashing lights of the big city, their limitless possibilities.[15] Two new twentieth-century media combine together here. Like neon advertising, commercial songs gradually came to define urban culture in the 1920s. Like neon advertising, popular hits tapped directly into the culture of the city, throbbing to the urban rhythm – 'staccato, not legato', as George Gershwin called it. In the words of Porter's contemporary Irving Berlin, these songs had to work in the everyday situation; they had to be 'easy to say' and 'easy to remember'.[16] But even if Porter's ballad is situated in the big city of the '30s, 'Down in the Depths' is significantly less egalitarian than Nelson Algren's neon fictions. The well-off singer complains that 'even' the janitor's wife has a perfect love life whereas he, living in a penthouse, is all alone. On one occasion when 'Down in the Depths' was performed on the radio, Porter replaced the janitor's wife with the more middle-class 'analyst's wife'. The producers of the show had called for this less snobbish choice of words. The 'neon rainbows' had to shine on an egalitarian city.[17]

Becoming Peggy Lee

The economic crisis was long over and the Second World War had ended with a victory when the American jazz star Peggy Lee wrote the number 'Neon Signs (Gonna Shine Like Neon, Too)'. Now, in 1949, the glow of the tubes was appearing in the title. And the mood of the song is a lot lighter than Porter's 'Down in the Depths'. The dialogue between the singer and the choir suggests a collective experience, imitating the fast movements of a pedestrian – and the lyrics of the song define the neon city as a place where you can be free. In the verses about the cinema and the dance hall, Peggy Lee sang that she wanted to escape housework – like 'mopping up the floor' – and she aimed to enjoy herself as much as she could ('I'm going to dance till they turn out the lights'). The dream of the song

Greyhound bus station sign at night, Columbia, South Carolina.

comes in the last line of the chorus. 'I'm going to shine like neon, too', the singer calls out with joy – and the choir echo this: 'We're going to shine like neon, too.'[18]

As in Nelson Algren's stories from the neon wilderness published shortly before, this recording was the product of an interaction between a city dweller in quite modest circumstances and the entertainment offered by the big city. In the case of Peggy Lee, however, the audience of the time were not treated to a slum story about poverty, drugs and suicide, but a life-affirming, passionate hymn to the possibilities of urban popular culture. The shining lights were a powerful metaphor for personal illumination, too. Anyone listening to Peggy Lee's song in the late '40s might have felt transported to Times Square, the all-American piazza as a pulsating island of urban vitality. The neon rainbows seen from above by Cole Porter's man in the penthouse seem to be shining down on and through this singer.

However, when Peggy Lee wrote this song, neon lights had for a long time meant something else. The public knew the lights of the violent, chaotic city from film noir movies. They possibly associated the illuminated advertisements with lifestyles that were a world away from the everyday reality of the suburban middle class. Peggy Lee sang about the lights that, three years previously in Frank Capra's hit film *It's a Wonderful Life,* had stood for the gloomy nightmare of Pottersville, with its coldness, suspicion and corruption. The perception of Times Square, as Louis Faurer's subtle photographs from this period show, now also increasingly signified a recognition of the threat to folks in the streets of a crisis-ridden metropolis.[19] With all its enjoyment of life, Peggy Lee's 'Neon Signs' could be read as a farewell to a vibrant city without the spectre of Pottersville and gloomy post-war sensibilities. It was also a belated hymn to the sophistication of popular Big Band jazz, blending together the vitality of popular culture of the 1930s with the equally glamorous appearance of theatres, cinemas and entertainment palaces lit by illuminated signs and letters. The fluid forms of the neon advertisements as much as the jazz beat seemed to embody a collective optimism standing out against the crisis of the Depression

– something that rapidly dated in the post-war period.[20] But Peggy Lee brought these times back to life once more.

In addition, with her neon hymn of a self-confident woman, the singer was moving into an area that was more and more defined by men. The neon city of the films and crime novels of the 1950s was the preserve of tough guys – or of prostitutes who were to become the property of the tough guys. Peggy Lee's 'Neon Lights', by contrast, represented a self-confident identification with female hedonism with no need of a protector. It was a song about her own life: Peggy Lee had been raised as Norma Deloris Egstrom in rural North Dakota during the economic crisis. Unlike Cole Porter, she had been down in the depths, and not just in the sense of being lovesick in a luxury penthouse. By the age of eleven she had already worked as a cleaner, cow milker and clothes washer.[21] In a bid to become a singer in Fargo, the nearest city, 160 km away, she had Americanized (or de-Scandinavianized) herself, changing her name to Peggy Lee, a new, snappy name advertising herself like a neon sign.[22] The recognition that this identity as an urban, sophisticated jazz singer was invented stayed with her even at the height of her popularity. When a man once asked her in a hotel lift whether she was Peggy Lee, the former Norma Deloris Egstrom, not at that point in her make-up, hairdo and stage clothes, answered – at least according to legend: 'Not yet, I'm not.'[23]

Just as in this anecdote, in Peggy Lee's song, actually mentioning the work the singer still has to break free from means the reality beyond the entertainment industry leaps out at you. As in the case of Nelson Algren, neon lights do not represent the dematerialized city but the real, physical one. And it was not by chance that Peggy Lee's song came out in a period when the image of the strong, go-getting women of the war years was replaced in the u.s. by the 1950s cliché of the stereotypical housewife and mother. The song looks back to the era of considerable female self-confidence – and not forwards to the period of the housewife trapped in the suburbs.[24]

Adamo and Adorno: Neon as Nothing

In the following years there was not much in the way of hedonistic hymns to flashing lights. The Dukes of Dixieland from New Orleans played the number 'Neon Love' in 1953. However, this piece of music did not sing the praises of the urban context but simply described the on-and-off mechanism of a neon advertisement – and one that, in any case, was located on an interstate highway, a long way from the urban jungle. 'Turn it on (turn it on) / Turn it off (turn it off)' is how the song went, the singer and the backing group making known their feelings towards a 'neon love' – so called simply because a certain object of affection was able to turn her feelings off like a 'sign on a u.s. route'.[25] In tune with this, the horns of the Dukes of Dixieland were imitating the traffic din of a multi-lane highway more than sophisticated urban jazz. The trade paper *Billboard* reckoned this single would make for 'some action' in New Orleans but it didn't have much chance anywhere else. The experts were right.[26]

Then, however, singers and songwriters discovered the potential of neon advertising for cultural criticism. This certainly made for more 'action'. Paul Simon and Art Garfunkel recorded 'Sound of Silence' in 1964, a song dealing with the flashing lights, the 'neon god they made', as a powerful image of commerce, idolatry and the breakdown in communication in American society.[27] Theodor W. Adorno had argued against the 'all-powerful neon-light style' in his *Philosophy of New Music* back in 1948.[28] Now criticism of the commercialization of culture had achieved popularity; criticism of the neon god had become chart-worthy.

On the other side of the Atlantic, Salvatore Adamo, the *chansonnier* born in Sicily and raised in Belgium, chimed in with the way things were going. With 'Le Néon' in 1967 he wrote an edgy, angry song about the modern urban landscape. His lyrics associate '*le néon*' and '*le néant*' (nothingness) – words sounding almost the same. He sings about himself in the first person out and about in an enormous city, later identified as New York. He describes himself as a *flâneur* who is becoming increasingly frustrated at his own insignificance and passivity, at his desperate search for hope, for a sympathetic soul '*au coeur du soir*'. As in the case of Alois Hergouth, the poet from Graz, post-war Broadway also stirs up intensely negative feelings in Belgium-based Adamo. The roar of the street at night seems to him like '*la ronde / des morts vivants*' – the dance of the living dead. The singer, becoming more and more belligerent, feels within himself the urge to destroy. He tries to get even with America, singing, like Adorno as it were, against the 'omnipresent neon-light style'. In the end we hear an aggressive, disjointed anti-neon song, its rhythm imitating the flicker of the tubes. This is far removed from jazz age hymns to pulsating lights and their promises of urban freedom and nightly revels. '*Broadway la blonde*' as portrayed by Adamo is just an open sore, a place that gets on your nerves.[29] Cultural criticism was now, coming to the end of the 1960s, at the heart of popular music. Far more popular than 'Le Néon' was the dreamy song Salvatore Adamo put on the B-side of this single: 'Une larme aux nuages' (A teardrop in the clouds).[30]

Country Lights

Alex Chilton was sixteen when he had his first big hit, 'The Letter', in 1966 with his band The Box Tops. Using modern long-distance transport as a metaphor, the song tells of a lover who doesn't think the 'fast train' is fast enough to get to his loved one. He needs 'a ticket for an aeroplane'.[31] The band's second single was likewise based on the metaphor of technology: 'The Neon Rainbow'. Written by country musician Carson Thompson, as was 'The Letter', it is a hymn to the bright, coloured lights of the city, lights that can warm the 'coldest nights'. Thompson composed a passionate number for Alex Chilton's youthful voice, singing with a power that seems to take off where Peggy Lee's enthusiasm left off.[32]

The song's bridge has an effect that is serious, culturally critical and typical of country music. The singer stops and reflects. The man who has just been praising the neon rainbow so passionately now sings about the fact that, by day, everything is different. When the neon advertisements are no longer shining, when the effects have been switched off, then – he sings – nobody speaks to anyone, nobody opens the door to anyone, the feeling of common humanity is nowhere to be found. Thus the neon lights are revealed to be cynical fictions. And the song's moral judgement on the 'neon rainbow' is that it is a lie – thus reading the luminous symbols like Simon and Garfunkel, like Adamo and Adorno, and in a similar way to the author John Kennedy Toole. The latter was the same age as Alex Chilton when, as a teenager from a small town in the Southern States in the 1950s, he put all his alienation into the writing of his novel, *The Neon Bible*.

In American music, as in this song by the Box Tops, Southern neon was to hang around a lot longer than the signs on Broadway. Cultural criticism based on the metaphor of neon has been a leitmotif of country music from Wayne Carson Thompson up to the present. In 'Neon Moon', for example, the ballad by the star duo Brooks and Dunn, the melancholy singer, like many melancholy singers before him, is sitting in a 'rundown bar' on the wrong side of the tracks, getting drunk in the glow of luminous tubes, seeing his 'broken dreams' carried away in this neon world.[33] Numerous songs before and after 'Neon Moon' take up the theme – or adapt it whenever the male singer sees the flashing light in the eyes of a passionate woman, the 'flashing, screaming, silent neon sign' standing for the seductive power of extra-marital affairs.[34] A long-term study shows that 75 per cent of successful country songs between 1960 and 1987 were love songs, the largest number being about an unhappy or lost love and the second largest group about being unfaithful. Here, according to the country music expert Curtis Ellison, we are dealing with very direct thematic connections between private, domestic concerns and the 'honky-tonk' of the city, represented by neon and responsible for tempting folks to be unfaithful.[35] So neon lights both the way that leads one astray and the thoughts of those with a broken heart.

There are two genres of the late twentieth and early twenty-first centuries in which neon has really prospered: one is light art, the other is country music. In country, there has remained a vital tension between the traditional anti-urbanism of an avowedly rural

America and the lights of urban entertainment. At the same time neon fulfils a similar role to that played in Nelson Algren's writing about the city of Chicago. It locates the songs in the world of the underprivileged – a world to which country music has always felt that it belonged, even when it had become completely commercialized. Like the hats, boots and trucks that Johnny Cash once identified as the clichéd accessories of the country pose, the metaphor of neon is an essential part of a music culture that continues to see itself as being underappreciated.[36]

The myth of 'neon women' also belongs to the folklore of country music. Songs on this theme are a million miles away from Peggy Lee's jazz classics from the late 1940s where the singer talks unabashedly about going out into the bright lights of the city. A few decades later, neon women in the conventional world of country music suffer a similar fate to their sisters in the nineteenth and early twentieth centuries. The sheer fact that they are out alone in the big city, one moment going through dark passages, another moment lit up by the pulsating lights, marked them out as immoral, as potential prostitutes.[37] Rita Canard, for instance, in 1974 sang a hesitant, bitter song called 'Neon Women'. In the ballad she confesses that she is a woman whose man could never get enough of neon women and she has therefore turned herself from being a 'stay at home girl' to becoming one of these 'neon women'. Now that she has lost her man for some time, she is on the street alone in the neon wilderness. As is only logical in the world of country music, she has gone directly from being a virtuous wife to a prostitute, waiting 'beneath the neon glow for strangers passing by'.[38] Two syllables and a noble gas are all it takes to describe her new fate. Only Rita Canard's unmistakable voice stops this neon woman from becoming a cliché.

Buzz Buzz, Beep Beep: Kraftwerk and XTC

He wanted to throw up whenever he saw a cow – this statement by a musician from punk band The Clash just about sums up the aesthetic of the late 1970s and early '80s.[39] Neon light, the metaphor for urban anonymity, coolness and the attractions of machines, the leitmotif in *Blade Runner*, was a far cry from dairy cattle. It stood for both aspects of modernity: the hard-edged love of punk for the ugly and for cool, techno sophistication.

The best example of the latter was the song 'Neonlicht', by the Düsseldorf band Kraftwerk. This track from their 1978 album *Die Mensch-Maschine*, like Peggy Lee's 'Neon Signs', evokes the experience of being out and about in the urban environment – in this case, with Kraftwerk's typical electronic layering, sound mixing and repetitions. The singer does not come over as either in a good mood like Peggy Lee or in a nervous state like Salvatore Adamo. He is neither melancholy like Rita Canard nor exhilarated like Alex Chilton. What the music suggests is a neutral piece of equipment. 'Neonlicht' describes, as unemotionally as possible, a moment in the urban landscape. '*Neonlicht / schimmerndes Neonlicht / und wenn die Nacht anbricht / ist diese Stadt aus Licht.*' (Neon light / shimmering neon light / and at fall of night / this town is all light.)[40] The reference here is to the attractive, seemingly dematerialized, cities of modernity. Band member Ralf Hütter once described as one of the main ideas of Kraftwerk that they tapped into the 'culture of Central Europe', something that had been destroyed by the Nazis in the 1930s. 'We are picking up the thread where it was left off', said Hütter, 'by continuing in the spirit of this culture.'[41] The model for this is the 'city of light' associated with the Weimar Republic, that is, the new ideas about architecture of Erich Mendelsohn, the experiments of Moholy-Nagy and the modernist ideas of utopian cities.

On the other hand, 'Neonlicht' could be read as an ode to the bright lights of capitalism. Kraftwerk played their number at concerts in the first decade of the twenty-first century with neon advertisements from the 1950s projected in the background – brand names such as '4711', 'Klosterfrau', 'Dujardin', 'Deutsche Bank' and 'Mercedes-Benz'.[42] In country music the metaphor of neon covered the grey area between would-be innocence and the corrupting force of modernity. In Kraftwerk's case it was the sign of a complete acceptance of technology and commercialization. But in

El Lissitzky, *Photogram, Superimposition, 1930*, black-and-white photograph.

the same way that neon was, internationally, associated more with fragile, colourful, sophisticated advertising tubes than with the cold light of anonymity, with their album *Die Mensch-Maschine* Kraftwerk were after a rather softer sound. The Düsseldorf musicians wanted to summon up something like 'soul' from their sound machines – similar to the flashing lights.[43]

The other extreme to Kraftwerk's cool sophistication also came out in 1978. The number 'Neon Shuffle', by the English band XTC, did not imitate the calm glow of neon tubes but their flickering on and off, the animated effects, the visual fragmentation of the environment. Driven by the staccato, hectic rhythm, Andy Partridge's strained voice invited his audience to join the dance, that is, the 'neon shuffle', urging them to make a 'noise', to take part in the 'dance for the human race' that would launch them into 'outer space'. The convulsive intensity of the music, however, runs counter to these invitations as it in fact shows the 'neon shuffle' to be an undanceable dance. Like various other numbers recorded by XTC in this period (songs about radios on the move, 'Science Friction', three-dimensional porno films and a world where 'Everything Is Buzz Buzz / Everything Is Beep Beep'), 'Neon Shuffle' riffs on a technology gone crazy. Unlike Kraftwerk, with their songs about the coherence and sophistication of machines, XTC worked according to the uninviting principle that the 'neon shuffle' would pierce the listener like a 'stick of bamboo'.[44] The chaotic end to the number dispels any illusion of there being a structured rhythm. XTC's bass-player Colin Moulding stored this final sequence on a separate tape and kept it in a box with the label: 'The Complete and Utter Destruction of Berlin by Bombers'.[45]

'Neon Shuffle' refers back to the 'Harlem Shuffle', a number by the American soul duo of the 1960s, Bob & Earl, recorded later by various artists and, given its groovy feeling for rhythm, the exact opposite of XTC's edginess. The 'Harlem Shuffle' is, in fact, an invitation to get up and dance – unlike 'Neon Shuffle', which is an invitation to give in to angst. It seems logical in this context that the album in which this new shuffle appeared was called *White Music*. This certainly did not give the audience soul and funk, the

African American forms of popular music that were good to dance to, but the self-conscious convulsions of white Britons.

In the late 1970s, a period of racist violence and right-wing extremism in Great Britain, an album title such as *White Music* was more than a little provocative.[46] One is tempted to draw more conclusions around the metaphor of neon as apparently being coded more 'white' than 'black'. Nelson Algren's neon wilderness had been a world of whites – Algren failed to react in his writing to the fact the African American population of Chicago grew at an enormous rate after 1940.[47] And in many other writings featuring neon lights, whether on Times Square or in stories about Asian cities, it is impossible to ignore the focus on white characters. Behind the metaphor of the bewildering neon city, either in the case of literary writers or of XTC, the anxieties of the middle class are also revealed. We are talking about white bourgeois observers who may have been uncomfortable with the new ethnic make-up of European and American cities and used neon as a metaphor for their own disquiet.

XTC's songs for *White Music*, however, had not originated in the capital but in a provincial milieu. The musicians (who did not intend their album title to refer to any ethnic identity) came from a declining, 'rusting' industrial town. In Swindon, their home town located between London and Bristol, railway works that had once made the place prosperous closed down in the 1970s. Swindon had seen better days.[48] As has happened so often in the cultural history of neon light, here too the metaphor turns up in the context of deindustrialization. Craft skills disappeared from these areas and with them the appreciation of manual labour, too.[49] Looking back nostalgically at neon was part of this process – either like artists and conservationists preserving the tubes or like Kraftwerk identifying themselves musically and metaphorically as inheritors of the industrial art of the pre-war avant-garde. XTC's 'Neon Shuffle', on the other hand, had nothing nostalgic about it. Instead, the band reflected on dysfunctional technology and their own dysfunctional sensibilities. Neon as metaphor oscillated between pop and punk, between being good to dance to and good to slit your wrists to.

This was where neon was at in the late 1970s as regards both the glow and the flicker: the prospect of a complete and utter capitulation to technology in the case of Kraftwerk, and in the case of XTC a destructive imitation of turning on and turning off.

Back to the Neon Wilderness

Ninety-eight years after William Ramsay and Morris Travers discovered the amazing glowing gas neon in their London laboratory, Peter Salisbury, Simon Jones, Nick McCabe and Richard Ashcroft met in a studio in London to work on their own kind of breakthrough – with as much concentration as the late nineteenth-century chemists. It was the autumn of 1996. The musicians had been through a stormy period: a court case (the jazz label Verve having forced them to change the name of their band, Verve, to *The* Verve), physical injury (a bouncer at a Paris concert club having broken guitarist Nick McCabe's finger) and rows and reconciliation (the band having split up shortly before and come back together again for recordings).[50]

In the studio, the hard-pressed musicians nevertheless produced one of the most successful and most highly rated music albums of the 1990s: *Urban Hymns*.[51] The most popular of the numbers, such as 'Bitter-Sweet Symphony', 'The Drugs Don't Work' and 'Lucky Man', in fact became urban anthems in a London that was just re-inventing itself during a period of enormous economic boom. Here the music of bands like The Verve, Oasis and Blur seemed to chime in perfectly with the new political and economic self-confidence of Great Britain.

The history of neon light also represents a history of the relations between popular culture and subversiveness. Writings from the casinos of Las Vegas, by hookers on Times Square or by female poets observing strippers in Bangkok not only reveal reactions to neon light but, more generally, the possibility of being exposed to the effects of pop culture and still producing independent, critical, rebellious works of fiction. Contrary to Adorno's image of totalitarian neon light, these narratives are based on an informed knowledge of the programmed lights of the city; they are based on subversiveness within, not outside, the culture of everyday life.

British pop music of the 1990s did not lend itself to such a reading. Anyone like Adamo and Adorno seeing contemporary society as Neon/Nothing, as totally stage-managed and devoid of content, would only feel confirmed in their view by the spectacle of Britpop. As the music historian John Harris shows in his study of the subject, *The Last Party*, politics, patriotism and pop culture went hand in hand in the United Kingdom during the Blair era. Musicians such as those of Oasis, from northern England, completely bought into economic success rather than keeping commerce at bay like the independent bands of earlier periods. Other performers, such as Blur singer Damon Albarn, accepted invitations from leading politicians.[52] Even The Verve, once thought of as the scourge of the mass entertainment business, saw a breakthrough thanks to the official recognition of Britpop. The band that had previously only been known to aficionados achieved the status of global superstars. And London, at the height of the boom generated by a globally successful financial services sector, discovered an ideal soundtrack in their 'urban hymns'.

But there's another angle to this pessimistic narrative. Salisbury, Jones, McCabe and Ashcroft spent nine months working on the recording of *Urban Hymns*. The last song to be recorded took one long night, between 6 p.m. and 5 a.m. And this sublime song stands out against the rousing hit numbers on the album. McCabe's guitar produces a continual droning sound, the drum coming in hesitatingly and Richard Ashcroft's voice drifting along against this background, blending into it, at times barely audible. The piece of music buzzes like a badly fitting neon tube. The title of the raw, poetic track is exactly the same as Nelson Algren's raw, poetic 1947 collection of stories: 'Neon Wilderness'.

The fact that this searching, meditative song is part of *Urban Hymns* seems only to confirm the seriousness of The Verve's urbanism. Possibly inspired by reading Nelson Algren's book, 'Neon Wilderness' creates an intoxicating, disorientating atmosphere, reminiscent of such urban characters as Algren's heroine Mary, whose view of things is almost totally conditioned by drugs, the rhythms of the jukebox and the flashing neon light. But 'Neon Wilderness' not only quotes Algren, the prototypical writer about losers, but also the author who, in his own day, missed the trends of his time, focusing on a moralizing lyricism of the slums in the era of ironic (not iconic) postmodernism. It seems typical of the cultural history of neon light that, of the songs on the million-seller album *Urban Hymns*, it is this very 'neon song' that appears to have not been particularly successful, having a dated sound and notable not for being in line with The Verve's usual hits but for an apparently aimless wandering through the sounds and moods of the city. For the music journalist Trevor Baker, 'Neon Wilderness' sounds all the way through like the end of a song and not like a song in itself. It seems to him like a two-and-a-half-minute outro, without a hook, without a chorus.[53] The number comes across as improvised, hardly made to last.

And yet rhymes and, accompanying them, clearly structured lines of lyrics, emerge from the droning. You can't catch many of them; others are more intelligible – two lines in particular. Here the singer, out and about in the city at night, is not thinking about his own life but the suffering of others. His eye is caught by 'someone else's distress / in a neon wilderness'.[54] Not much in this piece of music seems to hang together. But these lines comment, against a buzzing background, on the very history of neon light as a two-part story: of the lights themselves and of those who are out and about beneath their flickering. Light shows on Times Square and bodies being offered for sale; the flashing lights of Bangkok and the grotesque work of the strippers there; writing lit up in art museums and a girl being called a slag in Margate: we are flooded with the programmed effects and heading for a fate that can't be programmed. At least for two minutes and thirty-eight seconds until the next urban hymn begins.

REFERENCES

1 READING NEON

1 'A False Alarm from Rattlesnake Gulch', *Claude Neon News*, I/4 (November 1928), p. 10.
2 Arnold F. Hollemann, Egon Wiberg and Nils Wiberg, eds, *Lehrbuch der anorganischen Chemie* (Berlin, 1985), pp. 372–5.
3 Advertisements from Rudi Stern, *The New Let There Be Neon* [revd edn of *Let There Be Neon*, 1979] (Cincinnati, OH, 1988); Dusty Sprengnagel, *Neon World* (New York, 1999); *Plaste und Elaste: Leuchtreklame in der DDR* (Berlin, 2010); also author's observation. Note: neon signs with CAPITALS are shown as such, here and throughout, while advertising installations with lower- and upper-case lettering are shown in that style.
4 Michael F. Crowe, 'Neon Signs: Their Origin, Use, and Maintenance', APT *Bulletin*, XXIII/3 (1991), p. 34. In Shanghai the term *nihongdeng*, a phonetic borrowing of the original word 'neon', refers to all kinds of city lights, and thus is a general term similar to that used in English – see Hanchao Lu, *Beyond the Neon Lights: Everyday Shanghai in the Early Twentieth Century* (Berkeley, CA, 1999), p. 336.
5 Janet Ward, *Weimar Surfaces: Urban Culture in 1920s Germany* (Berkeley, CA, 2001), pp. 1–8.
6 See for example Harvey, who refers to the neon-decorated Piazza d'Italia in New Orleans: David Harvey, *The Condition of Postmodernity: An Enquiry into the Origins of Cultural Change* (Cambridge, MA, 1990), pp. 93–7.
7 Guy Debord, *The Society of the Spectacle*, trans. Donald Nicholson-Smith (New York, 1994); see also Biene Baumeister and Zwi Negator, '"Situationistische Revolutionstheorie" – Communistische Aktualität und linke Verblendung', in *Spektakel, Kunst, Gesellschaft: Guy Debord und die Situationistische*

Internationale, ed. Stephen Grigat, Johannes Grenzfurthner and Günther Friesinger (Berlin, 2006), pp. 116–18.

8 John Hannigan, *Fantasy City: Pleasure and Profit in the Postmodern Metropolis* (London, 1998), pp. 3–4.

9 Richard Sennett, *The Craftsman* (London, 2009), p. 9.

10 Hubert Dreyfus and Sean Dorrance Kelly, *All Things Shining: Reading the Western Classics to Find Meaning in a Secular Age* (New York, 2011), pp. 206–12.

11 Blake Eskin, 'On the Roof: Pepsi Degeneration', *New Yorker* (29 March 2004), p. 6; Louis M. Brill, 'The Pepsi-Cola Generation: Preserved in Neon for Now and Ever More', *SignWeb*, www.signweb.com, 20 February 2006, accessed 16 February 2011.

12 Fabian Wurm, *Signaturen der Nacht: Die Welt der Lichtwerbung* (Ludwigsburg, 2009), p. 83.

13 Crowe, 'Neon Signs', pp. 30–37.

14 Jessica O'Dwyer, 'When Neon Signs Were Art', *Americana*, XVII/2 (1989), p. 51.

15 Stern, *The New Let There Be Neon*, p. 91.

16 Margalit Fox, 'Rudi Stern, Artist Whose Medium Was Light, Dies at 69', *New York Times* Online, www.nytimes.com, 18 August 2006, accessed 16 February 2011.

17 Marlena Donahue, 'Neon Art Museum Exhibit: It's a Gas', *Los Angeles Times* (29 December 1984), p. F1.

18 Michael Webb, *The Magic of Neon* (Layton, UT, 1983), p. vii.

19 Dusty Sprengnagel and Georgia Illetschko, 'About the Author', in Sprengnagel, *Neon World*, p. 5.

20 Rudi Stern, 'Introduction', in Sprengnagel, *Neon World*, p. 3.

21 Sheila Swan and Peter Laufer, *Neon Nevada* (Reno, 1994), pp. 37–8.

22 Ibid., p. 41.

23 Ibid., p. 83.

24 Webb, *The Magic of Neon*, p. viii.

25 David Foster Wallace, 'Good Old Neon', in *Oblivion* (London, 2004), pp. 141–81.

26 John Kennedy Toole, *The Neon Bible* (New York, 1989), p. 32.

27 Nelson Algren, *The Neon Wilderness* [1947] (New York, 1986).

28 John D. MacDonald, *The Neon Jungle* (New York, 1953).

29 Mark McGarrity, *Neon Caesar* (New York, 1989); Tony Kenrick, *Neon Tough* (New York, 1988); James Lee Burke, *The Neon Rain* (New York, 1988); Dick Lochte, *The Neon Smile* (New York, 1955); Matt and Bonnie Taylor, *Neon Flamingo* (New York, 1987).

30 Sabine Deitmer, *NeonNächte* (Frankfurt, 1995).

31 Yusef Komunyakaa, *Neon Vernacular* (Middletown, CT, 1993);

Daniel Halpern, *Foreign Neon: Poems* (New York, 1991); Tony
Moffeit, *Neon Peppers* (Cherry Valley, NY, 1992); Lucien
Francoeur, *Neons in the Night* (Montreal, 1980); Michael
Salinger, *Neon* (Huron, OH, 2002).

32 August Kleinzahler, 'Poetics', *Live from the Hong Kong Nile
Club: Poems, 1975–2000* (New York, 2000), p. 35.

33 Dramaturgie/Kommunikation (Helena Huguet), 'In Neon von Julia
Kandzora', *Deutsches Theater: Spielplan*, www.deutschestheater.de,
accessed 16 February 2011.

34 Niels Carels, *Neon* (Amsterdam, 2000); Alois Hergouth, *Neon
und Psyche: Gedichte* (Graz, 1953).

35 Gilbert Sorrentino, 'Neon, Kulchur, etc.', *TriQuarterly*, XLIII (Fall
1978), pp. 299–308.

36 Cherie Currie with Tony O'Neill, *Neon Angel: A Memoir of a
Runaway* (New York, 2010).

37 Nick Pinkerton, 'Rebels of the Neon God: "Only Connect"',
Reverse Shot (Winter 2004), www.reverseshot.com, accessed 16
February 2011.

38 Denis Belloc, *Néons* (Paris, 1987).

39 Claude Pélieu, 'Neon Express', *Coca Neon/Polaroid Rainbow*
(Cherry Valley, NY, 1975), pp. 18–21.

40 Thomas Rosenlöcher, 'Die Neonikone', *Die Dresdner
Kunstausübung* (Frankfurt, 1996), p. 7.

41 Charles Plymell, 'In NYC', *neon poems* (Syracuse, NY, 1970),
pp. 12–13.

42 Mong-Lan, 'BANGKOK [neon lights]', *Antioch Review*, LXIII/1
(Winter 2005), p. 136.

43 Theodore Roszak, 'The Neon Telephone', *Michigan Quarterly
Review*, XXX/2 (1991), pp. 295–306; Dave Hickey, 'A Home in
the Neon', in *Air Guitar: Essays on Art and Democracy* (Los
Angeles, CA, 1997), pp. 18–24; Matthew O'Brien, *Beneath the
Neon: Life and Death in the Tunnels of Las Vegas* (Las Vegas,
NV, 2007); Lauren Langman, 'Neon Cages', in *Lifestyle Shopping:
The Subject of Consumption*, ed. Rob Shields (London, 1992),
pp. 41–82.

44 Theodor W. Adorno, *Philosophy of New Music* [1949], trans.
and ed. Robert Hullot-Kentor (Minneapolis, MN, and London,
2006), p. 16.

45 Library of Congress: SONIC Database, Recorded Sound Reference
Center, www.loc.gov, accessed 26 March 2011.

46 The references here are to songs with the word 'neon' in the title,
songs by bands and performers whose name contains the word

'neon', and songs from albums whose title refers to the noble gas (using iTunes Version 10.1.2.17, accessed 10 March 2011).

47 Arcade Fire, *The Neon Bible* (City Slang, 2007), CD.

48 Legs McNeil and Gillian McCain, *Please Kill Me: The Uncensored Oral History of Punk* (London, 1996).

49 'The Neon Judgement', *The Belgian Pop and Rock Archives: Bands and Artists*, http://houbi.com, December 2001, accessed 16 February 2011.

50 Simon and Garfunkel, 'The Sound of Silence', *Sounds of Silence* (Columbia Records, 1966), LP.

51 'Leon Spinks Biography', *Biography.com*, www.biography.com, accessed 16 February 2011.

52 Philip Whitfield, ed., *Marshall Illustrated Encyclopedia of Animals* (London, 1998), p. 525.

53 Dietmar Elger, 'Licht als Metapher – Kunst mit Neon', in *Lichtkunst aus Kunstlicht: Licht als Medium der Kunst im 20. und 21. Jahrhundert*, ed. Peter Weibel and Gregor Jansen (Ostfildern, 2006), p. 492.

54 Dietmar Elger, 'Licht als Metapher: Kunst und Neon', in *Licht und Raum: Elektrisches Licht in der Kunst des 20. Jahrhunderts*, ed. Michael Schwarz (Cologne, 1998), p. 64.

55 Ibid., p. 69.

56 Andrea Domesle, *Leucht-Schrift-Kunst: Holzer, Kosuth, Merz, Nannucci, Nauman* (Berlin, 1998), p. 165.

57 Elger, 'Licht als Metapher: Kunst und Neon', p. 62.

58 Jörg Heiser, 'Das geht alles von ihrer Zeit ab', *Süddeutsche Zeitung*, III/4 (December 2005), p. 18.

59 Katie Paterson, 'Vatnajokull (the sound of)', home page, www.katiepaterson.org, accessed 16 February 2011.

60 Charlotte Frank, 'Die Schwarzseher', *Süddeutsche Zeitung*, 23 (April 2008), p. 11.

61 See for instance: Wolfgang Schivelbusch, *Lichtblicke: Zur Geschichte der künstlichen Helligkeit im 19. Jahrhundert* [1983] (Frankfurt, 2004); Joachim Schlör, *Nachts in der grossen Stadt: Paris, Berlin, London, 1840–1930* [1991] (Munich, 1994); Elisabeth Bronfen, *Tiefer als der Tag gedacht: Eine Kulturgeschichte der Nacht* (Munich, 2008).

62 Andreas Bernard, *Die Geschichte des Fahrstuhls* (Frankfurt, 2006), p. 16.

63 See also Engell/Siegert/Vogl, who focus, among other things, on 'the relation between light and the "social machine"'; Lorenz Engell, Bernhard Siegert and Joseph Vogl, 'Editorial', *Archiv für*

Mediengeschichte 2: Licht und Leitung (Weimar, 2002), p. 7. This book concentrates on individual human beings rather than on parts of a machine.

2 ROSES ARE BLOOMING IN MANHATTAN

1 Morris W. Travers, 'William Ramsay', in *British Chemists*, ed. Alexander Findlay and William Hobson Mills (London, 1947), p. 165.
2 Morris W. Travers, *A Life of Sir William Ramsay* (London, 1956), pp. 175–9.
3 Ibid., pp. 175–9; Arnold F. Hollemann, Egon Wiberg and Nils Wiberg, eds, *Lehrbuch der anorganischen Chemie* (Berlin, 1985), pp. 372–3.
4 Mary Joe Nye, *Before Big Science: The Pursuit of Modern Chemistry and Physics, 1800–1940* (Cambridge, MA, 1999), p. xvi.
5 Christoph Asendorf, *Ströme und Strahlen: Das langsame Verschwinden der Materie um 1900* (Giessen, 1989), pp. 146–8.
6 David Knight, *Ideas in Chemistry: A History of the Science* (London, 2000), pp. 156–7.
7 Nye, *Before Big Science*, p. 27.
8 William Ramsay, 'Nobel Lecture. The Rare Gases of the Atmosphere: December 12, 1904', *Nobelprize.org: Nobel Prize in Chemistry*, http://nobelprize.org, accessed 12 March 2011.
9 Ibid.
10 William Ramsay, 'How Discoveries Are Made', in *Essays Biographical and Chemical* (London, 1908), p. 116.
11 William Ramsay, 'The Aurora Borealis', in *Essays Biographical and Chemical*, pp. 211–12.
12 Peter M. Kleine, 'Herrschaftslicht – Bürgerlicht – Stadtlicht? Historische Wegmarken', in *Stadtlicht Lichtkunst*, ed. Christoph Brockhaus (Cologne, 2004), p. 30.
13 Fabian Wurm, *Signaturen der Nacht: Die Welt der Lichtwerbung* (Ludwigsburg, 2009), p. 38.
14 Joachim Schlör, *Nachts in der grossen Stadt: Paris, Berlin, London, 1840–1930* [1991] (Munich, 1994), p. 68.
15 Wolfgang Schivelbusch, *Lichtblicke: Zur Geschichte der künstlichen Helligkeit im 19. Jahrhundert* [1983] (Frankfurt, 2004), p. 148.
16 Schlör, *Nachts in der grossen Stadt*, pp. 68–71.
17 John A. Jakle, *City Lights: Illuminating the American Night* (Baltimore, MD, 2001).

18 Janet Ward, *Weimar Surfaces: Urban Culture in 1920s Germany* (Berkeley, CA, 2001), p. 141.

19 Lewis A. Erenberg, *Steppin' Out: New York Nightlife and the Transformation of American Culture, 1890–1930* (Chicago, IL, 1984), p. xiv.

20 Jakle, *City Lights*, p. 199.

21 John A. Jakle and Keith A. Sculle, *Signs in America's Auto Age: Signatures of Landscape and Place* (Iowa City, 2004), pp. 14–15.

22 Stephen John Eskilson, 'America the Spectacle: Discourses of Color and Light, 1914–1934', dissertation, Brown University, 1995, microfilm, p. 9.

23 Wurm, *Signaturen der Nacht*, p. 45.

24 Günther Luxbacher, 'Das kommerzielle Licht: Lichtwerbung zwischen Elektroindustrie und Konsumgesellschaft vor dem Zweiten Weltkrieg', *Technikgeschichte*, 66 (1999), pp. 42–6.

25 Dirk Reinhardt, *Von der Reklame zum Marketing: Geschichte der Wirtschaftswerbung in Deutschland* (Berlin, 1993), pp. 323–4.

26 Anne Hoormann, *Lichtspiele: Zur Medienreflexion der Avantgarde in der Weimarer Republik* (Munich, 2003), pp. 247–9, 254.

27 Quoted in David E. Nye, *The American Technological Sublime* (Cambridge, MA, 1991), p. 187.

28 Vachel Lindsay, *The Congo and Other Poems* [1914] (Mineola, NY, 1992), p. 195.

29 Quoted in Rudi Stern, *The New Let There Be Neon* [revd edn of *Let There Be Neon*, 1979] (Cincinnati, OH, 1988), p. 79.

30 See for example Rebecca Solnit, *Wanderlust: A History of Walking* (London, 2001), pp. 202–4.

31 Hoormann, *Lichtspiele*, pp. 258–9.

32 Wilhelm Hausenstein, *Eine Stadt, auf nichts gebaut: Wilhelm Hausenstein über Berlin* (Berlin, 1984), pp. 7, 9.

33 Max Epstein, 'Berlin im Licht', *Weltbrille*, 7 (November 1928), p. 2.

34 Carl von Linde was working at the same time on a very similar project (see Michael F. Crowe, 'Neon Signs: Their Origin, Use, and Maintenance', *APT Bulletin*, XXIII/3 [1991], p. 31).

35 Rémi Baillot, *Georges Claude: Le Génie fourvoyé* (Les Ulis, 2010), pp. 141–3.

36 Walter E. Pittman, 'Energy from the Oceans: Georges Claude's Magnificent Failure', *Environmental Review*, VI/1 (Spring 1982), p. 3.

37 Quoted in Christine Blondel, 'Industrial Science as a "Show": A Case-study of Georges Claude', in *Expository Science: Forms*

and Functions of Popularisation, ed. Terry Shinn and Richard Whitley (*Sociology of the Sciences: A Yearbook*, Dordrecht, 1985), pp. 249–58; Baillot, *Georges Claude*, p. 13.

38 Pittman, 'Energy from the Oceans', p. 3.

39 Blondel, 'Industrial Science as a "Show"', p. 253; Baillot, *Georges Claude*, pp. 144–5.

40 Baillot, *Georges Claude*, p. 255.

41 Georges Claude, *Souvenirs et enseignements d'une expérience électorale* (Paris, 1932), pp. 76–8.

42 Pittman, 'Energy from the Oceans', p. 3.

43 Stern, *The New Let There Be Neon*, pp. 21–4; Georges Claude, *Ma vie et mes inventions* (Paris, 1957), p. 72.

44 Paul Möbius, *Die Neon-Leuchtröhren: ihre Fabrikation, Anwendung und Installation*, 2nd edn (Leipzig, 1938), p. 55.

45 Michael Webb, *The Magic of Neon* (Layton, UT, 1986), p. 54.

46 Möbius, *Die Neon-Leuchtröhren*, p. 55.

47 'Dutch Use Neon Lights to Grow Cucumbers and Strawberries', *New York Times* (15 February 1931), p. 26.

48 'Images Dance in Space, Heralding New Radio Era', *New York Times* (14 April 1929), p. 159.

49 Stern, *The New Let There Be Neon*, p. 23.

50 Hoormann, *Lichtspiele*, p. 250.

51 Stern, *The New Let There Be Neon*, p. 25.

52 Wurm, *Signaturen der Nacht*, p. 42.

53 Stern, *The New Let There Be Neon*, p. 23.

54 Andrea Domesle, *Leucht-Schrift-Kunst: Holzer, Kosuth, Merz, Nannucci, Nauman* (Berlin, 1998), pp. 39–40.

55 Reinhardt, *Von der Reklame zum Marketing*, p. 323.

56 Luxbacher, 'Das kommerzielle Licht', pp. 51–2.

57 *Claude Neon News*, II/5 (January 1930), p. 27.

58 Ibid., n. p.

59 Stern, *The New Let There Be Neon*, p. 24.

60 'Oil Concern to Light Stations by Neon Method', *Los Angeles Times* (14 July 1927), p. 10.

61 Tama Starr and Edward Hayman, *Signs and Wonders: The Spectacular Marketing of America* (New York, 1998), p. 82.

62 'Worcester Lawn Mowers', *Claude Neon News*, III/3 (September/October 1930), p. 9.

63 'Olympic Sign Constructed', *Los Angeles Times* (4 February 1931), p. A13.

64 Stern, *The New Let There Be Neon*, p. 158.

65 Samuel C. Miller and Donald G. Fink, *Neon Signs: Manufacture*

– *Installation – Maintenance* (New York, 1935), p. 1.
66 '50 Years of Electric Signs', *Signs of the Times* (May 1956), p. 26.
67 Stern, *The New Let There Be Neon*, p. 27.
68 Webb, *The Magic of Neon*, pp. vii, 54.
69 Reinhardt, *Von der Reklame zum Marketing*, pp. 327–8.
70 Miller and Fink, *Neon Signs*, p. 3.
71 'Newsboys Wear Neon Signs as Traffic Protection', *Los Angeles
Times* (31 August 1936), p. A1.
72 Stern, *The New Let There Be Neon*, pp. 24–8.
73 On the Jazz Age, see Ann Douglas, *Terrible Honesty: Mongrel
Manhattan in the 1920s* (New York, 1996).
74 Wolfgang Schivelbusch, *Licht, Schein und Wahn: Auftritte der
elektrischen Beleuchtung im 20. Jahrhundert* (Berlin, 1992), p. 67.
75 Miller and Fink, *Neon Signs*, pp. 4–5.
76 Starr and Hayman, *Signs and Wonders*, p. 92.
77 Lisa Mahar-Keplinger, *American Signs: Form and Meaning on
Route 66* (New York, 2002), p. 49; Darcy Tell, *Times Square
Spectacular: Lighting Up Broadway* (Washington, DC, 2007), p. 98.
78 Luxbacher, 'Das kommerzielle Licht', p. 52.
79 Walter Köhler und Robert Rompe, *Die elektrischen Leuchtröhren*
(Braunschweig, 1933), p. 54.
80 W. L. Schallreuter, *Neon Tube Practice* (London, 1939), p. 13.
81 *Claude Neon News*, II/1 (Mai 1929), p. 4.
82 Crowe, 'Neon Signs', p. 31.
83 Stern, *The New Let There Be Neon*, pp. 24–7.
84 Miller and Fink, *Neon Signs*, p. 5.
85 *Claude Neon News*, II/2 (July 1929), p. 23.
86 *Claude Neon News*, II/5 (January 1930), p. 6.
87 Ibid.
88 *Claude Neon News*, III/3 (September/October 1930), p. 9.
89 Ibid., p. 11.
90 *Claude Neon News*, I/5 (January 1929), p. 6.
91 *Claude Neon News*, I/1 (January 1928), p. 1.
92 Blondel, 'Industrial Science as a "Show"', p. 256.
93 'Georges Claude, Inventor, Dies', *New York Times* (24 May
1960), p. 37.
94 Eduard Farber, 'Claude, Georges', in *Dictionary of Scientific
Biography*, ed. Charles Coulston Gillispie, vol. III (New York,
1971), p. 299.
95 Guy Debord, *The Society of the Spectacle*, trans. Donald
Nicholson-Smith (New York, 1994), p. 13.
96 Ward, *Weimar Surfaces*, pp. 3–8.

97 Stern, *The New Let There Be Neon*, p. 36.

98 Ibid., p. 33.

99 Miller and Fink, *Neon Signs*, pp. 27–32.

100 Ibid., pp. 80–89.

101 See S. Gold, *Neon: A Handbook for Electrical Engineers, Neon Manufacturers, Sign Salesmen, and Advertisers* (London, 1934), p. 12; according to the *Oxford English Dictionary*, the word 'readability' was, however, first recorded as early as 1839.

102 Möbius, *Die Neon-Leuchtröhren*, pp. 56–9.

103 Miller and Fink, *Neon Signs*, p. 7.

104 J. B. Priestley, *Midnight on the Desert* (New York, 1937), p. 87.

105 Miller and Fink, *Neon Signs*, p. 2.

106 Ibid.

107 Meyer Berger, 'New Constellations on the Old White Way', *New York Times* (29 March 1936), p. SM12.

108 Jakle, *City Lights*, p. 204.

109 Tell, *Times Square Spectacular*, p. 101.

110 Berger, 'New Constellations', p. SM12.

111 Jakle, *City Lights*, pp. 204–5.

112 Starr and Hayman, *Signs and Wonders*, p. 130; Tell, *Times Square Spectacular*, pp. 106–14.

113 Tell, *Times Square Spectacular*, pp. 106–14.

114 Ibid., p. 108.

115 Ibid., pp. 105–11.

116 Ibid., p. 119.

117 Starr and Hayman, *Signs and Wonders*, p. 143.

118 James Traub, *The Devil's Playground: A Century of Pleasure and Profit in Times Square* (New York, 2004), p. 46.

119 Jakle, *City Lights*, p. 202.

120 Berger, 'New Constellations', p. 12.

121 Ibid.

122 Even at the annual fish show of the Tropical Fish Society of Brooklyn it was the neon tetras, newly discovered in 1937, that upstaged all the other types of fish, thanks to their luminosity ('New Fish Overshadow Guppys to Win Prize at Tropical Show', *New York Times* [29 August 1937], p. 35).

123 Samuel Lubell, 'What One Misses in Moscow', *New York Times* (24 June 1934), p. SM19.

124 Berger, 'New Constellations', p. 12.

125 Stern, *The New Let There Be Neon*, p. 121.

126 Schivelbusch, *Licht Schein und Wahn*, p. 104.

127 Reinhardt, *Von der Reklame zum Marketing*, pp. 327–8.

128 Antonia Linzbach, 'Transparente Schilder, fluoreszierende Papageien', in Fabian Wurm, *Signaturen der Nacht: Die Welt der Lichtwerbung* (Ludwigsburg, 2009), p. 69.

129 Hoormann, *Lichtspiele*, p. 299; Reinhardt, *Von der Reklame zum Marketing*, pp. 327–8.

130 Stern, *The New Let There Be Neon*, p. 24.

131 Gottfried Korff, 'Berliner Nächte: Zum Selbstbild urbaner Eigenschaften und Leidenschaften', in *Berlin: Blicke auf die deutsche Metropole*, ed. Gerhard Brunn und Jürgen Reulecke (Essen, 1989), pp. 92ff; see also Albrecht W. Thöne, *Das Licht der Arier: Licht-, Feuer- und Dunkelsymbolik des Nationalsozialismus* (Munich, 1979).

132 Reinhardt, *Von der Reklame zum Marketing*, p. 329.

133 'Aurora of Lights Dims out in City for the Duration', *New York Times* (29 April 1942), p. 10.

134 Ibid., p. 10.

135 'Great Signs Dark as Gay White Way Obeys Army Edict', *New York Times* (30 April 1942), p. 1.

136 Ibid., p. 1.

137 'Blackout Success Is Highly Praised', *New York Times* (2 May 1942), p. 15.

138 'Aurora of Lights', p. 10.

3 NEON WILDERNESS

1 Bettina Drew, *Nelson Algren: A Life on the Wild Side* (New York, 1989), pp. 157–69.

2 Nelson Algren, 'Introduction', *The Neon Wilderness* (New York, 1960), pp. 9–10.

3 Ibid., p. 10.

4 Mark J. Bouman, '"The Best Lighted City in the World": The Construction of a Nocturnal Landscape in Chicago', in *The American Cities and Technology Reader: Wilderness to Wired City*, ed. Gerrylynn K. Roberts (London, 1999), pp. 175, 181, 184.

5 See for example Alan Trachtenberg, *The Incorporation of America: Culture and Society in the Gilded Age* (New York, 1982), pp. 208–9.

6 Quoted in Harold L. Platt, *The Electric City: Energy and the Growth of the Chicago Area, 1880–1930* (Chicago, IL, 1991), p. 91.

7 Theodore Dreiser, *Journalism*, vol. I: *Newspaper Writings, 1892–1895*, ed. T. D. Nostwich (Philadelphia, PA, 1988), pp. 126, 137.

8 Trachtenberg, *The Incorporation of America*, pp. 210–11.
9 Stephen John Eskilson, '"A Century of Progress" Exposition, Chicago, 1933', in Dietrich Neumann, Kermit Swiler Champa, Werner Oechslin and Mary Woods, *Architektur der Nacht* (Munich, 2002), p. 164.
10 Rudi Stern, *The New Let There Be Neon* [revd edn of *Let There Be Neon*, 1979] (Cincinnati, OH, 1988), p. 27; John A. Jakle, *City Lights: Illuminating the American Night* (Baltimore, MD, 2001), pp. 162–3.
11 Eskilson, '"A Century of Progress" Exposition', pp. 164–5.
12 Nelson Algren, *Somebody in Boots* [1935] (New York, 1965), p. 235.
13 Ibid., p. 236.
14 Ibid., p. 238.
15 Ibid., p. 233.
16 Drew, *Nelson Algren*, p. 170; Mike Royko, 'Algren's Golden Pen', in *The Man with the Golden Arm: 50th Anniversary Critical Edition*, ed. William J. Savage Jr and Daniel Simon (New York, 1999), pp. 363–5.
17 Algren, *The Neon Wilderness*, n. p.
18 On the literary representation of slums and poverty, see Keith F. Gandal, *The Virtues of the Vicious: Jacob Riis, Stephen Crane, and the Spectacle of the Slum* (New York, 1997); Gavin Roger Jones, *American Hungers: The Problem of Poverty in American Literature, 1840–1945* (Princeton, NJ, 2008).
19 Anne Hoormann, *Lichtspiele: Zur Medienreflexion der Avantgarde in der Weimarer Republik* (Munich, 2003), p. 303.
20 Sibyl Moholy-Nagy in conversation with Studs Terkel, 1969. Quoted in *László Moholy-Nagy: Color in Transparency. Photographic Experiments in Color, 1934–1946*, ed. Jeannine Fiedler and Hattula Moholy-Nagy (Göttingen, 2006), p. 154.
21 Hoormann, *Lichtspiele*, p. 266.
22 Ibid., pp. 258–9.
23 Karen Bouchard and Dietrich Neumann, 'Simpson's Department Store, London, 1936', in Dietrich Neumann, Kermit Swiler Champa, Werner Oechslin und Mary Woods, *Architektur der Nacht* (Munich, 2002), p. 168.
24 Ibid., p. 168.
25 Arthur Shay, 'Remembering Nelson Algren', *Nelson Algren's Chicago* (Urbana, IL, 1988), p. xiv.
26 Carlo Rotella, *October Cities: The Redevelopment of Urban Literature* (Berkeley, CA, 1998), pp. 50–51.

27 Ted L. Clontz, *Wilderness City: The Post World War II American Urban Novel from Algren to Wideman* (New York, 2005), p. 22.
28 Quoted in Rotella, *October Cities*, p. 50.
29 Quoted in Shay, 'Remembering Nelson Algren', p. xxi.
30 Drew, *Nelson Algren*, p. 142.
31 Ibid., p. 174.
32 Ibid., pp. 178–80.
33 Rotella, *October Cities*, p. 52; see also Carlo Rotella, 'The Story of Decline and the October City', in *The Man with the Golden Arm*, ed. Savage and Simon, pp. 423–32.
34 Rotella, 'Story of Decline', pp. 427–8.
35 Quoted in Shay, 'Remembering Nelson Algren', p. xxii.
36 Nelson Algren, *Chicago: City on the Make* (Garden City, NY, 1951), pp. 91–2.
37 Ibid., p. 24.
38 Ibid., p. 30.
39 Fielder and *Time*, quoted in Lawrence Lipton, 'A Voyeur's View of the Wild Side: Nelson Algren and His Reviewers', in *The Man with the Golden Arm*, ed. Savage and Simon, p. 401; see also James R. Giles, *Confronting the Horror: The Novels of Nelson Algren* (Kent, OH, 1989).
40 Lipton, 'A Voyeur's View', pp. 407–8.
41 Rotella, *October Cities*, p. 59.
42 Shay, 'Remembering Nelson Algren', p. xxi.
43 Vito Zagarrio, 'It Is (Not) a Wonderful Life: For a Counter-reading of Frank Capra', in *Frank Capra: Authorship and the Studio System*, ed. Robert Sklar and Vito Zagarrio (Philadelphia, PA, 1998), pp. 64–94; *It's a Wonderful Life*, dir. Frank Capra (Liberty Films, 1946), film.
44 Stern, *The New Let There Be Neon*, pp. 122–5; Michael Webb, *The Magic of Neon* (Layton, UT, 1983), p. 34.
45 Elisabeth Bronfen, *Tiefer als der Tag gedacht: Eine Kulturgeschichte der Nacht* (Munich, 2008), pp. 432–3.
46 Stern, *The New Let There Be Neon*, pp. 27–8.
47 'Synagogue Marks Season', *New York Times* (26 December 1948), p. 43.
48 'Neon Converts to "Plastilux 500"', *New York Times* (30 May 1950), p. 28.
49 Elizabeth A. Wheeler, *Uncontained: Urban Fiction in Postwar America* (New Brunswick, NJ, 2001), pp. 9–11.
50 Jakle, *City Lights*, pp. 243–4.
51 'Skid Row Flares as Gaudy Nightmare in Neon Lights', *Los*

Angeles Times (18 April 1948), pp. A1, 8.

52 Stern, *The New Let There Be Neon*, p. 19.

53 'Bel-Air Area to Remain Free of Neon Lights', *Los Angeles Times* (3 September 1949), p. 1.

54 On Raymond Chandler and the neon history of Los Angeles, see William Brevda, 'The Double Nihilation of the Neon: Raymond Chandler's Los Angeles', *Texas Studies in Literature and Language*, XLI/1 (1999), pp. 71–102. See also Nathan Marsak and Nigel Cox, *Los Angeles Neon* (Atglen, PA, 2002).

55 John D. MacDonald, *The Neon Jungle* (New York, 1953), pp. 5–6.

56 Leonard Cassuto, *Hard-Boiled Sentimentality: The Secret History of American Crime Stories* (New York, 2009), p. 121.

57 Ibid., pp. 167–8.

58 William Brevda, 'The Rainbow Sign of Nelson Algren', *Texas Studies in Literature and Language*, XLIV/4 (2002), pp. 393–413.

59 Drew, *Nelson Algren*, p. 261.

60 Ibid., p. 262.

61 Foster Hirsch, *Otto Preminger: The Man Who Would Be King* (New York, 2007), pp. 234–6; *The Man with the Golden Arm*, dir. Otto Preminger (Otto Preminger Films, 1955), film.

62 Frankie meets an important representative of the music industry in a bare, minimalist skyscraper. The audition – when Frankie, new to drumming, fails to make his mark – also does not take place in a bar but in a soulless, all-purpose hall. Looking at the all-American consumer goods, in the company of the woman who may well bring him a new future, the attractions and latest labour-saving devices on show in the shop window are coolly presented, and not advertised with words up in flashing lights.

63 Dimendberg points out the distinction between 'centripetal space' (that of the neon wilderness) and 'centrifugal space' (that of the 'road movie', which was very successful in the period after film noir). See Edward Dimendberg, *Film Noir and the Spaces of Modernity* (Cambridge, MA, 2004), p. 255.

64 Michael Johns, *Moment of Grace: The American City in the 1950s* (Berkeley, CA, 2002), pp. 43–4.

65 Algren, 'Introduction', pp. 11–12.

66 Ibid., p. 13.

67 Ibid., p. 14.

68 Kurt Vonnegut, 'Algren as I Knew Him', in *The Man with the Golden Arm*, ed. Savage and Simon, pp. 367–70.

4 LAS VEGAS: CITY OF LIGHTS

1 Dave Hickey, 'A Home in the Neon', *Air Guitar: Essays on Art and Democracy* (Los Angeles, 1997), p. 19; Charles F. Barnard, *The Magic Sign: The Electric Art/Architecture of Las Vegas* (Cincinnati, OH, 1993), p. 84.
2 Lisa Mahar-Keplinger, *American Signs: Form and Meaning on Route 66* (New York, 2002), p. 161.
3 Barnard, *The Magic Sign*, pp. 64–78.
4 Alan Hess, *Viva Las Vegas: After-Hours Architecture* (San Francisco, 1993), p. 74.
5 Hickey, 'A Home in the Neon', p. 19.
6 Martino Stierli, *Las Vegas im Rückspiegel: Die Stadt in Theorie, Fotografie und Film* (Zürich, 2010), pp. 90ff.
7 Hickey, 'A Home in the Neon', p. 23.
8 Ibid., p. 52. In a discussion on Las Vegas arranged for an exhibition catalogue; Hickey nevertheless declared that, in any case, the word authenticity had no meaning for him; Hickey et al., 'The Players', *The Magic Hour: The Convergence of Art and Las Vegas*, ed. Alex Farquharson (Ostfildern, 2001), p. 42.
9 Laura Bieger, *Ästhetik der Immersion: Raum-Erleben zwischen Welt und Bild. Las Vegas, Washington und die White City* (Bielefeld, 2007), p. 179.
10 Bieger, *Ästhetik der Immersion*, p. 123.
11 *Casino*, dir. Martin Scorsese (Universal Pictures, 1995), film.
12 Hal Rothman, *Neon Metropolis: How Las Vegas Started the Twenty-first Century* (London, 2003), pp. xxviii, 3.
13 Mark Gottdiener, Claudia C. Collins and David R. Dickens, *Las Vegas: The Social Production of an All-American City* (Malden, MA, 1999), p. 260; Rothman, *Neon Metropolis*, p. 264.
14 Rothman, *Neon Metropolis*, p. xxv; see also Hal Rothman and Mike Davis, eds, *The Grit beneath the Glitter: Tales from the Real Las Vegas* (Berkeley, MA, 2002).
15 John O'Brien, *Leaving Las Vegas* [1990] (New York, 1995). Charles Bock's Las Vegas novel, *Beautiful Children*, published in 2008, on the other hand, manages completely to capture the polyphonic quality of the city and to convey some of the energy of the neon era as well as the social transformations of the late twentieth century. Tellingly, in Bock's novel it is not an intellectual who reveals the huge changes to the city but a small boy (underprivileged as is typical of the Algren tradition), who accompanies his aunt on a local bus along the Strip, observing

through the 'darkened windows of public transportation' the changes that have occurred since the explosion of neon palaces. Charles Bock, *Beautiful Children* (New York, 2008), p. 65. See also, on the background to this first great city novel about Southern Nevada: Charles McGrath, 'What Happened in Vegas Stayed in ~~Vegas~~ His Novel', *New York Times Magazine*, www.nytimes.com, 27 January 2008, accessed 18 March 2011.

16 These, according to Hickey, are the rules of democracy – and this, he claims, is what traditionally minded academics have never been able to get their heads round, as they have been used to 'in-depth analysis' rather than the superficially egalitarian culture of this city. They have therefore always been looking for the 'hidden Las Vegas', something that does not exist in the city of superficiality (Hickey, 'A Home in the Neon', p. 21).

17 Robert Venturi, Denise Scott Brown and Steven Izenour, *Learning from Las Vegas* (Cambridge, MA, 1972), p. xii.

18 Stierli, *Las Vegas im Rückspiegel*, p. 28.

19 Barnard, *The Magic Sign*, pp. 67–9.

20 Venturi, Scott Brown and Izenour, *Learning from Las Vegas*, pp. xi–xii.

21 Stierli, *Las Vegas im Rückspiegel*, p. 15. See also, from the point of view of reception and cultural history, Aron Vinegar and Michael J. Golec, eds, *Relearning from Las Vegas* (Minneapolis, MN, 2009).

22 Carl A. Zimring, '"Neon, Junk, and Ruined Landscape": Competing Visions of America's Roadsides and the Highway Beautification Act of 1965', in *The World beyond the Windshield: Roads and Landscapes in the United States and Europe*, ed. Christof Mauch and Thomas Zeller (Athens, OH, 2008), pp. 94–107.

23 Venturi, Scott Brown and Izenour, *Learning from Las Vegas*, p. 116.

24 Ibid., p. 18.

25 Ibid., pp. 80–81.

26 Stierli, *Las Vegas im Rückspiegel*, p. 16.

27 Venturi, Scott Brown and Izenour, *Learning from Las Vegas*, pp. 161–2.

28 Ibid., p. xvii.

29 Ibid., p. xvi.

30 Stierli here refers to Umberto Eco's distinction between the 'apocalyptic' and the 'integrated' (in relation to expressions of popular culture), opposites in the debate about Las Vegas (p. 88). See also Umberto Eco, 'Apocalyptic and Integrated',

in *Apocalypse Postponed/Umberto Eco*, ed. Robert Lumley (Bloomington, IN, 1994).

31 Hess, *Viva Las Vegas*, p. 10.

32 John Chase, *Glitter Stucco and Dumpster Diving: Reflections on Building Production in the Vernacular City* (New York, 2000); see also Barnard, *The Magic Sign*, pp. 17–19.

33 Barnard, *The Magic Sign*, p. 189.

34 Peter Bexte, 'Wolken über Las Vegas', *Archiv für Mediengeschichte*, 5 (2005), pp. 131–7.

35 Ibid., p. 133.

36 Calum Storrie, *The Delirious Museum: A Journey from the Louvre to Las Vegas* (London, 2006), p. 13.

37 Ken Cooper, '"Zero Pays the House": The Las Vegas Novel and Atomic Roulette', *Contemporary Literature*, XXXIII/3 (1992), pp. 530–31.

38 Ibid., p. 543.

39 Katharine Best and Katharine Hillyer, *Las Vegas: Playtown USA* (New York, 1955), p. 3.

40 Ibid., pp. 135–9, 178.

41 Ed Reid and Ovid Demaris, *The Green Felt Jungle* (New York, 1963), p. 1.

42 Ed Reid, *Las Vegas: City without Clocks* (Englewood Cliffs, NJ, 1961), p. 17.

43 'Behind these shocking facts', according to the authors of the introduction, 'is the true story of Las Vegas, a story now told for the first time' (Reid and Demaris, *The Green Felt Jungle*, p. 13).

44 Barnard, *The Magic Sign*, pp. 17, 88, 94.

45 David E. Nye, *The American Technological Sublime* (Cambridge, MA, 1991), pp. 295–6.

46 Jakle, *City Lights*, p. 248.

47 Bruce Bégout, *Zeropolis: The Experience of Las Vegas* (London, 2003), p. 13.

48 Ibid., pp. 62–4.

49 Ibid., p. 119.

50 Ibid., p. 13. His compatriot and colleague Jean Baudrillard came to the conclusion, on the neon signs in Nevada, that it is wrong to think about nuances in this case at all. Here all there is is a '*confusion prodigeuse des effets*'. Jean Baudrillard, *Amérique* [1986] (Paris, 2000), pp. 147–8.

51 Mike Davis, *Dead Cities and Other Tales* (New York, 2002), pp. 86–100.

52 Marianne DeKoven, *Utopia Limited: The Sixties and the*

Emergence of the Postmodern (Durham, NC, 2004), p. 92.
53 Quoted in Michael E. Staub, 'Setting up the Seventies: Black Panthers, New Journalism, and the Rewriting of the Sixties', in *The Seventies: The Age of Glitter in Popular Culture*, ed. Shelton Waldrep (New York, 2000), p. 22.
54 Hunter S. Thompson, *Fear and Loathing in Las Vegas: A Savage Journey to the Heart of the American Dream* [1971] (New York, 1998), p. 4.
55 Ibid., p. 27.
56 Ibid., p. 47.
57 John Gregory Dunne, *Vegas: A Memoir of a Dark Season* (New York, 1974), p. 5.
58 Ibid., p. 25.
59 Ibid., pp. 173–4.
60 Ibid., p. 25.
61 Ibid., p. 19.
62 Ibid., pp. 131, 159–60, 174, 191.
63 Ibid., 19.
64 Joan Didion, 'Marrying Absurd' [1967], in *Literary Las Vegas: Portraits of America's Most Fabulous City*, ed. Mike Tronnes (Edinburgh, 1995), pp. 162–5; see also Joan Didion, *Slouching towards Bethlehem* (New York, 1968).
65 Didion, 'Marrying Absurd', p. 164.
66 Joan Didion, *Play It as It Lays* [1970] (New York, 2005), p. 171.
67 Hal Rothman, 'Las Vegas and the American Psyche, Past and Present', *Pacific Historical Review*, LXX/4 (2001), pp. 627–40.
68 Marc Weingarten, *The Gang That Wouldn't Write Straight: Wolfe, Thompson, Didion, and the New Journalism Revolution* (New York, 2006), pp. 245–51; Paul Perry, *Fear and Loathing: The Strange and Terrible Saga of Hunter S. Thompson* (New York, 1992), pp. 158–9.
69 Tom Wolfe, *The Kandy-Kolored Tangerine-Flake Streamline Baby* (New York, 1965), p. 8.
70 Ibid., p. 11.
71 Ibid., p. 8.
72 Weingarten, *The Gang*, pp. 2–3.
73 Ibid., p. 99.
74 Wolfe, *Kandy-Kolored*, p. 19.
75 Ibid., p. 27.
76 Ibid., p. xvii.

5 GREEN FINGERS

1 Anne Wilkes Tucker, 'So Intelligent, . . . So Angry, and Having
   Such Passion for the World', in Anne Wilkes Tucker with Lisa
   Hostetler and Kathleen V. Jameson, *Louis Faurer* (London, 2002),
   p. 24.
2 Lisa Hostetler, 'Louis Faurer and Film Noir', in *Louis Faurer*,
   p. 61.
3 Lisa Hostetler, *Street Seen: The Psychological Gesture in
   American Photography, 1940–1959* (Munich, 2010), p. 83.
4 Darcy Tell, *Times Square Spectacular: Lighting Up Broadway*
   (Washington, DC, 2007), p. 128; cf. Tama Starr and Edward
   Hayman (*Signs and Wonders: The Spectacular Marketing of
   America*, New York, 1998), who point out that clothing the
   naked statues had been planned right from the start (p. 149).
5 Starr and Hayman, *Signs and Wonders*, p. 146.
6 Tell, *Times Square Spectacular*, p. 128; Rudi Stern, *The New Let
   There Be Neon* [revd edn of *Let There Be Neon*, 1979]
   (Cincinnati, OH, 1988), p. 139.
7 Tell, *Times Square Spectacular*, pp. 128–31.
8 Tucker, 'So Intelligent', pp. 13–47.
9 Otto Hofmann-Wellenhof, 'Nachwort', in *Neon und Psyche:
   Gedichte, Alois Hergouth* (Graz, 1953), p. 63.
10 Ibid.
11 Siegfried Kracauer, *The Salaried Masses: Duty and Distraction
   in Weimar Germany* [1929], trans. Quintin Hoare (London and
   New York, 1998), p. 93.
12 Theodor W. Adorno, *Philosophy of New Music* [1949], trans.
   and ed. Robert Hullot-Kentor (Minneapolis, MN, and London,
   2006), p. 16.
13 Vladimir Nabokov, 'On a Book Entitled *Lolita*', in *Lolita* [1955]
   (London, 2000), p. 312.
14 Ibid., p. 282.
15 Ibid., p. 285.
16 Stern, *The New Let There Be Neon*, p. 65. The historian of Times
   Square, Darcy Tell, points out that the new products and services
   in the 1950s – cough syrup, health insurance, air conditioning,
   airlines – were less suitable for dramatic representation than,
   for example, the alcoholic drinks of more hedonistic periods
   (Tell, *Times Square Spectacular*, p. 131).
17 The term Times Square refers not just to the actual square, but to
   an area of five blocks between 42nd and 47th Street. Lynne B.

Sagalyn, *Times Square Roulette: Remaking the City Icon* (Cambridge, MA, 2001), pp. 51–2.

18 Laurence Senelick, 'Private Parts in Public Places', in *Inventing Times Square: Commerce and Culture at the Crossroads of the World*, ed. William R. Taylor (Baltimore, MD, 1996), pp. 337ff.

19 Ibid., pp. 340–41.

20 Alexander J. Reichl, *Reconstructing Times Square: Politics and Culture in Urban Development* (Lawrence, KS, 1999), p. 57.

21 Tell, *Times Square Spectacular*, p. 134.

22 Quoted in Arnold Rampersad, *The Life of Langston Hughes*, vol. II (New York, 1986), p. 194.

23 Langston Hughes, 'Juke Box Love Song', in *Selected Poems of Langston Hughes* (New York, 1969), p. 227.

24 Langston Hughes, 'Neon Signs', in *Selected Poems*, pp. 232–3.

25 See, for example: Robert O'Brien Hokanson, 'Jazzing It Up: The Be-bop Modernism of Langston Hughes', *Mosaic*, XXXI/4 (1998), pp. 61–82.

26 Frank O'Hara's poems about Times Square (particularly 'A Step Away From Them'), however, like Hughes's poems, show a clear enthusiasm for neon. See Frank O'Hara, *Lunch Poems* (San Francisco, CA, 1964).

27 James Traub, *The Devil's Playground: A Century of Pleasure and Profit in Times Square* (New York, 2004), pp. 114–16.

28 Lisa Phillips, 'Beat Culture: America Revisioned', in *Beat Culture and the New America, 1950–1965*, ed. Lisa Phillips (New York, 1995), p. 33.

29 Traub, *The Devil's Playground*, pp. 114–16.

30 Jack Kerouac, *Visions of Cody* (New York, 1972), p. 75.

31 Charles Plymell, 'In NYC', in *neon poems* (Syracuse, NY, 1970), pp. 12–13.

32 John Rechy, *City of Night* [1962] (New York, 1988), p. 30. Rechy's novel has been described by critics as one of the most important literary documents on sexual subcultures. It is notable that the narrator is quite clearly detached from the 'City of Night' in which he is a prostitute. Unlike Nelson Algren, who quite consciously sought out the company of the down and out of the neon wilderness, the narrator does not associate with anyone, neither with the clients nor with the other prostitutes. The key metaphor of his own identity, *City of Night* makes clear again and again, is not the light of the neon signs on Times Square and elsewhere, but the equally lit-up Texas sky: 'clear, magic, electric blue' (p. 10).

33 Denis Belloc, *Néons* [1987] (Boston, 1991), p. 87.

34 Ibid., p. 87.

35 Marguerite Duras saw in Belloc an advance in realism – *Néons* is, as it were, written by the body. This reading ignores the consciously constructed perspective on the position of the narrator in the urban environment, not only reflecting the rhythms of neon, but positively pursuing them and in the end, as an artist, composing himself. See James S. Williams, 'All Her Sons: Marguerite Duras, Antiliterature, and the Outside', *Yale French Studies*, 90 (1996), p. 50.

36 Sylvère Lotringer, 'Jane Dickson', *BOMBSITE*, online edition of *BOMB Magazine*, 60 (Summer 1997), http://bombsite.com, accessed 19 March 2011.

37 Gary Indiana, 'Real Estate', in *Life under Neon: Paintings and Drawings of Times Square, 1981–1988*, ed. Jane Dickson, exh. cat., Goldie Paley Gallery/Moore College of Art and Design (Philadelphia, PA, 1989), p. 4.

38 Reichl, *Reconstructing Times Square*, pp. 60–61.

39 Bart Eeckhout, 'The Postsexual City? Times Square in the Age of Virtual Reproduction', in *Taking Up Space: New Approaches to American History*, ed. Anke Ortlepp and Christoph Ribbat (Trier, 2004), pp. 207–8.

40 Quoted in Laurence Senelick, 'Private Parts in Public Places', p. 352.

41 Starr and Hayman, *Signs and Wonders*, pp. 252–3.

42 M. Christine Boyer, 'Twice-told Stories: The Double Erasure of Times Square', in *The Unknown City: Contesting Architecture and Social Space*, ed. Iain Borden et al. (Cambridge, MA, 2001), pp. 30–52.

43 Delany associates his book with the concept of 'queer space', forming sexual identities running counter to the architecture defining the city. See for example Dianne Chisholm, *Queer Constellations: Subcultural Space in the Wake of the City* (Minneapolis, MN, 2004), pp. 29–30.

44 Samuel R. Delany, *Times Square Red, Times Square Blue* (New York, 1999), p. 146.

45 Ibid., pp. 198–9.

46 Ibid., p. 123.

47 Michael Webb, '"So wie heute, nur übersteigert": Die glaubhafte Anti-Utopie von *Blade Runner*', in *Filmarchitektur: Von Metropolis bis Blade Runner*, ed. Dietrich Neumann (Munich, 1996), pp. 44–7.

48 *Blade Runner*, dir. Ridley Scott (Warner Brothers, 1982), film.

49 Norman M. Klein, 'Building *Blade Runner*', *Social Text*, 28 (1991), pp. 147–9.

50 See for example Giuliana Bruno, 'Ramble City: Postmodernism and *Blade Runner*', *October*, 41 (1987), pp. 61–74.

51 Matt Hills, 'Academic Textual Poachers: *Blade Runner* as Cult Canonical Movie', in *The Blade Runner Experience: The Legacy of a Science Fiction Classic*, ed. Will Brooker (London, 2005), p. 131.

52 *Schlitz Gusto*, home page, Joseph Schlitz Brewing Company, www.schlitzgusto.com, accessed 11 March 2011.

53 Nicholas Christopher, *Somewhere in the Night: Film Noir and the American City* (New York, 1998), pp. 234–5.

54 See also, on *Blade Runner* as a film of 'repressed sexuality': Kyle J. Novak, 'Bondage, Bestiality, and Bionics: Sexual Fetishism in Ridley Scott's *Blade Runner*', *Valley Humanities Review: Current Issue*, www.lvc.edu, 29 April 2010, accessed 11 March 2011.

55 Scott Bukatman, *Blade Runner* (London, 1997), p. 61.

56 Timothy Yu, 'Oriental Cities, Postmodern Futures: *Naked Lunch, Blade Runner*, and *Neuromancer*', MELUS, XXXIII/4 (2008), pp. 45–71.

57 Stern, *The New Let There Be Neon*, p. 81.

58 Dusty Sprengnagel, *Neon World* (New York, 1999), p. 113.

59 Daniel Halpern, 'Foreign Neon', *Foreign Neon: Poems* (New York, 1991), pp. 3–4; Frank Tuohy, 'Nocturne with Neon Lights', in *The Collected Stories* (New York, 1984), pp. 285–95.

60 Peter Bialobrzeski, *Neontigers* (Ostfildern, 2003); *Lost in Translation*, dir. Sofia Coppola (Focus Features, 2003), film.

61 Homay King, *Lost in Translation: Orientalism, Cinema, and the Enigmatic Signifier* (Durham, NC, 2010), p. 163.

62 Suji Kwock Kim, 'Montage with Neon, Bok Choi, Gasoline, Lovers and Strangers', in *Notes from the Divided Country* (Baton Rouge, LA, 2003), pp. 35–7.

63 Pei-Chia Lan, 'Working in a Neon Cage: Bodily Labor of Cosmetics Saleswomen in Taiwan', *Feminist Studies*, XXIX/1 (2003), pp. 21–45.

64 Mong-Lan, 'BANGKOK [neon lights]', *The Antioch Review*, LXIII/1 (Winter 2005), p. 136.

65 Dietmar Kreutzer, 'Vorwort', in *Plaste und Elaste: Leuchtreklame in der DDR* (Berlin, 2010), p. 13.

66 Quoted in Kreutzer, 'Vorwort', p. 14; see also Christoph Gunkel, 'Es werde Licht: Leuchtreklame in der DDR', *Spiegel Online: Einestages*, http://einestages.spiegel.de, 16 September 2010, accessed 11 March 2011.

6 ART FROM TUBES

1 'Sculpture: A Times Square of the Mind', *Time* Online, www.time.com, 18 March 1966, accessed 25 March 2011; Tom Wolfe, 'The New Life Out There: Electrographic Architecture', *New York Magazine*, 1/36 (December 1968), pp. 47–8.
2 Wolfe, 'The New Life', pp. 47–8.
3 Tama Starr and Edward Hayman, *Signs and Wonders: The Spectacular Marketing of America* (New York, 1998), p. 215.
4 Martino Stierli, *Las Vegas im Rückspiegel: Die Stadt in Theorie, Fotografie und Film* (Zürich, 2010), pp. 84–5; Charles F. Barnard, *The Magic Sign: The Electric Art/Architecture of Las Vegas* (Cincinnati, OH, 1993), p. 103.
5 Michael Webb, *The Magic of Neon* (Layton, UT, 1983), p. 73.
6 Ibid., pp. 10–20.
7 Ibid., p. 16.
8 Alan Hess, *Googie: Fifties Coffee Shop Architecture* (San Francisco, CA, 1985), pp. 29, 67, 120–21.
9 Ibid., pp. 102–96.
10 Jon C. Teaford, 'The City', in *A Companion to 20th-century America*, ed. Stephen J. Whitfield (Oxford, 2004), pp. 206–11; Michael Johns, *Moment of Grace: The American City in the 1950s* (Berkeley, CA, 2002), pp. 20–25.
11 Joshua Shannon, *The Disappearance of Objects: New York Art and the Rise of the Postmodern City* (New Haven, CT, 2009), pp. 4–7, 79–80, 285–6.
12 Ibid., p. 5.
13 Dave Hickey, 'The Luminous Body: Sourceless Illumination as a Metaphor for Grace', in *Light in Architecture and Art: The Work of Dan Flavin*, ed. Jeffrey Kopie (Marfa, TX, 2002), p. 154.
14 Quoted in Rudi Stern, *The New Let There Be Neon* [revd edn of *Let There Be Neon*, 1979] (Cincinnati, OH, 1988), p. 102.
15 Sam Hunter, *Chryssa* (Stuttgart, 1974), pp. 15–19; 'Sculpture: A Times Square of the Mind'.
16 Stephen Antonakos, 'A Statement by the Artist', in *Stephen Antonakos: Neons and Drawings*, exh. cat., Rose Art Museum, Brandeis University (Waltham, MA, 1986), p. 10.
17 Andrea Domesle, *Leucht-Schrift-Kunst: Holzer, Kosuth, Merz, Nannucci, Nauman* (Berlin, 1998), pp. 297–8.
18 Webb, *The Magic of Neon*, pp. 76–7.
19 Quoted in Dietmar Elger, 'Licht als Metapher: Kunst und Neon',

in *Licht und Raum: Elektrisches Licht in der Kunst des 20. Jahrhunderts*, ed. Michael Schwarz (Cologne, 1998), pp. 62–3.

20 S. Conrad Lienhardt, 'Tears for St Francis: Eine Lichtinstallation für die Pfarrkirche St Franziskus in Steyr/Oberösterreich', in *Keith Sonnier: Skulptur Licht Raum*, ed. Wolfgang Häusler and Conrad Lienhardt (Ostfildern, 2002), pp. 61–2.

21 Domesle, *Leucht-Schrift-Kunst*, pp. 118–20.

22 Elger, 'Licht als Metapher: Kunst und Neon', pp. 62, 75.

23 Konrad Bitterli, 'Werkspuren und Schnittstellen: Sonniers Schaffen zwischen alltäglicher Funktion und künstlerischer Autonomie', in *Keith Sonnier: Skulptur Licht Raum*, pp. 8–9.

24 Stern, *The New Let There Be Neon*, pp. 98–119.

25 Webb, *The Magic of Neon*, pp. 74–5.

26 Stern, *The New Let There Be Neon*, p. 118.

27 Ibid., p. 91.

28 Peter Weibel, 'Zur Entwicklung der Lichtkunst', in *Lichtkunst aus Kunstlicht: Licht als Medium der Kunst im 20. und 21. Jahrhundert*, ed. Peter Weibel and Gregor Jansen (Ostfildern, 2006), p. 113.

29 Dan Flavin, '". . . in Daylight or Cool White": An Autobiographical Sketch', in Michael Govan and Tiffany Bell, *Dan Flavin: A Retrospective* (New Haven, CT, 2004), pp. 189–91.

30 Quoted in Michael Govan, 'Irony and Light', in Govan and Bell, *Dan Flavin*, p. 29.

31 Flavin, '". . . in Daylight"', pp. 189–90.

32 Phyllis Tuchman, 'Dan Flavin Interviewed by Phyllis Tuchman', in Govan and Bell, *Dan Flavin*, pp. 192–4.

33 Govan, 'Irony and Light', p. 34; Angela Vettese, 'Dan Flavin: Light as a Fact and Light as a Sign', in Angela Vettese, Giuseppe Panza di Biumo and Mattioli Laura Rossi, *Dan Flavin: Rooms of Light: Works of the Panza Collection from Villa Panza, Varese and the Solomon R. Guggenheim Museum, New York* (Milano, 2004), p. 27; see also Joachim Pissaro, 'Dan Flavin's Epiphany', in *It Is What It Is: Writings on Dan Flavin Since 1964*, ed. Paula Feldman and Karsten Schubert (London, 2004), pp. 240–44; Tiffany Bell, 'Working Strategies', in *Light in Architecture and Art: The Work of Dan Flavin*, ed. Jeffrey Kopie (Marfa, TX, 2002), pp. 111–26.

34 David Bourdon, 'Art: Dan Flavin', in *It Is What It Is*, ed. Feldman and Schubert, pp. 23–4.

35 Hilton Kramer, 'Art: More Aluminum, Less Symbolism', in *It Is What It Is*, ed. Feldman and Schubert, p. 36.

36 Pepe Karmel, 'Outrageous in the Sixties, but Seeming Serene in the 90s', in *It Is What It Is*, ed. Feldman and Schubert, p. 202.

37 Jeffrey Weiss, 'Preface', in Govan and Bell, *Dan Flavin*, p. 10; Hal Foster, 'Dan Flavin and the Catastrophe of Minimalism', in *Dan Flavin: New Light*, ed. Jeffrey Weiss (New Haven, CT, 2006), p. 143.

38 Quoted in Vettese, 'Dan Flavin: Light as a Fact', p. 23; Govan, 'Irony and Light', pp. 100–03.

39 Lili Lakich, *Neon Lovers Glow in the Dark*, exh. cat., Museum of Neon Art, Los Angeles (1986), p. 6.

40 Ibid., p. 18.

41 Ibid., p. 34.

42 Ibid., p. 16.

43 Lili Lakich, 'What's New in Neon', *Los Angeles Times* Online, http://articles.latimes.com, 19 January 1986, accessed 25 March 2011.

44 Lakich, *Neon Lovers*, p. 18.

45 Ibid., p. 8.

46 Ibid., p. 18.

47 Bell, 'Working Strategies', p. 113.

48 Tuchman, 'Dan Flavin Interviewed by Phyllis Tuchman', p. 194.

49 Hickey, 'The Luminous Body', p. 157.

50 Gregor Jansen and Andreas F. Beitin, 'Der Stoff aus dem die Leuchten sind: Die Leuchtstoffröhre als minimalistisches Prinzip in der Lichtkunst', in *Lichtkunst aus Kunstlicht*, ed. Weibel and Jansen, p. 530.

51 Tuchman, 'Dan Flavin Interviewed by Phyllis Tuchman', p. 194.

52 Joseph D. Ketner II, 'Elusive Signs: Bruce Nauman Works with Light', in *Elusive Signs: Bruce Nauman Works with Light*, ed. Joseph D. Ketner II (Cambridge, MA, 2006), p. 37.

53 Brenda Richardson, ed., *Bruce Nauman: Neons*, exh. cat., Baltimore Museum of Art (1983), p. 27.

54 Ibid., p. 19.

55 Michele De Angelus, 'Interview with Bruce Nauman, May 27 and 30, 1980', in *Please Pay Attention Please: Bruce Nauman's Words: Writings and Interviews*, ed. Janet Kraynak (Cambridge, MA, 2003), p. 252.

56 Richardson, ed., *Bruce Nauman*, p. 19.

57 Ketner, 'Elusive Signs', p. 17.

58 Richardson, ed., *Bruce Nauman*, p. 38.

59 Ketner, 'Elusive Signs', p. 17.

60 De Angelus, 'Interview with Bruce Nauman', p. 238.

61 Ibid., p. 231.

62 Catherine Nichols, 'Sprache', in *Bruce Nauman: Ein Lesebuch*, ed. Eugen Blume et al. (Cologne, 2010), p. 295.

63 Richardson, ed., *Bruce Nauman*, p. 20.

64 Domesle, *Leucht-Schrift-Kunst*, p. 85; Elger, 'Licht als Metapher: Kunst und Neon', pp. 74–5.

65 Elger, 'Licht als Metapher: Kunst mit Neon', pp. 502–3.

66 Domesle, *Leucht-Schrift-Kunst*, p. 62.

67 Ibid.

68 Joseph Kosuth, *No Exit* (Ostfildern, 1991), p. 18.

69 Domesle, *Leucht-Schrift-Kunst*, p. 102.

70 Anne M. Wagner, 'Nauman's Body of Sculpture', in Constance M. Lewallen, *A Rose Has No Teeth: Bruce Nauman in the 1960s* (Berkeley, CA, 2007), p. 139.

71 Eugen Blume, 'Bruce Nauman: Live or Die – oder: Die Ausmessung des Seins', *Bruce Nauman. Live or Die* (Cologne, 2010), p. 15.

72 Catherine Nichols, 'Cowboy', in *Bruce Nauman: Ein Lesebuch*, pp. 53–6.

73 De Angelus, 'Interview with Bruce Nauman', p. 266.

74 Fiona Hamilton, 'Margate Regenerating with Help of Tracey Emin and J.M.W. Turner', *The Times: The Sunday Times* Online, http://entertainment.timesonline.co.uk, 9 May 2009, accessed 25 March 2011.

75 Carl Freedman, 'The Turn of the Screw: Tracey Emin in Conversation with Carl Freedman', in *Tracey Emin: Works, 1963–2006*, ed. Honey Luard (New York, 2006), p. 328.

76 Ibid., p. 328.

77 Tracey Emin, 'Edited Transcription of "Why I Never Became a Dancer", 1995', in Neal Brown, *Tracey Emin (Tate Modern Art)* (London, 2006), pp. 78–9; see also the chapter 'Why I Never Became a Dancer' in Tracey Emin, *Strangeland* (London, 2005), pp. 42–6.

78 Tracey Emin, 'Tracey Emin CV Part 1', in *Tracey Emin*, ed. Luard, pp. 146–7.

79 Gregor Jansen, 'Nichts Neues unter der Sonne: Zur negativen Ästhetik künstlichen Lichts', in *Lichtkunst aus Kunstlicht: Licht als Medium der Kunst im 20. und 21. Jahrhundert*, ed. Peter Weibel and Gregor Jansen (Ostfildern, 2006), p. 648.

80 Rosemary Betterton, 'Why Is My Art Not as Good as Me? Femininity, Feminism and "Life-Drawing" in Tracey Emin's Art', in *The Art of Tracey Emin*, ed. Chris Townsend (London, 2002), pp. 29–30.

81 Rudi Fuchs, 'Fuzzy Sex', in Andrea Rose, Toby Forward, Rudi Fuchs, *Tracey Emin: Borrowed Light* (London, 2007), pp. 26–8.
82 Brown, *Tracey Emin*, pp. 40–41.
83 Emin also took on the peepshow, the key institution of the neon world: in 1996 she lived and worked completely naked for three and a half weeks in a Stockholm museum. Observers could watch her through sixteen lenses. But the naked Emin under observation was not a passive object as she was working on her paintings (Brown, *Tracey Emin*, p. 87).
84 Anne Hoormann, 'Licht-Kunst am Bau: Zur Virtualisierung der Architektur', *Archiv für Mediengeschichte*, 2 (2002), pp. 223–4.
85 Söke Dinkla, 'Strategien der Identifikation: Lichtkunst im öffentlichen Raum', *Am Rande des Lichts – Inmitten des Lichts: Lichtkunst und Lichtprojekte im öffentlichen Raum Nordrhein-Westfalens*, ed. Söke Dinkla (Cologne, 2004), p. 15.
86 Hamilton, 'Margate Regenerating'.
87 'Tracey Emin's New Neon – The Big Switch On!', *YouTube*, www.youtube.com, 30 April 2010, accessed 25 March 2011.

7 LISTENING TO NEON

1 Dusty Sprengnagel, *Neon World* (New York, 1999), p. 126.
2 Max Celko, 'Zukunftsvisionen aus Licht', *Du*, 796 (May 2009), p. 21
3 Michael Webb, *The Magic of Neon* (Layton, UT, 1983), p. 58.
4 The title, according to the band, did not refer to John Kennedy Toole's novel of the same name: see Josh Modell, 'Interview: Win Butler of Arcade Fire', AV *Club: Music: Interview*, www.avclub.com, 14 March 2007, accessed 23 March 2011.
5 Silverchair, *Neon Ballroom* (Sony, 1999), CD.
6 Ben Ratliff, 'Exuberant Rural Rhythms of Black Brazilian Culture', *New York Times* Online, http://nytimes.com, 2 August 1996, accessed 11 March 2011; Tico da Costa, 'Paixão Neon', *Brazil Encanto* (Music of the World, 1990), CD.
7 Jürgen Teipel, *Verschwende deine Jugend: Ein Doku-Roman über den deutschen Punk und New Wave* (Frankfurt, 2001), p. 115.
8 John Mayer, 'Neon', *Where the Light Is: John Mayer Live in Los Angeles* (Columbia, 2008), CD.
9 Neon Stereo Vs Marcie, 'F*ck Me Baby' (System Recordings, 2007), EP.
10 Judith Lang Zaimont, *Neon Rhythm: Chamber Music of Judith Lang Zaimont* (Arabesque Recordings, 1996), CD; no author (Judith

Lang Zaimont), 'Artist Biography', home page, www.jzaimont.com, accessed 23 March 2011.

11 'Big Ali: Neon Music', *YouTube*, www.youtube.com, 6 December 2009, accessed 25 March 2011.

12 William Mcbrien, *Cole Porter: A Biography* (New York, 1998), pp. 201–2.

13 Morris Dickstein, *Dancing in the Dark: A Cultural History of the Great Depression* (New York, 2009), pp. 374–5.

14 Cole Porter, 'Down in the Depths', *Red, Hot and Blue* [1936] (Chrysalis, 1990), CD.

15 Dickstein, *Dancing in the Dark*, pp. 374–5.

16 Michael Johns, *Moment of Grace: The American City in the 1950s* (Berkeley, CA, 2002), p. 26.

17 McBrien, *Cole Porter*, pp. 201–2.

18 Peggy Lee and The Jud Conlon Singers, 'Neon Signs (I'm Gonna Shine Like Neon, Too)' (Capitol Records, 1949), vinyl, single.

19 Lisa Hostetler, 'Louis Faurer and Film Noir', *Louis Faurer*, pp. 49–61.

20 Dickstein, *Dancing in the Dark*, pp. 436–7.

21 Peggy Lee, *Miss Peggy Lee: An Autobiography* (London, 2002), p. 15.

22 Ibid., p. 36.

23 Peter Richmond, *Fever: The Life and Music of Miss Peggy Lee* (New York, 2006), p. 3.

24 Ibid., pp. 7–9.

25 Dukes of Dixieland, 'Tra-La-La-La / Neon Love' (Okeh, 1953), vinyl, single.

26 'Top Rhythm and Blues Records: Record Reviews, Popular: The Dukes of Dixieland', *Billboard* (7 February 1953), p. 46.

27 Simon and Garfunkel, 'The Sound of Silence', *Sounds of Silence* (Columbia Records, 1966), vinyl, LP.

28 Theodor W. Adorno, *Philosophy of New Music* [1949], trans. and ed. Robert Hullot-Kentor (Minneapolis, MN, 2006), p. 16.

29 Salvatore Adamo, 'Le Néon / Une larme aux nuages' (Electrola, 1967), vinyl, single.

30 Adamo, 'Le Néon'.

31 The Box Tops, 'The Letter / Happy Times' (Mala, 1967), vinyl, single.

32 The Box Tops, 'The Neon Rainbow / Everything I Am' (Mala, 1967), vinyl, single.

33 Brooks and Dunn, 'Neon Moon', *Brand New Man* (Arista, 1991), CD.

34 Johnny Duncan, 'Stranger / Flashing, Screaming, Silent Neon Sign' (Columbia, 1976), vinyl, single.

35 Curtis W. Ellison, *Country Music Culture: From Hard Times to Heaven* (Jackson, MS, 1995), p. 67.

36 Bill C. Malone, *Don't Get Above Your Raisin': Country Music and the Southern Working Class* (Urbana, IL, 2002), pp. 254–5.

37 Rebecca Solnit, *Wanderlust: A History of Walking* (London, 2001), pp. 236–9.

38 Rita Canard, 'Neon Women / Tear Store' (Juldane, 1974), vinyl, single.

39 Teipel, *Verschwende deine Jugend*, pp. 89–90.

40 Kraftwerk, 'Neonlicht', *Die Mensch-Maschine* (Kling Klang, 1978), vinyl, LP.

41 Pascal Bussy, *Neonlicht: Die Kraftwerk Story* (Berlin, 2005), p. 32.

42 'Kraftwerk: Neonlicht (Neon Light) Live', *YouTube*, www.youtube.com, 22 April 2008, accessed 26 March 2011.

43 Bussy, *Neonlicht*, p. 105.

44 XTC, 'Neon Shuffle', *White Music* (Virgin, 1978), vinyl, LP.

45 Neville Farmer and XTC, *XTC: Song Stories – The Exclusive Authorized Story behind the Music* (New York, 1998), p. 34.

46 Ibid., pp. 14–15.

47 Jon C. Teaford, 'The City', in *A Companion to 20th-century America*, ed. Stephen J. Whitfield (Oxford, 2004), p. 207.

48 Farmer and XTC, *XTC: Song Stories*, pp. 4–5.

49 See also Carlo Rotella, *Good with Their Hands: Boxers, Bluesmen, and Other Characters from the Rust Belt* (Berkeley, CA, 2002).

50 Colin Larkin, 'Verve', *The Virgin Encyclopedia of Indie and New Wave* (London, 1998), p. 459.

51 The Verve, *Urban Hymns* (Virgin, 1997), CD.

52 John Harris, *The Last Party: Britpop, Blair, and the Demise of English Rock* (London, 2004), pp. xiii–xv.

53 Trevor Baker, *Richard Ashcroft: The Verve, Burning Money and the Human Condition* (Church Stretton, 2008), p. 108.

54 The Verve, 'Neon Wilderness', *Urban Hymns* (Virgin, 1997), CD.

BIBLIOGRAPHY

Adamo, Salvatore, 'Le Néon / Une larme aux nuages' (Electrola, 1967), vinyl, single

Adorno, Theodor W., *Philosophy of New Music* [1949], trans. and ed. Robert Hullot-Kentor (Minneapolis, MN, and London, 2006)

Algren, Nelson, *Chicago: City on the Make* (Garden City, NY, 1951)

——, *Entrapment and Other Writings* (New York and London, 2009)

——, 'Introduction', *The Neon Wilderness* (New York, 1960), pp. 9–14

——, *The Neon Wilderness* [1947] (New York, 1986)

——, *Somebody in Boots* [1935] (New York, 1965)

Antonakos, Stephen, 'A Statement by the Artist', *Stephen Antonakos: Neons and Drawings*, exh. cat., Rose Art Museum, Brandeis University (Waltham, MA, 1986), p. 10

Arcade Fire, *The Neon Bible* (City Slang, 2007), CD

Asendorf, Christoph, *Ströme und Strahlen: Das langsame Verschwinden der Materie um 1900* (Giessen, 1989)

'Aurora of Lights Dims Out in City for the Duration', *New York Times* (29 April 1942), p. 10

Baillot, Rémi, *Georges Claude: Le Génie fourvoyé* (Les Ulis, 2010)

Baker, Trevor, *Richard Ashcroft: The Verve, Burning Money and the Human Condition* (Church Stretton, 2008)

Barnard, Charles F., *The Magic Sign: The Electric Art/Architecture of Las Vegas* (Cincinnati, OH, 1993)

Baudrillard, Jean, *Amérique* [1986] (Paris, 2000)

Baumeister, Biene, and Zwi Negator, 'Situationistische Revolutionstheorie – Communistische Aktualität und linke Verblendung', in *Spektakel, Kunst, Gesellschaft: Guy Debord und die Situationistische Internationale*, ed. Stephan Grigat, Johannes Grenzfurthner and Günther Friesinger (Berlin, 2006), pp. 5–35

Bégout, Bruce, *Zeropolis: The Experience of Las Vegas* (London, 2003)

'Bel-Air Area to Remain Free of Neon Lights', *Los Angeles Times*
(3 September 1949), p. 1

Bell, Tiffany, 'Working Strategies', in *Light in Architecture and Art:
The Work of Dan Flavin*, ed. Jeffrey Kopie (Marfa, TX, 2002),
pp. 111–26

Belloc, Denis, *Neons* (Boston, MA, 1991)

——, *Néons* (Paris, 1987)

Benjamin, Walter, 'The Work of Art in the Age of Mechanical
Reproduction', in *Illuminations*, ed. Hannah Arendt, trans. Harry
Zohn (London, 1992), pp. 211–44.

Berger, Meyer, 'New Constellations on the Old White Way', *New York
Times* (29 March 1936), p. SM12

Bernard, Andreas, *Die Geschichte des Fahrstuhls* (Frankfurt, 2006)

Best, Katharine, and Katharine Hillyer, *Las Vegas: Playtown USA* (New
York, 1955)

Betterton, Rosemary, 'Why Is My Art Not as Good as Me? Femininity,
Feminism and "Life-Drawing" in Tracey Emin's Art', in *The Art
of Tracey Emin*, ed. Chris Townsend (London, 2002), pp. 23–39

Bexte, Peter, 'Wolken über Las Vegas', *Archiv für Mediengeschichte*,
5 (2005), pp. 131–7

Bialobrzeski, Peter, *Neontigers* (Ostfildern, 2004)

Bieger, Laura, *Ästhetik der Immersion: Raum-Erleben zwischen Welt
und Bild. Las Vegas, Washington und die White City* (Bielefeld,
2007)

'Big Ali: Neon Music', *YouTube*, www.youtube.com, 6 December 2009,
accessed 25 March 2011

'Biografie von László Moholy-Nagy', in *László Moholy-Nagy: Color in
Transparency. Photographic Experiments in Color, 1934–1946*,
ed. Jeannine Fiedler and Hattula Moholy-Nagy (Göttingen,
2006), pp. 202–3

Bitterli, Konrad, 'Werkspuren und Schnittstellen: Sonniers Schaffen
zwischen alltäglicher Funktion und künstlerischer Autonomie', in
Keith Sonnier: Skulptur Licht Raum, ed. Wolfgang Häusler and
Conrad Lienhardt (Ostfildern, 2002), pp. 7–18

'Blackout Success Is Highly Praised', *New York Times* (2 May 1942), p. 15

Blade Runner, dir. Ridley Scott (Warner Brothers, 1982), film

Blondel, Christine, 'Industrial Science as a "Show": A Case-study of
Georges Claude', in *Expository Science: Forms and Functions of
Popularisation*, ed. Terry Shinn and Richard Whitley (Dordrecht,
1985), pp. 249–58

Blume, Eugen, 'Bruce Nauman: Live or Die – oder: Die Ausmessung des
Seins', *Bruce Nauman: Live or Die* (Cologne, 2010), pp. 9–53

Bock, Charles, *Beautiful Children* (New York, 2008)

Bouchard, Karen, and Dietrich Neumann, 'Simpson's Department Store, London, 1936', in Dietrich Neumann et al., *Architektur der Nacht* (Munich, 2002), p. 168

Bouman, Mark J., '"The Best Lighted City in the World": The Construction of a Nocturnal Landscape in Chicago', in *The American Cities and Technology Reader: Wilderness to Wired City*, ed. Gerrylynn K. Roberts (London, 1999), pp. 173–87

Bourdon, David, 'Art: Dan Flavin', in *It Is What It Is: Writings on Dan Flavin Since 1964*, ed. Paula Feldman and Karsten Schubert (London, 2004), pp. 22–4

Box Tops, The, 'The Letter / Happy Times' (Mala, 1967), vinyl, single

——, 'The Neon Rainbow / Everything I Am' (Mala, 1967), vinyl, single

Boyer, M. Christine, 'Twice-told Stories: The Double Erasure of Times Square', in *The Unknown City: Contesting Architecture and Social Space*, ed. Iain Borden et al. (Cambridge, MA, 2001), pp. 30–52

Brevda, William, 'The Double Nihilation of the Neon: Raymond Chandler's Los Angeles', *Texas Studies in Literature and Language*, XLI/1 (1999), pp. 71–102

——, 'The Rainbow Sign of Nelson Algren', *Texas Studies in Literature and Language*, XLIV/4 (2002), pp. 393–413

Brill, Louis M., 'The Pepsi-Cola Generation: Preserved in Neon for Now and Ever More', *SignWeb*, www.signweb.com, 20 February 2006, accessed 16 February 2011

Bronfen, Elisabeth, *Tiefer als der Tag gedacht: Eine Kulturgeschichte der Nacht* (Munich, 2008)

Brooks and Dunn, 'Neon Moon', *Brand New Man* (Arista, 1991), CD

Brown, Neal, *Tracey Emin (Tate Modern Art)* (London, 2006)

Bruno, Giuliana, 'Ramble City: Postmodernism and *Blade Runner*', *October*, 41 (1987), pp. 61–74

Bukatman, Scott, *Blade Runner* (London, 1997)

Burke, James Lee, *The Neon Rain* (New York, 1988)

Bussy, Pascal, *Neonlicht: Die Kraftwerk Story* (Berlin, 2005)

Canard, Rita, 'Neon Women / Tear Store' (Juldane, 1974), vinyl, single

Carels, Niels, *Neon* (Amsterdam, 2000)

Casino, dir. Martin Scorsese (Universal Pictures, 1995), film

Cassuto, Leonard, *Hard-Boiled Sentimentality: The Secret History of American Crime Stories* (New York, 2009)

Celko, Max, 'Zukunftsvisionen aus Licht', *Du*, 796 (May 2009), pp. 20–24

Chase, John, *Glitter Stucco and Dumpster Diving: Reflections on Building Production in the Vernacular City* (New York, 2000)

Chisholm, Dianne, *Queer Constellations: Subcultural Space in the Wake of the City* (Minneapolis, MN, 2004)

Christopher, Nicholas, *Somewhere in the Night: Film Noir and the American City* (New York, 1998)

Claude, Georges, *Ma vie et mes inventions* (Paris, 1957)

——, *Souvenirs et enseignements d'une expérience électorale* (Paris, 1932)

Claude Neon News, I/I (January 1928)–III/3 (September/October 1930)

Clontz, Ted L., *Wilderness City: The Post World War II American Urban Novel from Algren to Wideman* (New York, 2005)

Cooper, Ken, '"Zero Pays the House": The Las Vegas Novel and Atomic Roulette', *Contemporary Literature*, XXXIII/3 (1992), pp. 528–44

Crowe, Michael F., 'Neon Signs: Their Origin, Use, and Maintenance', APT *Bulletin*, XXIII/3 (1991), pp. 30–37

Currie, Cherie, with Tony O'Neill, *Neon Angel: A Memoir of a Runaway* (New York, 2010)

Da Costa, Tico, 'Paixão Neon', *Brazil Encanto* (Music of the World, 1990), CD

Davis, Mike, *Dead Cities and Other Tales* (New York, 2002)

De Angelus, Michele, 'Interview with Bruce Nauman, May 27 and 30, 1980', in *Please Pay Attention Please: Bruce Nauman's Words: Writings and Interviews*, ed. Janet Kraynak (Cambridge, MA, 2003), pp. 197–295

Debord, Guy, *The Society of the Spectacle*, trans. Donald Nicholson-Smith (New York, 1994)

Deitmer, Sabine, *NeonNächte* (Frankfurt, 1995)

DeKoven, Marianne, *Utopia Limited: The Sixties and the Emergence of the Postmodern* (Durham, NC, 2004)

Delany, Samuel R., *Times Square Red, Times Square Blue* (New York, 1999)

Deutsches Historisches Museum, www.dhm.de, accessed 16 February 2011

Dickstein, Morris, *Dancing in the Dark: A Cultural History of the Great Depression* (New York, 2009)

Didion, Joan, *Play It as It Lays* [1970] (New York, 2005)

——, *Slouching towards Bethlehem* (New York, 1968)

Dimendberg, Edward, *Film Noir and the Spaces of Modernity* (Cambridge, MA, 2004)

Dinkla, Söke, 'Strategien der Identifikation: Lichtkunst im öffentlichen Raum', in *Am Rande des Lichts – Inmitten des Lichts: Lichtkunst und Lichtprojekte im öffentlichen Raum Nordrhein-Westfalens*, ed. Söke Dinkla (Cologne, 2004), pp. 12–17

Domesle, Andrea, *Leucht-Schrift-Kunst: Holzer, Kosuth, Merz, Nannucci, Nauman* (Berlin, 1998)

Donahue, Marlena, 'Neon Art Museum Exhibit: It's a Gas', *Los Angeles Times* (29 December 1984), p. F1

Douglas, Ann, *Terrible Honesty: Mongrel Manhattan in the 1920s* (New York, 1996)

Dramaturgie/Kommunikation (Helena Huguet), 'In Neon von Julia Kandzora', Spielplan, *Deutsches Theater*, www.deutschestheater.de, accessed 16 February 2011

Dreiser, Theodore, *Journalism, Volume One: Newspaper Writings, 1892–1895*, ed. T. D. Nostwich (Philadelphia, PA, 1988)

Drew, Bettina, *Nelson Algren: A Life on the Wild Side* (New York, 1989)

Dreyfus, Hubert, and Sean Dorrance Kelly, *All Things Shining: Reading the Western Classics to Find Meaning in a Secular Age* (New York, 2011)

Dukes of Dixieland, 'Tra-La-La-La / Neon Love' (Okeh, 1953), vinyl, single

Duncan, Johnny, 'Stranger / Flashing, Screaming, Silent Neon Sign' (Columbia, 1976), vinyl, single

Dunne, John Gregory, *Vegas: A Memoir of a Dark Season* (New York, 1974)

'Dutch Use Neon Lights to Grow Cucumbers and Strawberries', *New York Times* (15 February 1931), p. 26

Eco, Umberto, 'Apocalyptic and Integrated', in *Apocalypse Postponed/ Umberto Eco*, ed. Robert Lumley (Bloomington, IN, 1994)

Eeckhout, Bart, 'The Postsexual City? Times Square in the Age of Virtual Reproduction', in *Taking Up Space: New Approaches to American History*, ed. Anke Ortlepp and Christoph Ribbat (Trier, 2004), pp. 199–216

Elger, Dietmar, 'Licht als Metapher – Kunst mit Neon', in *Lichtkunst aus Kunstlicht: Licht als Medium der Kunst im 20. und 21. Jahrhundert*, ed. Peter Weibel and Gregor Jansen (Ostfildern, 2006), pp. 490–505

——, 'Licht als Metapher: Kunst und Neon', in *Licht und Raum: Elektrisches Licht in der Kunst des 20. Jahrhunderts*, ed. Michael Schwarz (Cologne, 1998), pp. 62–75

Ellison, Curtis W., *Country Music Culture: From Hard Times to Heaven* (Jackson, MS, 1995)

Emin, Tracey, 'Edited Transcription of "Why I Never Became a Dancer", 1995', in Neal Brown, *Tracey Emin (Tate Modern Art)* (London, 2006), pp. 78–9

——, *Strangeland* (London, 2005)

——, 'Tracey Emin CV Part I', in *Tracey Emin: Works, 1963–2006*,
    ed. Honey Luard (New York, 2006), pp. 146–7
Engell, Lorenz, Bernhard Siegert and Joseph Vogl, 'Editorial', in *Licht
    und Leitung*, ed. Lorenz Engell, Bernhard Siegert, Joseph Vogl,
    Archiv für Mediengeschichte, 2 (2002), pp. 5–7
Epstein, Max, 'Berlin im Licht', *Weltbrille*, 7 (November 1928), p. 2
Erenberg, Lewis A., *Steppin' Out: New York Nightlife and the Trans-
    formation of American Culture, 1890–1930* (Chicago, IL, 1984)
Eskilson, Stephen John, '"A Century of Progress" Exposition, Chicago,
    1933', in Dietrich Neumann et al., *Architektur der Nacht*
    (Munich, 2002), pp. 164–5
——, 'America the Spectacle: Discourses of Color and Light,
    1914–1934', dissertation, Brown University, 1995, microfilm
Eskin, Blake, 'On the Roof: Pepsi Degeneration', *The New Yorker* (29
    March 2004), p. 6
Farber, Eduard, 'Claude, Georges', in *Dictionary of Scientific
    Biography*, ed. Charles Coulston Gillispie, vol. III (New York,
    1971), p. 299
Farmer, Neville, and XTC, *XTC: Song Stories – The Exclusive Authorized
    Story behind the Music* (New York, 1998)
Fiedler, Jeannine, and Hattula Moholy-Nagy, *László Moholy-Nagy: Color
    in Transparency. Photographic Experiments in Color, 1934–1946*
    (Göttingen, 2006)
'Fifty Years of Electric Signs', *Signs of the Times* (May 1956),
    pp. 17–80
Flavin, Dan, '". . . in Daylight or Cool White": An Autobiographical
    Sketch', in Michael Govan and Tiffany Bell, *Dan Flavin:
    A Retrospective* (New Haven, CT, 2004), pp. 189–91
Foster, Hal, 'Dan Flavin and the Catastrophe of Minimalism', in *Dan
    Flavin: New Light*, ed. Jeffrey Weiss (New Haven, CT, 2006),
    pp. 133–51
Fox, Margalit, 'Rudi Stern, Artist Whose Medium Was Light, Dies at 69',
    New York Times Online, www.nytimes.com, 18 August 2006,
    accessed 16 February 2011
Francoeur, Lucien, *Neons in the Night* (Montreal, 1980)
Frank, Charlotte, 'Die Schwarzseher', *Süddeutsche Zeitung* (23 April 2008),
    p. 11
Freedman, Carl, 'The Turn of the Screw: Tracey Emin in Conversation
    with Carl Freedman', in *Tracey Emin: Works, 1963–2006*,
    ed. Honey Luard (New York, 2006), pp. 327–33
Freiwillige Selbstkontrolle, 'Im Westen nix Neues', *Teilnehmende
    Beobachtung* (ZickZack, 1981), vinyl, EP

Fuchs, Rudi, 'Fuzzy Sex', in Andrea Rose, Toby Forward and Rudi
    Fuchs, *Tracey Emin: Borrowed Light* (London, 2007), pp. 22–9
Gandal, Keith F., *The Virtues of the Vicious: Jacob Riis, Stephen Crane,
    and the Spectacle of the Slum* (New York, 1997)
'Georges Claude, Inventor, Dies', *New York Times* (24 May 1960), p. 37
Giles, James R., *Confronting the Horror: The Novels of Nelson Algren*
    (Kent, OH, 1989)
Gold, S., *Neon: A Handbook for Electrical Engineers, Neon
    Manufacturers, Sign Salesmen, and Advertisers* (London, 1934)
Gossart, Ewa, 'Berlin wird Weltstadt: Lichtreklame als Medium der
    urbanen Selbstinszenierung', in *Berlin im Licht*, ed. Franziska
    Nentwig et al. (Berlin, 2008), pp. 45–59
Gottdiener, Mark, Claudia C. Collins and David R. Dickens, *Las Vegas:
    The Social Production of an All-American City* (Malden, MA, 1999)
Govan, Michael, 'Irony and Light', in Michael Govan and Tiffany Bell,
    Dan Flavin: A Retrospective (New Haven, CT, 2004), pp. 19–107
'Great Signs Dark as Gay White Way Obeys Army Edict', *New York
    Times* (30 April 1942), p. 1
Gunkel, Christoph, 'Es werde Licht: Leuchtreklame in der DDR', *Spiegel
    Online: Einestages*, http://einestages.spiegel.de, 16 September
    2010, accessed 11 March 2011
Halpern, Daniel, *Foreign Neon: Poems* (New York, 1991)
Hamilton, Fiona, 'Margate Regenerating with Help of Tracey Emin and
    J.M.W. Turner', *The Times: The Sunday Times* Online,
    http://entertainment.timesonline.co.uk, 9 May 2009, accessed 25
    March 2011
Hannigan, John, *Fantasy City: Pleasure and Profit in the Postmodern
    Metropolis* (London, 1998)
Harris, John, *The Last Party: Britpop, Blair, and the Demise of English
    Rock* (London, 2004)
Harvey, David, *The Condition of Postmodernity: An Enquiry into the
    Origins of Cultural Change* (Cambridge, MA, 1990)
Hausenstein, Wilhelm, *Eine Stadt, auf nichts gebaut: Wilhelm
    Hausenstein über Berlin* (Berlin, 1984)
Hawthorne, Nathaniel, *The Scarlet Letter* [1850] (New York, 2000)
Heiser, Jörg, 'Das geht alles von ihrer Zeit ab', *Süddeutsche Zeitung*,
    III/4 (December 2005), p. 18
Hergouth, Alois, *Neon und Psyche: Gedichte* (Graz, 1953)
Hess, Alan, *Googie: Fifties Coffee Shop Architecture* (San Francisco,
    CA, 1985)
——, *Viva Las Vegas: After-Hours Architecture* (San Francisco,
    CA, 1993)

Hickey, Dave, et al., *Air Guitar: Essays on Art and Democracy* (Los Angeles, CA, 1997)
——, 'The Luminous Body: Sourceless Illumination as a Metaphor for Grace', in *Light in Architecture and Art: The Work of Dan Flavin*, ed. Jeffrey Kopie (Marfa, TX, 2002), pp. 147–58
——, 'The Players', in *The Magic Hour: The Convergence of Art and Las Vegas*, ed. Alex Farquharson (Ostfildern, 2001), pp. 40–50
Hills, Matt, 'Academic Textual Poachers: *Blade Runner* as Cult Canonical Movie', in *The Blade Runner Experience: The Legacy of a Science Fiction Classic*, ed. Will Brooker (London, 2005), pp. 124–41
Hirsch, Foster, *Otto Preminger: The Man Who Would Be King* (New York, 2007)
Hofmann-Wellenhof, Otto, 'Nachwort', in *Neon und Psyche: Gedichte, Alois Hergouth* (Graz, 1953), p. 63.
Hokanson, Robert O'Brien, 'Jazzing It Up: The Be-bop Modernism of Langston Hughes', *Mosaic*, XXXI/4 (1998), pp. 61–82
Hollmann, Arnold F., Egon Wiberg and Nils Wiberg, *Lehrbuch der anorganischen Chemie* (Berlin, 1985)
Hoormann, Anne, 'Licht-Kunst am Bau: Zur Virtualisierung der Architektur', *Archiv für Mediengeschichte*, 2 (2002), pp. 213–26
——, *Lichtspiele: Zur Medienreflexion der Avantgarde in der Weimarer Republik* (Munich, 2003)
Hostetler, Lisa, 'Louis Faurer and Film Noir', in Anne Wilkes Tucker et al., *Louis Faurer* (London, 2002), pp. 49–61
——, *Street Seen: The Psychological Gesture in American Photography, 1940–1959* (Munich, 2010)
Hughes, Langston, *Selected Poems of Langston Hughes* (New York, 1969)
Hunter, Sam, *Chryssa* (Stuttgart, 1974)
'Images Dance in Space, Heralding New Radio Era', *New York Times* (14 April 1929), p. 15
Indiana, Gary, 'Real Estate', in *Life under Neon: Paintings and Drawings of Times Square, 1981–1988*, ed. Jane Dickson, exh. cat., Goldie Paley Gallery/Moore College of Art and Design (Philadelphia, PA, 1989), p. 4
It's a Wonderful Life, dir. Frank Capra (Liberty Films, 1946), film iTunes Version 10.1.2.17 (10 March 2011)
Jakle, John A., *City Lights: Illuminating the American Night* (Baltimore, MD, 2001)
——, and Keith A. Sculle, *Signs in America's Auto Age: Signatures of Landscape and Place* (Iowa City, 2004)
Jansen, Gregor, 'Nichts Neues unter der Sonne: Zur negativen Ästhetik künstlichen Lichts', in *Lichtkunst aus Kunstlicht: Licht als*

Medium der Kunst im 20. und 21. Jahrhundert, ed. Peter Weibel and Gregor Jansen (Ostfildern, 2006), pp. 626–55

——, and Andreas F. Beitin, 'Der Stoff aus dem die Leuchten sind: Die Leuchtstoffröhre als minimalistisches Prinzip in der Lichtkunst', in *Lichtkunst aus Kunstlicht: Licht als Medium der Kunst im 20. und 21. Jahrhundert*, ed. Peter Weibel and Gregor Jansen (Ostfildern, 2006), pp. 527–38

Johns, Michael, *Moment of Grace: The American City in the 1950s* (Berkeley, CA, 2002)

Jones, Gavin Roger, *American Hungers: The Problem of Poverty in American Literature, 1840–1945* (Princeton, NJ, 2008)

Karmel, Pepe, 'Outrageous in the Sixties, but Seeming Serene in the 90s', in *It Is What It Is: Writings on Dan Flavin Since 1964*, ed. Paula Feldman and Karsten Schubert (London, 2004), pp. 202–5

Kenrick, Tony, *Neon Tough* (New York, 1988)

Kerouac, Jack, *Visions of Cody* (New York, 1972)

Kesten, Hermann, 'Die Lichtreklame', in *Anthologie jüngster Lyrik: Neue Folge*, ed. Willi Fehse and Klaus Mann (Hamburg, 1929), p. 105

Ketner, Joseph D. II, 'Elusive Signs: Bruce Nauman Works with Light', in *Elusive Signs: Bruce Nauman Works with Light*, ed. Joseph D. Ketner II (Cambridge, MA, 2006), pp. 15–37

Kim, Suji Kwock, *Notes from the Divided Country* (Baton Rouge, LA, 2003)

King, Homay, *Lost in Translation: Orientalism, Cinema, and the Enigmatic Signifier* (Durham, NC, 2010)

Klein, Norman M., 'Building *Blade Runner*', *Social Text*, 28 (1991), pp. 147–52

Kleine, Peter M., 'Herrschaftslicht – Bürgerlicht – Stadtlicht? Historische Wegmarken', in *Stadtlicht Lichtkunst*, ed. Christoph Brockhaus (Cologne, 2004), pp. 26–41

Kleinzahler, August, 'Poetics', *Live from the Hong Kong Nile Club: Poems, 1975–2000* (New York, 2000), p. 35

Knight, David, *Ideas in Chemistry: A History of the Science* (London, 2000)

Köhler, Walter, and Robert Rompe, *Die elektrischen Leuchtröhren* (Braunschweig, 1933)

Komunyakaa, Yusef, *Neon Vernacular* (Middletown, CT, 1993)

Korff, Gottfried, 'Berliner Nächte: Zum Selbstbild urbaner Eigenschaften und Leidenschaften', in *Berlin: Blicke auf die deutsche Metropole*, ed. Gerhard Brunn und Jürgen Reulecke (Essen, 1989), pp. 71–103

Kosuth, Joseph, *No Exit* (Ostfildern, 1991)

Kracauer, Siegfried, *The Salaried Masses: Duty and Distraction in Weimar Germany* [1929], trans. Quintin Hoare (London and New York, 1998), p. 93

Kraftwerk, 'Neonlicht', *Die Mensch-Maschine* (Kling Klang, 1978), vinyl, LP

——, 'Neonlicht (Neon Light) Live', *YouTube*, www.youtube.com, 22 April 2008, accessed 26 March 2011

Kramer, Hilton, 'Art: More Aluminum, Less Symbolism', in *It Is What It Is: Writings on Dan Flavin Since 1964*, ed. Paula Feldman and Karsten Schubert (London, 2004), p. 36

Kreutzer, Dietmar, 'Vorwort', in *Plaste und Elaste: Leuchtreklame in der DDR* (Berlin, 2010), pp. 7–17

Kuhrau, Sven, 'Berlin soll leuchten! Der Kurfürstendamm und die City West im Kalten Krieg', in *Berlin im Licht*, ed. Franziska Nentwig et al. (Berlin, 2008), pp. 83–95

Lakich, Lili, *Neon Lovers Glow in the Dark*, exh. cat., Museum of Neon Art, Los Angeles (1986)

——, 'What's New in Neon', *Los Angeles Times* Online, http://articles.latimes.com, 19 January 1986, accessed 25 March 2011

Lan, Pei-Chia, 'Working in a Neon Cage: Bodily Labor of Cosmetics Saleswomen in Taiwan', *Feminist Studies*, XXIX/1 (2003), pp. 21–45

Langman, Lauren, 'Neon Cages', in *Lifestyle Shopping: The Subject of Consumption*, ed. Rob Shields (London, 1992), pp. 41–82

Larkin, Colin, 'Verve', *The Virgin Encyclopedia of Indie and New Wave* (London, 1998)

Lee, Peggy, *Miss Peggy Lee: An Autobiography* (London, 2002)

——, and The Jud Conlon Singers, 'Neon Signs (I'm Gonna Shine Like Neon, Too)' (Capitol Records, 1949), vinyl, single

Lienhardt, Conrad, 'Tears for St Francis: Eine Lichtinstallation für die Pfarrkirche St. Franziskus in Steyr/Oberösterreich', in *Keith Sonnier: Skulptur Licht Raum*, ed. Wolfgang Häusler and Conrad Lienhardt (Ostfildern, 2002), pp. 61–2

Lindsay, Vachel, *The Congo and Other Poems* [1914] (Mineola, NY, 1992)

Linzbach, Antonia, 'Transparente Schilder, fluoreszierende Papageien', in Fabian Wurm, *Signaturen der Nacht: Die Welt der Lichtwerbung* (Ludwigsburg, 2009), pp. 68–71

Lipton, Lawrence, 'A Voyeur's View of the Wild Side: Nelson Algren and His Reviewers', in *The Man with the Golden Arm: 50th Anniversary Critical Edition*, ed. William J. Savage Jr and Daniel Simon (New York, 1999), pp. 399–410

Lochte, Dick, *The Neon Smile* (New York, 1995)

Lost in Translation, dir. Sofia Coppola (Focus Features, 2003), film

Lotringer, Sylvère, 'Jane Dickson', BOMBSITE; online edition of BOMB *Magazine*, 60 (Summer 1997), http://bombsite.com, accessed 19 March 2011

Lu, Hanchao, *Beyond the Neon Lights: Everyday Shanghai in the Early Twentieth Century* (Berkeley, CA, 1999)

Lubell, Samuel, 'What One Misses in Moscow', *New York Times* (24 June 1934), p. 19

Luxbacher, Günther, 'Das kommerzielle Licht: Lichtwerbung zwischen Elektroindustrie und Konsumgesellschaft vor dem Zweiten Weltkrieg', *Technikgeschichte*, 66 (1999), pp. 33–59

McBrien, William, *Cole Porter: A Biography* (New York, 1998)

MacDonald, John D., *The Neon Jungle* (New York, 1953)

McGarrity, Mark, *Neon Caesar* (New York, 1989)

McGrath, Charles, 'What Happened in Vegas Stayed in ~~Vegas~~ His Novel', *New York Times Magazine*, www.nytimes.com, 27 January 2008, accessed 18 March 2011

McNeil, Legs, and Gillian McCain, *Please Kill Me: The Uncensored Oral History of Punk* (London, 1996)

Mahar-Keplinger, Lisa, *American Signs: Form and Meaning on Route 66* (New York, 2002)

Malone, Bill C., *Don't Get Above Your Raisin': Country Music and the Southern Working Class* (Urbana, IL, 2002)

Man with the Golden Arm, The, dir. Otto Preminger (Otto Preminger Films, 1955), film

Marsak, Nathan, and Nigel Cox, *Los Angeles Neon* (Atglen, PA, 2002)

Mayer, John, 'Neon', *Where the Light Is: John Mayer Live in Los Angeles* (Columbia, 2008), CD

Meinecke, Thomas, *Lob der Kybernetik: Songtexte, 1980–2007* (Frankfurt, 2007)

Mendelsohn, Erich, *Amerika: Bilderbuch eines Architekten* (Berlin, 1926)

Miller, Samuel C., and Donald G. Fink, *Neon Signs: Manufacture – Installation – Maintenance* (New York, 1935)

Möbius, Paul, *Die Neon-Leuchtröhren: ihre Fabrikation, Anwendung und Installation* (Leipzig, 1938)

Modell, Josh, 'Interview: Win Butler of Arcade Fire', AV *Club: Music: Interview*, www.avclub.com, 14 March 2007, accessed 23 March 2011

Moffeit, Tony, *Neon Peppers* (Cherry Valley, NY, 1992)

Mong-Lan, 'BANGKOK [neon lights]', *The Antioch Review*, LXIII/1 (Winter 2005), p. 136

Nabokov, Vladimir, *Lolita* [1955] (London, 2000)

——, 'On a Book Entitled *Lolita*', *Lolita* [1955] (London, 2000), pp. 311–17

'Neon Converts to "Plastilux 500"', *New York Times* (30 May 1950), p. 28

'Neon Judgement, The', Bands and Artists, *The Belgian Pop and Rock Archives*, http://houbi.com, December 2001, accessed 16 February 2011

Neon Stereo Vs Marcie, 'F*ck Me Baby' (System Recordings, 2007), vinyl, EP

Neumann, Dietrich, 'Blau-Gold-Haus, Cologne, 1952', in Dietrich Neumann et al., *Architektur der Nacht* (Munich, 2002), p. 183

'New Fish Overshadow Guppys to Win Prize at Tropical Show', *New York Times* (29 August 1937), p. 35

'Newsboys Wear Neon Signs as Traffic Protection', *Los Angeles Times* (31 August 1936), p. A1

Nichols, Catherine, 'Cowboy', in *Bruce Nauman: Ein Lesebuch*, ed. Eugen Blume et al. (Cologne, 2010), pp. 53–6

——, 'Sprache', in *Bruce Nauman: Ein Lesebuch*, ed. Eugen Blume et al. (Cologne, 2010), pp. 295–8

Novak, Kyle J., 'Bondage, Bestiality, and Bionics: Sexual Fetishism in Ridley Scott's *Blade Runner*', *Valley Humanities Review: Current Issue*, www.lvc.edu, 29 April 2010, accessed 11 March 2011

Nye, David E., *The American Technological Sublime* (Cambridge, MA, 1991)

Nye, Mary Joe, *Before Big Science: The Pursuit of Modern Chemistry and Physics, 1800–1940* (Cambridge, MA, 1999)

O'Brien, John, *Leaving Las Vegas* [1990] (New York, 1995)

O'Brien, Matthew, *Beneath the Neon: Life and Death in the Tunnels of Las Vegas* (Las Vegas, NV, 2007)

O'Dwyer, Jessica, 'When Neon Signs Were Art', *Americana*, XVII/2 (1989), pp. 50–55

O'Hara, Frank, *Lunch Poems* (San Francisco, CA, 1964)

'Oil Concern to Light Stations by Neon Method', *Los Angeles Times* (14 July 1927), p. 10

'Olympic Sign Constructed', *Los Angeles Times* (4 February 1931), p. A13

Paterson, Katie, 'Vatnajokull (the sound of)', home page, www.katiepaterson.org, accessed 16 February 2011

Pélieu, Claude, 'Neon Express', *Coca Neon / Polaroid Rainbow* (Cherry Valley, NY, 1975), pp. 18–21

Perry, Paul, *Fear and Loathing: The Strange and Terrible Saga of Hunter S. Thompson* (New York, 1992)

Phillips, Lisa, 'Beat Culture: America Revisioned', *Beat Culture and the New America, 1950–1965*, ed. Lisa Phillips, exh. cat., Whitney Museum, New York (1995), pp. 23–40

Pinkerton, Nick, 'Rebels of the Neon God: "Only Connect"', *Reverse Shot* (Winter 2004), www.reverseshot.com, accessed 16 February 2011

Pissaro, Joachim, 'Dan Flavin's Epiphany', in *It Is What It Is: Writings on Dan Flavin Since 1964*, ed. Paula Feldman and Karsten Schubert (London, 2004), pp. 240–44

Pittman, Walter E., 'Energy from the Oceans: Georges Claude's Magnificent Failure', *Environmental Review*, VI/1 (Spring 1982), pp. 2–13

Plaste und Elaste: Leuchtreklame in der DDR (Berlin, 2010)

Platt, Harold L., *The Electric City: Energy and the Growth of the Chicago Area, 1880–1930* (Chicago, IL, 1991)

Plymell, Charles, 'In NYC', *neon poems* (Syracuse, NY, 1970), pp. 12–13

Porter, Cole, 'Down in the Depths', *Red, Hot and Blue* [1936] (Chrysalis, 1990), CD

Priestley, J. B., *Midnight on the Desert* (New York, 1937)

'Punk, Pop, Rock: Die Neue Deutsche Welle und das Kino', Zeughauskino, *Deutsches Historisches Museum*, www.dhm.de, accessed 16 February 2011

Rampersad, Arnold, *The Life of Langston Hughes*, vol. II (New York, 1986)

Ramsay, William, 'The Aurora Borealis', *Essays Biographical and Chemical* (London, 1908), pp. 205–25

——, 'How Discoveries Are Made', *Essays Biographical and Chemical* (London, 1908), pp. 115–28

——, 'Nobel Lecture. The Rare Gases of the Atmosphere: December 12, 1904', *Nobelprize.org: Nobel Prize in Chemistry*, The Official Web Site of the Nobel Prize, http://nobelprize.org, accessed 12 March 2011

Ratliff, Ben, 'Exuberant Rural Rhythms of Black Brazilian Culture', *New York Times* Online, http://nytimes.com, 2 August 1996, accessed 11 March 2011

Rechy, John, *City of Night* [1962] (New York, 1988)

——, *Nacht in der Stadt* (Berlin, 2001)

Reichl, Alexander J., *Reconstructing Times Square: Politics and Culture in Urban Development* (Lawrence, KS, 1999)

Reid, Ed, *Las Vegas: City Without Clocks* (Englewood Cliffs, NJ, 1961)

——, and Ovid Demaris, *The Green Felt Jungle* (New York, 1963)

Reinhardt, Dirk, *Von der Reklame zum Marketing: Geschichte der Wirtschaftswerbung in Deutschland* (Berlin, 1993)

'Reklameschlacht um einen Cologneer Autoturm', *DIE ZEIT* Online, www.zeit.de, 22 March 1963, accessed 19 March 2011

Richardson, Brenda, ed., *Bruce Nauman: Neons* (Baltimore, MD, 1983)

Richmond, Peter, *Fever: The Life and Music of Miss Peggy Lee* (New York, 2006)

Rosenlöcher, Thomas, 'Die Neonikone', *Die Dresdner Kunstausübung* (Frankfurt, 1996), p. 7

Roszak, Theodore, 'The Neon Telephone', *Michigan Quarterly Review*, XXX/2 (1991), pp. 295–306

Rotella, Carlo, *Good with Their Hands: Boxers, Bluesmen, and Other Characters from the Rust Belt* (Berkeley, CA, 2002)

——, *October Cities: The Redevelopment of Urban Literature* (Berkeley, CA, 1998)

——, 'The Story of Decline and the October City', *The Man with the Golden Arm: 50th Anniversary Critical Edition*, ed. William J. Savage Jr and Daniel Simon (New York, 1999), pp. 423–32

Rothman, Hal, 'Las Vegas and the American Psyche, Past and Present', *Pacific Historical Review*, LXX/4 (2001), pp. 627–40

——, *Neon Metropolis: How Las Vegas Started the Twenty-first Century* (London, 2003)

——, and Mike Davis, eds, *The Grit beneath the Glitter: Tales from the Real Las Vegas* (Berkeley, CA, 2002)

Royko, Mike, 'Algren's Golden Pen', *The Man with the Golden Arm: 50th Anniversary Critical Edition*, ed. William J. Savage Jr and Daniel Simon (New York, 1999), pp. 363–5

Sagalyn, Lynne B., *Times Square Roulette: Remaking the City Icon* (Cambridge, MA, 2001)

Salinger, Michael, *Neon* (Huron, OH, 2002)

Schallreuter, W. L., *Neon Tube Practice* (London, 1939)

Schivelbusch, Wolfgang, *Licht, Schein und Wahn: Auftritte der elektrischen Beleuchtung im 20. Jahrhundert* (Berlin, 1992)

——, *Lichtblicke: Zur Geschichte der künstlichen Helligkeit im 19. Jahrhundert* [1983] (Frankfurt, 2004)

Schlitz Gusto, home page, Joseph Schlitz Brewing Company, www.schlitzgusto.com, accessed 11 March 2011

Schlör, Joachim, *Nachts in der grossen Stadt: Paris, Berlin, London, 1840–1930* [1991] (Munich, 1994)

'Sculpture: A Times Square of the Mind', *Time* Online, www.time.com, 18 March 1966, accessed 25 March 2011

Senelick, Laurence, 'Private Parts in Public Places', in *Inventing Times Square: Commerce and Culture at the Crossroads of the World*, ed. William R. Taylor (Baltimore, MD, 1996), pp. 329–70

Sennett, Richard, *The Craftsman* (London, 2009)

Shannon, Joshua, *The Disappearance of Objects: New York Art and the Rise of the Postmodern City* (New Haven, CT, 2009)

Shay, Arthur, 'Remembering Nelson Algren', *Nelson Algren's Chicago* (Urbana, IL, 1988), pp. ix–xxii

Silverchair, *Neon Ballroom* (Sony, 1999), CD

Simon and Garfunkel, 'The Sound of Silence', *Sounds of Silence* (Columbia Records, 1965), CD

'Skid Row Flares as Gaudy Nightmare in Neon Lights', *Los Angeles Times* (18 April 1948), pp. A1, 8

Solnit, Rebecca, *Wanderlust: A History of Walking* (London, 2001)

SONIC Database, Library of Congress, Recorded Sound Reference Center, www.loc.gov, accessed 26 March 2011

Sorrentino, Gilbert, 'Neon, Kulchur, etc.', *TriQuarterly*, 43 (Fall 1978), pp. 299–308

'Spinks, Leon: Biography', *Biography.com*, www.biography.com, accessed 16 February 2011

Sprengnagel, Dusty, *Neon World* (New York, 1999)

Starr, Tama, and Edward Hayman, *Signs and Wonders: The Spectacular Marketing of America* (New York, 1998)

Staub, Michael E., 'Setting up the Seventies: Black Panthers, New Journalism, and the Rewriting of the Sixties', in *The Seventies: The Age of Glitter in Popular Culture*, ed. Shelton Waldrep (New York, 2000), pp. 19–40

Stern, Rudi, 'Introduction', in Dusty Sprengnagel, *Neon World* (New York, 1999), p. 3

——, *The New Let There Be Neon* [revd edn of *Let There Be Neon*, 1979] (Cincinnati, OH, 1988)

Stierli, Martino, *Las Vegas im Rückspiegel: Die Stadt in Theorie, Fotografie und Film* (Zürich, 2010)

Storrie, Calum, *The Delirious Museum: A Journey from the Louvre to Las Vegas* (London, 2006)

Swan, Sheila, and Peter Laufer, *Neon Nevada* (Reno, NV, 1994)

'Synagogue Marks Season', *New York Times* (26 December 1948), p. 43

Taylor, Matt, and Bonnie Taylor, *Neon Flamingo* (New York, 1987)

Teaford, Jon C., 'The City', in *A Companion to 20th-century America*, ed. Stephen J. Whitfield (Oxford, 2004), pp. 198–212

Teipel, Jürgen, *Verschwende deine Jugend: Ein Doku-Roman über den deutschen Punk und New Wave* (Frankfurt, 2001)

Tell, Darcy, *Times Square Spectacular: Lighting Up Broadway* (Washington, DC, 2007)

Thompson, Hunter S., *Fear and Loathing in Las Vegas: A Savage Journey to the Heart of the American Dream* [1971] (New York, 1998)

Thöne, Albrecht W., *Das Licht der Arier: Licht-, Feuer- und Dunkelsymbolik des Nationalsozialismus* (Munich, 1979)

Toole, John Kennedy, *The Neon Bible* (New York, 1989)

'Top Rhythm and Blues Records: Record Reviews, Popular: The Dukes of Dixieland', *Billboard* (7 February 1953), p. 46

'Tracey Emin's New Neon – The Big Switch On!', *YouTube*, www.youtube.com, 30 April 2010, accessed 25 March 2011

Trachtenberg, Alan, *The Incorporation of America: Culture and Society in the Gilded Age* (New York, 1982)

Traub, James, *The Devil's Playground: A Century of Pleasure and Profit in Times Square* (New York, 2004)

Travers, Morris W., *A Life of Sir William Ramsay* (London, 1956)

——, 'William Ramsay', in *British Chemists*, ed. Alexander Findlay and William Hobson Mills (London, 1947), pp. 146–75

Tuchman, Phyllis, 'Dan Flavin Interviewed by Phyllis Tuchman', in Michael Govan and Tiffany Bell, *Dan Flavin: A Retrospective* (New Haven, CT, 2004), pp. 192–4

Tucker, Anne Wilkes, 'So Intelligent . . . So Angry, and Having Such Passion for the World', *Louis Faurer* (London, 2002), pp. 13–47

Tuohy, Frank, 'Nocturne with Neon Lights', *The Collected Stories* (New York, 1984), pp. 285–95

Venturi, Robert, Denise Scott Brown and Steven Izenour, *Learning from Las Vegas* (Cambridge, MA, 1972)

Verve, The, *Urban Hymns* (Virgin, 1997), CD

Vettese, Angela, 'Dan Flavin: Light as a Fact and Light as a Sign', in Angela Vettese et al., *Dan Flavin: Rooms of Light: Works of the Panza Collection from Villa Panza, Varese and the Solomon R. Guggenheim Museum, New York* (Milano, 2004), pp. 23–32

Vinegar, Aron, and Michael J. Golec, eds, *Relearning from Las Vegas* (Minneapolis, MN, 2009)

Vonnegut, Kurt, 'Algren as I Knew Him', in *The Man with the Golden Arm: 50th Anniversary Critical Edition*, ed. William J. Savage Jr and Daniel Simon (New York, 1999), pp. 367–70

Wagner, Anne M., 'Nauman's Body of Sculpture', in Constance M. Lewallen, *A Rose Has No Teeth: Bruce Nauman in the 1960s* (Berkeley, CA, 2007), pp. 119–39

Wallace, David Foster, 'Good Old Neon', *Oblivion* (London, 2004), pp. 141–81

Ward, Janet, *Weimar Surfaces: Urban Visual Culture in 1920s Germany* (Berkeley, CA, 2001)

Webb, Michael, *The Magic of Neon* (Layton, UT, 1983)

——, '"So wie heute, nur übersteigert": Die glaubhafte Anti-Utopie von *Blade Runner*', in *Filmarchitektur: Von Metropolis bis Blade Runner*, ed. Dietrich Neumann (Munich, 1996), pp. 44–7

Weibel, Peter, 'Zur Entwicklung der Lichtkunst', in *Lichtkunst aus Kunstlicht: Licht als Medium der Kunst im 20. und 21. Jahrhundert*, ed. Peter Weibel and Gregor Jansen (Ostfildern, 2006), pp. 86–223

Weingarten, Marc, *The Gang That Wouldn't Write Straight: Wolfe, Thompson, Didion, and the New Journalism Revolution* (New York, 2006)

Weiss, Jeffrey, 'Preface', in Michael Govan and Tiffany Bell, *Dan Flavin: A Retrospective* (New Haven, CT, 2004), pp. 10–11

Wheeler, Elizabeth A., *Uncontained: Urban Fiction in Postwar America* (New Brunswick, NJ, 2001)

Whitfield, Philip, *Marshall Illustrated Encyclopedia of Animals* (London, 1998)

Williams, James S., 'All Her Sons: Marguerite Duras, Antiliterature, and the Outside', *Yale French Studies*, 90 (1996), pp. 47–70

Wolfe, Tom, *The Kandy-Kolored Tangerine-Flake Streamline Baby* (New York, 1965)

——, 'The New Life Out There: Electrographic Architecture', *New York Magazine*, 1/36 (December 1968), pp. 47–50

Wurm, Fabian, *Signaturen der Nacht: Die Welt der Lichtwerbung* (Ludwigsburg, 2009)

XTC, 'Neon Shuffle', *White Music* (Virgin, 1978), vinyl, LP

Yu, Timothy, 'Oriental Cities, Postmodern Futures: *Naked Lunch, Blade Runner*, and *Neuromancer*', MELUS, XXXIII/4 (2008), pp. 45–71

Zagarrio, Vito, 'It Is (Not) a Wonderful Life: For a Counter-reading of Frank Capra', in *Frank Capra: Authorship and the Studio System*, ed. Robert Sklar and Vito Zagarrio (Philadelphia, PA, 1998), pp. 64–94

Zaimont, Judith Lang, 'Artist Biography', home page, www.jzaimont.com, accessed 23 March 2011

——, *Neon Rhythm: Chamber Music of Judith Lang Zaimont* (Arabesque Recordings, 1996), CD

Zentrum für Internationale Lichtkunst Unna: Die Sammlung (Cologne, 2004)

Zimring, Carl A., '"Neon, Junk, and Ruined Landscape": Competing Visions of America's Roadsides and the Highway Beautification Act of 1965', in *The World Beyond the Windshield: Roads and Landscapes in the United States and Europe*, ed. Christof Mauch and Thomas Zeller (Athens, OH, 2008), pp. 94–107

ACKNOWLEDGEMENTS

My research on the cultural history of neon began during my tenure as a Humboldt/Lynen Fellow at MIT and Boston University. I am grateful to the Alexander von Humboldt Foundation and to my hosts William Uricchio (MIT) and John Paul Riquelme (BU). The idea for this book emerged from inspiring collaborations with the photographers Peter Bialobrzeski and Andreas Schmidt, projects that Markus Hartmann at Hatje Cantz made possible in the first place. Without Thomas Schaber's and Michael Leaman's generous interest, this book wouldn't exist. I would also like to thank Tea Janković in Basel and particularly Julia Huneke in Paderborn for helping things along. My research profited from conversations with Bill Brown, Bill Decker, Jörn Glasenapp, Robert Kanigel, Maureen McLane, Nils Plath and Änne Söll, as well as from presenting this project to audiences in Basel, Strasbourg, Freiburg, Cologne, Williamsburg (Virginia) and Stillwater (Oklahoma). Finally, I would like to acknowledge support from the Karol, Ilja and Ina Schermuly Association for Making Life Interesting.

PHOTO
ACKNOWLEDGEMENTS

The author and publishers wish to express their thanks to the below sources of illustrative material and/or permission to reproduce it.

Photo Ion Abbott © Jane Dickson: p. 114; The Art Institute of Chicago © Mark Faurer: p. 102; photo Jeff Atherton © Lili Lakich: p. 137; © Charles F. Barnard: p. 90; Ella Cisneros, New York © VG Bild-Kunst: p. 146; photo Everett Collection/Rex Features: p. 29; © 1981 by Fawcett Books, from *The Neon Jungle* by John D. MacDonald, used by permission of Fawcett Books, a division of Random House, Inc.: p. 71; © Estate of Dan Flavin, VG Bild-Kunst, Bonn 2011: p. 127; © Friedrich Christian Flick Collection im Hamburger Bahnhof/VG Bild-Kunst, Bonn 2011: p. 140; photos Carol M. Highsmith: pp. 78, 79, 86, 94, 95, 97; photo James Jarche: p. 14; photo © Pierre Jehan/Roger-Viollet: p. 32; photo Billy Jim: p. 126; photo © Kodak Collection/NMEM/Science and Society Picture Library, all rights reserved: p. 14; photo Francois Kollar: p. 6; Library of Congress, Washington, DC (Historic American Buildings Survey): pp. 9, 154; Library of Congress, Washington, DC (Historic American Engineering Record): p. 69; Library of Congress, Washington, DC (Prints and Photographs Division – Carol M. Highsmith's America in the Carol M. Highsmith Archive): pp. 78, 79, 86, 94, 95, 97; photo Roman März: p. 140; © Hattula Moholy-Nagy: pp. 52, 61; photo Don Payne © Charles F. Barnard: p. 89; photo Roger-Viollet/Rex Features: p. 6; Science Museum, London (photo © Science Museum/Science and Society Picture Library, all rights reserved): p. 22; © Stadtarchiv Rostock: p. 123; collection Stedelijk Museum Amsterdam (© Stedelijk Museum Amsterdam/VG Bild-Kunst, Bonn 2011): p. 147; photo Martin Stupich: p. 69; photo John Vachon: p. 89.

INDEX

217

94, 134, 138, 141, 143, 149,
154, 156, 167

Fargo, North Dakota 157
fast-food restaurants 129, 134
    McDonald's 97, 129
Faurer, Louis 101–3, 113, 122, 156
    Bus No. 7 102
Fiedler, Leslie 64, 75
film 16, 30, 60, 66–7, 73–4, 101,
    117–19, 121, 145, 156–7
    cartoons 83
    the city in 74, 118–20, 156–7
    film noir 67, 74, 119, 156
    see also cinema
flâneur 30, 99, 115, 119, 151, 158
Flavin, Dan 132–6, 138–9, 141,
    143, 152
    *the diagonal of May 25, 1963
    (to Constantin Brancusi) 126*
Florida 135
Fonseque, Jacques 34
Fontana, Lucio 18, 132
Ford, Harrison 119
France 39–40
Frank, Robert 101
Fremont Street, Las Vegas 78–9
Freud, Sigmund 143

gambling, gambler 11, 21, 58, 62,
    81–2, 84–5, 87–9, 91, 93
gas lamps 26–7, 54
German Democratic Republic
    (GDR) *see* East Germany
Germany 16–17, 28, 30, 34–5, 39,
    42–3, 48–50, 53, 60, 83, 118,
    121, 123–4, 135
    East Germany 8, 122–5
Gershwin, George 154
Giáp, Võ Nguyên 18
Ginsberg, Allen 110–11
Gitlin, Todd 92

glamour 13, 36, 50, 66, 106, 147
glass blowing *see* craft
Gold, S. 42–3
Graz, Austria 104, 106, 159
Great Britain *see* Britain
Great Depression, the 35, 45,
    39–40, 54, 153–4, 156–7

Halpern, Daniel 16, 121
Harlem, New York City 110–11,
    164
Havana, Cuba 35
Hawaii 105–6
hedonism 78, 81, 87, 91, 157–8
helium 7–8, 23
Hell, Richard 18
Hergouth, Alois 16, 104–8, 110, 159
Hess, Alan 85
Hickey, Dave 17, 77, 80–81, 87,
    91, 100, 130, 139
high culture 71, 81, 143
Hollywood 36, 45, 66, 72–3, 75,
    83, 118, 136
homeless people 17, 55, 63–4
Hong Kong 8, 120
Hoormann, Anne 28, 49, 148
Hoover, Herbert 44
Hopper, Edward 113
Howells, William Dean 29
Hughes, Langston 110–11, 113
Hungary 60
hyper-reality 40

Iceland 19, 25
immigration 56, 62, 65, 118
Indiana, Gary 115
intellectuals (academics, writers,
    artists) 15, 17, 20, 23, 29, 33,
    64, 80, 82–3, 92, 99, 121,
    141–42, 148
Italy 49
Ito, Atsuhiro 151